Inspired!

Inspired!

TAKE YOUR PRODUCT DREAM
FROM CONCEPT TO SHELF

Vik Venkatraman

WILEY

John Wiley & Sons, Inc.

Published by John Wiley & Sons, Inc., Hoboken, New Jersey.
Published simultaneously in Canada.

For general information on our other products and services or for technical support, please contact our Customer Care Department within the United States at (800) 762-2974, outside the United States at (317) 572-3993 or fax (317) 572-4002.

Wiley also publishes its books in a variety of electronic formats. Some content that appears in print may not be available in electronic books. For more information about Wiley products, visit our web site at www.wiley.com.

Library of Congress Cataloging-in-Publication Data:
Venkatraman, Vik.
    Inspired! : take your product dream from concept to shelf / Vik Venkatraman.
        p. cm.
    Includes index.
    ISBN 978-0-470-63845-3 (cloth); ISBN 978-0-470-93376-3 (ebk);
    ISBN 978-0-470-93377-0 (ebk); ISBN 978-0-470-93378-7 (ebk)
        1. New products—Marketing.   2. Product management.   I. Title.
    HF5415.153.V45   2010
    658.5'75—dc22

                                                                    2010032276

Printed in the United States of America

10 9 8 7 6 5 4 3 2 1

To all the friends I've made launching products,
to New York City, where anything can be made to happen,
and to you, my dear reader (and customer for this product),
without whom nothing would be possible.
Thank you.

Contents

PHASE III ROLLOUT

Preface

I took the road less traveled by, and that has made all the difference.
—Robert Frost

It was late at night in a smoky room slightly off the beaten path in New York City. My heart was pounding. I was meeting for the first time with a New York City beverage distributor—pitching him on why he should take my product. I had poured my heart into creating this product, and stretched myself past my limit to do so. Making this deal could be the difference between affording a new pair of shoes or a new pair of socks—the difference between telling my family that I made it happen or that I didn't—the difference between epic success and epic failure. Distributors like him were more than just customers—they were powerbrokers, gatekeepers to the success that waited on the retail shelves in my city. He represented tremendous potential for my new beverage product, and was as a result rather intimidating.

I sat anxiously with my sales advisor as we poured out samples for people in the room, casually discussing the benefits of the product to consumers, as well as our hopes to partner with this distributor to get our word out across New York City. I ask them:

"What do you think? Can we make a deal?"

Silence. There were two partners at this distributorship, and they stared at me as if they expected me to crumble under their glare. I knew they liked my juice, since they smiled when they were drinking it. But they said nothing, lest they give away their position. This was a negotiation that had the potential to get them an excellent product, and they wanted to be sure they extracted the best possible pricing and terms from me.

"We think your price is too high." They thought my terms were too steep too. I wanted them to pay me up front! Three or four cigarettes had already been smoked during this meeting—the smoke blown in my face, and I'm certain, sticking to my clothes.

"I'll give you 60 days," I said, surprising them with my generous broadening in terms. "And I'll put an incentive program together for your accounts and your salespeople. Free cases for key accounts, and commission-style dollars to your people." I was no expert, but I could talk the talk. I knew exactly which buttons to push, and was waiting for my opening.

"Lock it down." My sales advisor whispers in my ear, after working through some math. "You still net 25 percent after incentives." That's what I was waiting for. Too many young product launchers make the mistake of over-promoting and poorly managing cash flow and I was determined to be different.

"I can reduce the price by 50 cents if you'll pick up the pallet now. I've got another meeting to get to, and can't dance with you guys all night." And we shook on it.

That was how I launched my product in New York City, and probably one of the most exciting moments of my life.

Hopefully, through this book, we'll do the same for you.

Why I Wrote This Book

Each year, more than 10,000 new products are brought to market. Most product launchers are doing so for the first time or are new to the industries in which they launch the product. These launchers approach the market as bold consumers with a great idea. They start with what they want to make and go from there. Some of them are creating a product for themselves, others just for fun. They work really hard designing, making, producing a product, and then work really hard to sell it. They pour their soul and all their money into their precious product.

Sometimes these product launchers are able to make it, and sometimes they aren't. Sometimes people like the product, and sometimes they don't. Every now and then, one or two products are able to make local or regional successes for themselves. The majority of the time, they fail. In fact, over 90 percent of them go out of business in a few years.

Why does this happen? It isn't because product launchers are not intelligent or not hard-working, or because the products they created were bad or faulty. It is most likely because they didn't plan properly, didn't design the product as well as they could, and didn't go to market in the most effective way. They didn't know who the key players were, so they spread their resources thin trying to work on everything, and trying to spend money on all different channels. By the time they are done, they are exhausted from doing everything at once, and undercapitalized because they spent money in 10 different directions. When there are as many product launches in the market as there are, a competitor that runs a little better quickly outpaces them and they soon fall away.

What would have happened if they had a road map to a successful product launch? How might they have made decisions differently if they had insight from of the leading players in the industry? How might their inspiration be directed if they could hear firsthand from those who had walked in the footsteps before them?

If you think that you want to create a product and set it free to wander store shelves and win the hearts of consumers—you're in the right place. If you've got a great idea or two that you've always wanted to put in front of customers but never knew how, this book will guide you along. If you've got a product in front of you, but don't quite know how to make the system work for you, I'll show you what I and my friends have learned in our adventures launching products.

If you follow the suggestions and examples in this book, not only will your product become a reality, but you will put it on at least one shelf. If you play your cards correctly, you can put it on dozens of shelves and get it into the hands of a few consumers.

Who Am I?

Like you, I once had the dream to put my product in front of my consumer. Unlike many similar products that tried and failed to share my shelf, I did it. I did it on a modest budget, which would have undoubtedly been smaller had I read this book first. While I might be something of an expert now, I certainly was not when I got started.

My first business was a web and graphics design firm, when I learned that aesthetics and design can be the difference between a successful concept and one that fails. As a brand manager for a hugely successful energy drink brand, I learned that successful brands can be built on a single well-designed product, and that execution is everything. As a management consultant, I learned that relationships are as important to the sale as the idea and the execution, and that clean communications make the difference between confusion and understanding.

Along the way, I did a smattering of other things. I bartended at a happening spot in New York City—the kind of place where people start dancing on the bar after midnight. I taught calculus. I got an engineering degree with honors from Columbia University. I ran a pet store. I hosted art gallery openings. Through all of these jobs I learned a very important thing—all people are emotionally driven, which counterintuitively allows well-run businesses to be math and data-driven.

Naïvely thinking I understood the world, I tried starting a few companies. I got together with a group of guys to create a new kind of entertainment company: The World Breakdancing League, which would turn breakdancing into a competitive league sport. Together we created an innovative and entertaining product that was far ahead of its time, organized teams, and got in front of the guys at major sporting arenas and TV networks. But within a few years, our product (that is, a team) fell apart. Lesson learned—work harder to make sure the founding team is on the same page. Tired of the entertainment space, where success was dictated by power brokers and luck, I realized that I had always wanted to create real, tangible products that people could hold and love. As such, I created Star Power, an exotic fruit juices company, and the first to bottle and sell starfruit juice in the United States. In the same vein, I also created V Bespoke, a new kind of custom-tailored clothing concept that would try to change the way people thought about clothing retail.

Creating something new is never easy or straightforward; when I started, I only knew that I had a great idea for a product and that I would do whatever it took to get it in front of my customer. I would let them decide my fate—be it success or failure.

And I struggled. I screwed up my product before I got it right. I spent a long time building a supply chain I ended up not using. I botched sales. I made some enemies. I made some great friends and also learned some tough lessons from people I should not have trusted. I wasted time and capital chasing opportunities written in the fog.

Many of the examples in this book draw from the experiences I had trying to get my product from concept to shelf quickly, effectively, and on a dime. If I am able to help *you* save a few weeks of your valuable time, a few thousand dollars, or raising capital that you don't need yet in exchange for stock that you don't yet want to lose, then I've done my job. You can thank me later.

Why You Should Keep Reading . . .

In this book, we're going to talk about how to test and learn, how to build great relationships in your industry, and ultimately, how to turn your dream product into a company that is lucrative and satisfying to you, and valuable to your customer.

Every step of the way, I'm going to refer to a methodical approach to new relationships and key decisions we'll call the *Inspired Method.* It involves a mutually exclusive, comprehensively exhaustive (MECE) analysis of key players, key variables, and key details—or as close as we can get with information readily available—to help make fully informed decisions.

This might mean doing a lot of research before selecting an important business partner, studying an industry (or many industries) before building product features, or surveying lots of customers before deciding on a marketing approach. It definitely means getting a ton of information from vendors before negotiating with them, and ultimately, to be sure that the end product and the end process that we build is optimal and sustainable.

I'm going to start at the top, assuming that you have not yet come up with the product you want to launch, that you have no specialized skills, and that you want to spend as little money and time as possible. I'll assume that you don't necessarily have a great sense of what makes a product cool, and that you may not even have any personal skills that are going to help you manufacture or sell your product. If you've got some of this in your bag, great. If not—that's okay, too.

While doing so, I'm going to arm you with scripts and documents that I've used and share interviews with some of the coolest people I've met. Along the way, I'll give you exercises (that you really should do), ways to apply the Inspired Method, and challenges at the end of the chapter that will really make you question some of your basic assumptions of life:

- *Exercises:* Often, a chapter will dip into areas in which you will need to do homework, or tactical steps that need to be in place for you to be able to make a reasoned decision or learn more about the topic at hand. Some are more involved than others, and I insist that each time one of these pops up, make the time to do it. Otherwise, you risk being uninformed and potentially missing opportunities.
- *Apply the Inspired/Launch Method:* As you continue reading, you will see this method pop up on occasion as we work through the various challenges you might face as you create and launch your product. While difficult, and sometimes time intensive, launching a product on your own is very feasible and something you will absolutely accomplish by the time you finish this book. Taking the time to make calculated decisions through the Inspired Method is sure to save you both headache and cash, allowing you the space to enjoy your accomplishment.
- *Challenges:* Launching a product is going to take all your resolve. At the end of each chapter, I'll challenge you to do something that might take you just a little bit out of your comfort zone. They might be fun to read, but I'll suggest you actually go do them.

If you take the time to listen to this advice and do these exercises, application methods, and challenges, I'm confident that you will find yourself putting a product on the shelf in no time. Plus, you will save as much time, money, and heartache as possible. Trust me—this is insight that I wish I had known when starting my project.

Author's Note

I've opted to use the subject "he" throughout the text. This is not intended as sexist language, but simply for grammar consistency.

Let's Get Started

In *Inspired! Take Your Product Dream from Concept to Shelf,* I'm going to *inspire* you come up with your concept and then we'll move through developing your concept and cobbling together a prototype. Once

Table P.1: Eight-Month Target Product Launch Time Line

	Month 0	Month 1	Month 2	Month 3	Month 4	Month 5	Month 6	Month 7	Month 8
Ideation	Think about what you want to make								
Concept Testing		Figure out what's going to work							
Prototyping				Hold it in your hand.					
Supply Chain Plan						Build team and source suppliers			
Sales and Production								Sell it. Make it. Repeat.	
Planning for success			Business Planning		Startup Financing		Set and achieve milestones		

you know exactly what you need, we'll start thinking about the supply chain—who's going to make it, who's going to buy it, and how you get your stuff from factory to retailer. We're going to be thinking about our customer the whole time, why they need our product, and how best to communicate that to them. We'll also learn how to launch a web site and a blog, and discover some interesting marketing ideas. As we push through the sell, we'll make sure we've got the right team around us, a way to get capital, and an airtight plan for growth. In Table P.1, I suggest an eight-month plan that takes us through this entire process so that you can take your product from idea to shelf.

If all of this seems looks like a lot of work, don't feel daunted. We're going to get a lot of help, meet some interesting people, outsource the difficult work to the experts, and build a product and company that we can be truly proud of.

To make your job easier, I've put up some materials and documents on the website at www.wiley.com/go/venkatraman. Its all material I've used (some of it more than once) to help get an idea off the ground. Consider it my gift to you for checking out my book.

You are about to embark on the most fulfilling journey of your life. Let's get started.

Acknowledgments

First and foremost, I want to thank my mother and father for encouraging me unconditionally during my formative years to believe that anything is possible, and my brother for challenging me when it was not. Without you, I might not have dared.

I want to thank my friends for their curious spectatorship and sustained support in my various projects, and my braintrust for their constructive devil's advocacy. Without you, I might never have taken the plunge.

I have a special thanks for my friend Nikhil Gutha for believing in my book strongly enough to introduce me to the team at John Wiley & Sons, and to Pamela Van Geissen, my editor, for her passionate endorsement that got the green light. Without you, I might never have become an author.

Thanks of course to the editing, copywriting, business, and literary talents at John Wiley & Sons for helping me to take a cool concept and make a finished book. Without you, my product might not shine as brightly on its shelf.

Finally, thanks to you, my reader, not for just reading my book, but to take the gentle push it offers to create your dreams and live an inspired life.

PHASE I

DEVELOPMENT

CHAPTER 1

Develop the Idea

Nations may rise and fall, but an idea lives on. Ideas have endurance without death.

—John F. Kennedy

The path to being a product creator starts with wanting more. Wanting more satisfaction out of our work, more control over our time, or more money. It grows with curiosity. Curiosity about what happens outside our cubicle, away from our desk, and elsewhere in society. Curiosity about what is really possible, and what we are really capable of. These emotions ignite with a spark. A light bulb goes off in our heads. Suddenly, we have an idea that might help or entertain people. The idea refines itself and takes the shape of a product: an object that holds the power to simultaneously solve a problem and make money.

The new shoes you want to make for style or comfort, the new snack you want to make for taste and health, the new toy you want to make for decoration and entertainment—are all within reach. Every successful product around you started as a concept, many of them created and brought to market by people just like you.

Whether you want to rescue yourself from unemployment (or from employment), see your ideas come to life, or find a way to help and entertain the people around you, creating and developing your product idea can help make that happen.

Overview

Before we get into the longer discussion of creating and selling your product, let's start with the definition of *product*. It is, admittedly, a bit of a catchall. When we use it in this book, a product is an item that is packaged and labeled for sale. It could be on a shelf in a brick and mortar retailer, or it could be for sale online. It is probably labeled with a UPC code. It is a standardized and producible object. It is scalable, salable, and tangible.

In general, the products business is a crowded, competitive space. It can be complex because of the multiple moving touch points between you and your customer and daunting in the scope of events that you will need to manage.

Starting slow, thinking through investments, and trying to spend as little capital as we initially can, we build this complexity piece by piece, only engaging new players once we know what their role will be. For example, although you can make your formula in your kitchen or at your desk, you will eventually benefit from a supplier to create and pack your product. Although you can sell your product on your web site or in your living room, you will eventually need a network of brokers, distributors, and retailers to really scale. Each of these players comes with trade-offs—their own set of intricacies, rules, expectations, and best practices. These reasons (and not always a quality of the product itself) are why the failure rate on new product introductions, especially by new or inexperienced companies is more than 90 percent.

However, with this book in hand, you will be armed with the kind of knowledge most product entrepreneurs don't have, and you should be well prepared to penetrate a notoriously thorny world. And why not?—established products bring with them a lucrative and long-term revenue stream. In the case of a sale, a very favorable valuation, often four to six times revenue. That means if you are able to work your way up to, for example, $1 million in revenue for the year, you could sell your company for $4 million to $6 million.

An established product is also a direct line to customers, and is a way to communicate a message unlike any other channel. Success can bring the ability to affect society and tackle social problems, as well as personal recognition and empowerment. That next great idea that you're sitting on is a lottery ticket that lets you pick the numbers as they roll.

The successful products company understands branding, marketing, design, and the messages that matter to their customer. It also understand their partners and suppliers, and build great relationships. Getting through retailers involves street level sales, incentives and promotions, support, and exclusivity. It is nearly impossible for one person to do alone and part-time, but not at all unachievable to leverage your available labor if planned properly.

I did it. And I'm going to show you how.

Keep in mind that even a cleverly engineered supply chain is not enough. The products business is capital intensive. Your manufacturer is going to have minimum production volumes that could be in the truckloads. This book will walk through some negotiation strategies that work, but keep in mind that you will likely have to finance your first order alone. Production should not occupy your whole wallet either, as sales and marketing expenses should be in the plan as well. Although this book will focus on getting your concept to a shelf, every product entrepreneur should have more than a cursory understanding of the costs involved.

Start with Yourself

You are special, but not unique. The experiences and insight that you have developed over the course of your life are yours, but likely similar to a larger group of people. In addition, it is likely that the things you need are commonly needed by your group. Perhaps you already know what kind of product you want to make. Perhaps you even have an idea of what it would look like and what features you would like it to have. Then again, you may have picked up this book exactly to get that kind of inspiration.

Ideas are fluid things—they can change shapes in your head and be very slippery to nail down, even when you think you have a pretty solid concept. For many people I know, this is a big stumbling block—you cannot very well act on a concept and bring it to life without putting it on paper in a way that lets you understand yourself better. A mind map is one tool that enables you to lay out an idea in all its interconnected glory.

How do you create and use a mind map? Stephen Zhu, vice president and co-founder of XMind, recently launched a digital product called XMind in China. It's mind-mapping software—and to create it, Stephen had to become something of a mind-mapping expert. He says the best way to mind map, if there is such a thing, is to proceed without limitations. Let the creative sparkle work out first, then organize your thoughts, and finally format the map so that it's easy to refer back to.

I have found that XMind is easy to use. It helps to clarify your thinking by offering a digital place to vent. But the biggest mistake I've seen people make is to get caught up in the organization and formatting of the process before all their ideas get out. Don't let that happen to you.

The first exercise in this chapter will get you started on laying out all your random thoughts about your concept. Don't worry too much about whether it makes sense or where it goes; just get into the concept map and lay everything out. Take a peek at Figure 1.1 to see how I did.

Depending on your area of interest, expertise, or skill, you might choose one industry and category in which to launch your product. For example, in looking at my mind map, I might realize that I have some consulting skills and really want to help small businesses, or that I know many young professionals and have always wanted to create electronics. If you don't already have a product in mind, selecting this type of segment from your network and the industry you want to play in could be the most influential decisions you make. (We will get into this in Chapter 2, and will start industry selection in the next exercise.)

When you haven't yet found inspiration in a current product, see if you can identify a customer you have access to. Are you part of a group of people who share a hobby or passion? Most of us are, even if we don't think of it that way. If you work in an office, everyone there has that in common with you. If you are a member of a gym or play a sport, those are both groups of people who share a very specific pastime. Even seasonal hobbies like snowboarding the winter or jogging in the spring can come with large groups of people who are all interested in similar things. Once you figure out where that group of people is for you, start figuring out what they need. Loiter and talk to people in your gym, join a runners' club, poll people in your social group about what they might need.

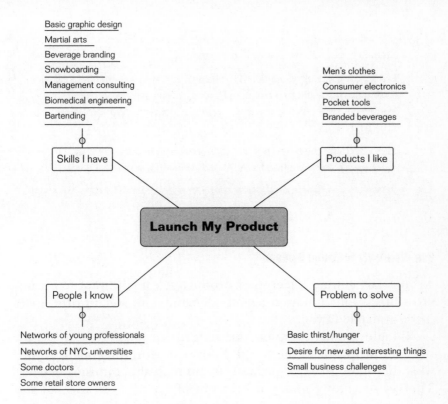

Basic graphic design
Martial arts
Beverage branding
Snowboarding
Management consulting
Biomedical engineering
Bartending

Men's clothes
Consumer electronics
Pocket tools
Branded beverages

Skills I have

Products I like

Launch My Product

People I know

Problem to solve

Networks of young professionals
Networks of NYC universities
Some doctors
Some retail store owners

Basic thirst/hunger
Desire for new and interesting things
Small business challenges

Figure 1.1 Launch My Product—Sample Mind Map

Exercise: Mind Mapping

Before you read any further, grab a pencil and try this exercise. Let's map out your interests and skills in a quick diagram that could help you get thinking about what you bring to the table.

Put your product in the middle (if you know what it is, great; if not, don't worry) and list around it all the things about you that could help. Skills you have either from hobbies or past work count, as do the people (both individuals and social groups) that you know. Also, think a bit about why people want this product—what problem do you want to solve for them that will make them want to purchase this from you?

Now, look back at your map. How many of your own skills and experiences seem apropos to your product idea? Depending on your personal and professional background, you may have a lot of content to learn. The product launchers I've met fall into one of two categories:

1. Professionals with decades of relevant industry experience who are flexing the full might of a platinum Rolodex to get their product out.
2. People who are chasing a passion without substantial work experience in their field.

I happen to be the latter, but am not necessarily endorsing either.
By the way, if you wanted to try XMind, check out www.xmind.net/.

Use Web Tools to Gauge Demand

As you start getting a feel for a product you might want to create, cross-check your intuition against demand with some of the tools made available to you.

Google Trends channels the zeitgeist of arguably the biggest demand processor in the world. Every moment, someone is typing what they want into Google, and we can read about it using Trends. The key to getting usable insight out of Trends is to test not the name or category of your potential product, but the question key-words that your customers might be thinking about.

When I was trying to come up with my product, I went to Trends to see how some of my different proposed selling points stacked up. I wanted my product to be a starfruit juice (based some-what on some antioxidant reading I had been doing at the time), but a quick test on Trends confirmed that people were not really searching for starfruit. They didn't know about it yet. People *were* frequently and reliably searching for antioxidants and Vitamin C, however. While this does not necessarily mean they want to buy them, it's definitely an indicator of demand. They had recently been much more likely than in the past to be searching for super-fruits. And this was not only true in the United States but in many major markets around the world. Given that my juice was going to be rich in antioxidants and Vitamin C, and was itself a superfruit, I was feeling confident that my product had merit, and in my ability to capture some web traffic.

Exercise: Break It Down

Before we get into the real nuts and bolts of your project, do you already have an inkling of what category or product type you want to work on? Using only your gut feel, look at Table 1.1 and cross off all the categories that you *don't* want to create a product in. Circle the ones you might be interested in.

Table 1.1: Product Categories

Product Category	Product Type	Super Type	Types of Products
Automotive Parts	Specialized	Hardgood	Parts, Tools & Equipment, Accessories
Baby Food and Supplies	Food/Bev/Chem	Consumable	Nursery, Feeding, Foods
Baby Supplies	Specialized	Hardgood	Nursery, Feeding, Gear
Beauty	Food/Bev/Chem	Consumable	Fragrance, Skin and Hair Care, Bath—high-end brands sold in department stores
Books	Specialized	Content	Books, Calendars, Card Decks
Camera & Photo	Electronics	Hardgood	Digital Cameras, Camcorders, Telescopes
Cell Phones	Electronics	Hardgood	Phones
Cell Phone Accessories	Electronics	Hardgood	Fashion Accessories, Batteries
Clothing & Accessories	Fashion	Hardgood	Outerwear, Athletic Wear, Innerwear, Belts, Handbags, Wallets, Sunglasses
Collectibles	Entertainment	Hardgood	Coins, Stamps, Cards
Consumer Electronics	Electronics	Hardgood	TVs, CD Players, Car Audio, GPS

(continued)

Exercise: Break It Down *(continued)*

Product Category	Product Type	Super Type	Types of Products
DVDs and Videos	Entertainment	Content	Movies and TV shows, Blu-Ray
Furniture	Specialized	Hardgood	Indoor Furniture
Gourmet Foods	Food/Bev/Chem	Consumable	Meat & Seafood, Chocolate, Desserts, Gift Baskets
Grocery	Food/Bev/Chem	Consumable	Beverages, Breakfast, Canned Goods, Household Supplies, Snacks
Health & Personal Care	Food/Bev/Chem	Consumable	First Aid, Nutrition, Hair Removal, Beauty brands sold in discount stores or drugstores
Home & Garden	Small Items	Hardgood	Furniture, Bedding, Vacuums, Pet Supplies, Gardening Tools
Home Improvement	Specialized	Hardgood	Hand & Power Tools, Landscaping, Plumbing, Electrical, Building Materials, Appliance Parts
Industrial & Scientific	Specialized	Hardgood	Lab Equipment & Supplies, Industrial Materials, Power Transmission and Electronic Components, Sanitation, & Janitorial Supplies
Jewelry	Fashion	Hardgood	All Jewelry
Kitchen	Small Items	Hardgood	Small Appliances, Utensils, Tableware

Motorcycle & ATV Parts	Specialized	Hardgood	Parts, Tools & Equipment, Accessories
Music	Entertainment	Content	CDs, Cassettes, Vinyl
Musical Instruments	Specialized	Hardgood	Guitars, Orchestra, Recording Equipment
Office Supplies	Small Items	Consumable	Pens, Pencils, Stationery, Paper, Supplies
Personal Computers	Electronics	Hardgood	Desktops, Laptops, Drives, Storage
Pet Food	Food/Bev/Chem	Consumable	Dog, Cat, Fish Food
Pet Supplies	Small Items	Hardgood	Pet Supplies
Shoes	Fashion	Hardgood	Shoes, Boots, Sandals, Slippers
Software	Electronics	Hardgood	Business, Media Education, Utility, Security, and Children's Software
Sporting Goods	Specialized	Hardgood	Sports Equipment, Bikes, Tents, Fan Gear
Toys & Games	Entertainment	Hardgood	Infant & Preschool, Learning & Exploration Toys, Ride-ons, Action Figures, Dolls, Board Games, Arts & Crafts, Hobbies, Furniture
Video Games	Entertainment	Content	Console Games, PC Games, and Accessories
Watches	Specialized	Hardgood	All Watches
Video Gaming Hardware	Electronics	Hardgood	Game Consoles

Source: Amazon.com.

While search is one decent indicator of popularity, conversation is another. Twitter search is a quick and effective way to see what people are tweeting on a particular topic. To continue my example, I saw that many people were discussing how much they loved starfruit. It turned out that while many had not yet heard of it, there were pockets of people happily exclaiming their love for starfruit. However, for my other terms that I thought were working well on Google, a Twitter search only brought up tweets of people hawking one product or another. It seems that other savvy web marketers saw that people were searching for popular ideas and saturated the conversation with them. This is bound to happen—it takes effort to stay ahead of the wave. Also, a quick search on news and blog articles for your item or for your category will help you see what the mainstream media and experts are saying about your category. Finally, make sure you get on to Amazon and see if something like your product already exists.

Through the methods outlined here, you should get a fair sense of what the market will think of your product. The live conversations you have will let you get personal opinions from those near you. Google will tell you what people are looking for, and a Twitter search will let you in on what they're discussing. The experts can tell you whether they agree with Google Trends, synthesis of the information. When you put that all together, you should have an idea of your product's features and selling points, even if you don't know what it is yet.

Indeed, for a while, I had not yet planned a specific beverage, and wanted to learn more about the category. I realized that my product would be all-natural or organic, it would need to emphasize the Vitamin C, and downplay the sugar content. With that in mind, I could get to the details later.

Exercise: What's Out There?

Whether or not you have a product in mind yet, get on to your computer and check out what kind of demand exists for your (or any) product.

- Google Trends: google.com/trends
- Twitter Search: search.twitter.com/
- News and Blog Search: news.google.com/ and blogsearch.google.com/
- Amazon Product Search: amazon.com/
- Bonus: USPTO Search: Look for TESS on uspto.gov/

Capture Inspiration

Now that you have a sense of the demand for a product, search yourself for inspiration. Even a product in high demand will take passion, hard work, and investment. Let's be sure to find something you can stand behind. What needs do you want to fill? Perhaps you wish to bring people a product they enjoy at a better price and compete on value. Perhaps you wish to create a more premium product and offer it to customers who value it. Perhaps you wish to create a new category and decide for yourself what is or is not premium.

Just as important as the product you are trying to produce is your rationale for doing so. Do you want to have your own business to run, or do you just want to be an inventor? Do you want to build a global brand or do you want to create a local cash cow? Do you want to create a lean and invisible machine, or a vehicle to employ all your family members as it brings you fame and fortune?

The important decision that you will likely need to make soonest is whether you want to create a source of immediate income, or create something valuable but perhaps not high income that you could sell one day for a large sum of money.

There are benefits to both, of course, but it can be challenging to do both at the same time. If you are keeping the money you make as income, it cannot also be reinvested into your company to create a growing brand. There are limitations as well—if you don't have the preexisting savings or the access to capital to create a longer-term brand, you have to play the brutal Venture Capital game much earlier on.

Carter Reum, the founder of Veev (the first and best Açai spirit) and a guy whose opinion I respect tremendously put it really well:

> With only a few exceptions, if you are starting your business without extensive access to capital ($2 to $5 million), then plan your business as a cash flow generator until you are a bit larger, a bit more experienced, and better networked with that kind of capital source. If you have the access to capital and the stomach to suffer through the downtimes that will inevitably strike, then strive to build a brand that you can one day sell to make a tidy sum.
>
> Otherwise, you will spend not enough capital to build a brand, and won't have enough cash flow left to live on. Projects fail when the founder runs out of cash because he didn't plan his venture properly at the beginning.

A Note on Wealth

Most of us aren't sitting on millions of dollars. If you are, call me. I have an investment idea for you. (Just kidding.) Many of us don't have personal access to those who do either. For now, don't worry about it. We are each richer than we think and better connected than we know—and will learn firsthand how a great idea can open doors.

We're going to spend more time on fundraising and financing in Chapter 8. For now, just keep in mind that while starting a business can be bootstrapped, running a products business nearly always requires capital.

A Difficult Game

There are many challenges standing between you and product success celebrity. While launching a product is not at all impossible, I would be remiss if I did not point out the difficulties up front.

Failure Rate: In this past year, entrepreneurs like you will have brought thousands of new products to market. In a few years, less than 10 percent will survive. Sometimes products fail because they are not that good, but often it is because the product is poorly planned and inadequately merchandised. With the help of this book, we'll get you moving with a sound strategy, an innovative product, and attractive packaging. Whether or not your business implodes after that will be less a matter of chance and more a reflection of your foresight and tenacity.

Supply Risk: Whether your product is filtered water or remote-controlled toy cars, you will need to get your raw material from somewhere. You'll buy these raw materials from a supplier, and once you do, you'll depend on that supplier to reliably get you the same stuff from then on. You depend on a supplier and face risks on the availability, quality, and price of your product, as well as logistical risks around shipping time and changing policy (that is, minimum orders, or input commodity price). You might also face political risks in the country you choose suppliers from as well as currency fluctuations (if it's somewhere other than your home country). There are various strategies for mitigating supply risk, and we'll cover them together. However, keep in mind that just because you finally get your product right, you cannot forget about your suppliers or their businesses.

Aesthetic Challenges: Creating a great product alone is not enough. The marketplace is crowded with applicants for the Next Big Thing, and you're no different (yet). A customer selecting a product for the first time does not know anything yet about your brand. Your product needs to speak for itself, it needs to stand out while being consistent, grab attention without being garish, and communicate a message that is in line with yours—all without you there. When bootstrapping a product launch, it is likely that you will not initially have the luxury of creating several packages and testing them. You are going to have to trust yourself and create something, and hope that the market finds it appealing. We'll discuss later in this book a few good ways to get the most out of your packaging and hopefully save you some painful iteration.

Tiered Customer Challenges: When your product and package are shiny and complete, you now have to get them in front of your customer. While you could set up a stand in front of your house or a web site and sell directly to your customer, chances are that you want to experience the scale that comes with the products business. There is a vast network of power players between you and your consumer and you will have to meet them all. Across the country, millions of consumers go to thousands of stores to shop. These stores (or accounts, for you) in turn buy their goods from hundreds of distributors, who deliver all sorts of product to them. These distributors have the ability to buy your product, and put you in front of many more customers than you could hope to find on your own. Together, we will show them that your product is an innovative new product and has promises of success.

Cash Flow Challenges: Before tremendous demand pulls your product off a store's shelves, this business is a sales-heavy business. Just as hard as you sell to your distributor, they have to sell to their accounts (with your help). The accounts then use every trick they have to sell hard to customers, as your newer product carries higher margins for them. Since everyone thinks they are doing each other a service by taking on this risk, there are typically credit terms all along the way. Accounts won't pay your distributor for 30 days, and in turn, the distributor will try not to pay you for 30 days. In practice, these 30 days easily stretch out to 45 or 60 days. This means if you don't have a few months of working capital and inventory to match, you might have to dig deep into the pockets of yourself and others to stay afloat while waiting for payment.

Brand Inertia: Brands don't build themselves. Not only will you have to have clever marketing and advertising, but presence and consistency across an ever-growing number of channels. You will have to compete not only for your customer's dollars, but their thoughts as well. Through the merits of your product and your message, you will need to guide your product from unknown to one that people demand. It can take time, resources, and skillful execution of a valuable product to get a brand moving. If you're a lone entrepreneur like I was when starting Star Power, this will likely be your largest challenge. However, with a good product, patience, and the resilience not to quit when the going gets slow, you too, will build yourself a thriving young brand.

If you are not yet dissuaded, then perhaps you'll succeed in this business.

Overcoming Obstacles

In addition to some of the general challenges of a products business, there are a few important considerations for the product itself. If the product is wrong, even flawless business execution may not save you.

Too many product launchers that I know make the same mistakes again and again. While it is possible for some of the bigger products companies around to make these errors and get away with it, it's tougher for the startup because we are often under much more scrutiny and much higher expectation from our customer. In my experience, I've seen three main reasons that products fail—besides just being run poorly.

Failure Reason 1—A Cool, but Useless Product: If the inspiration for your product started as "Wouldn't it be really cool if . . ." think really carefully about your market. Would it be really cool to have a piece of computer hardware that allowed you to share smells around the Web, or allowed users to smell web sites? Yes, it could be cool, but it would be very expensive and you would get assaulted by smells from your computer. If you product doesn't seem to solve a pressing issue, it probably doesn't.

Failure Reason 2—An Insignificant Market: Then there are products so specialized that they cater to a market of one. There are times when a product launcher looks at his customer and fits his needs too closely. I once wanted to design a new kind of wallet designed to fit over a Moleskine notebook. While the exercise started innocently enough, I soon started imagining it especially for people who carry it everywhere and also carry very little in their wallet, who are in the college student life stage, and are hipsters. They also need to like the product at all. This customer probably exists, but there aren't going to be enough to even pay your mobile phone bill. As you think through your target audience, make sure it's sizable enough to contribute a meaningful amount of money toward your retirement fund.

Failure Reason 3—An Nonproducible Product: Finally, there is the *nonproducible* product. There are some parts too intricate for a mold to make, and some products too complex for people to assemble. While it is often tough to know this ahead of time, pay attention to the part of the next chapter in which we seek feedback and partnerships from manufacturing facilities for your product. If they say it can't be done, or that it will be prohibitively expensive to do, you probably should start over.

That said, there are many challenges that look and feel like the preceding that can ultimately be overcome. A cool product might

> ### Apply the Inspired Launch Method
>
> 1. List: Collect a list as exhaustive as possible within a reasonable time frame. First make a list of industries you might want to be in and then of the products you might want to make.
> 2. Test: Test the options against your skills and vision, and your customers' and partners' feedback.
> 3. Cull: Eliminate options that aren't going to work. Be aggressive.
> 4. Pick and negotiate—Select the one to three items that make the most sense, while taking steps to reduce costs and improve benefits if possible.
> 5. Adapt: As circumstances change, repeat steps 1 to 4.

sell with great marketing, a tiny market might expand with a few tweaks to the product, and an nonproducible item in one factory might already be flying down the conveyor in another.

Summary

It's time to get excited. All of us have had that aha moment when we just knew that we have just had a brilliant idea. We're going to nail it down, map it out, understand ourselves, and make it happen. We're going to be purposeful and avoid common pitfalls by making careful, calculated, well-informed decisions. And along the way, we're also going to have a blast while we make some money.

> ### ❗ Challenge: Inner Strength
>
> Go to your local shopping mall (or any other reasonably popular place). As you walk around, get firm eye contact with strangers walking around the mall. Don't break eye contact until they do. Don't make any silly faces (unless you feel like it) and feel free to get into conversations with people you see. Don't get put off if people look funnily at you.
>
> Over the course of one to two hours, see how many people you can engage in this little game, and see how many you are able to keep eye contact with until they drop it.

It's natural to feel a bit uneasy, as society has conditioned us into a certain type of meekness. This kind of uneasiness can trigger our most instinctual fight-or-flight response. Please don't get into any fights—this exercise is meant to simulate the feeling you are going to have each time you meet with someone you need—whether a potential partner, investor, or customer (all of whom are nearly the same thing for a start-up product).

CHAPTER

2

Create Your Product

When I consider my opportunities, I marvel at my moderation.
—Lord Clive of India

It was a cold and blustery afternoon up in the mountains in the eastern United States. I had just returned from a six-hour snowboarding adventure that had left me both fatigued and invigorated. While Frosted Flakes–sized snow was falling all around us, I was enjoying a hot shower in a comfortable mountain cabin.

As I wipe the steam from the mirror, a health food magazine in the corner of the room catches my eye. I'm a guy who loves to eat—and at this point in my life, I had been voraciously trying all sorts of food in an effort to find more interesting, healthier, more exciting options. The cover story was about new exotic fruits, and how some of these were considerably healthier for us than others: A concept that had recently been coined as *superfruits*. The article discussed everything from lychee to prickly pear to the goji berry, but what caught my eye was a reference to a fascinating fruit called the starfruit. It was shaped literally like a star, rich in antioxidants and Vitamin C, low in sugar, and wildly exotic. I had never heard of it before, which only intrigued me more.

When I returned from the mountains I went in search of this fruit. While you might now be able to walk into any supermarket and pick one up, at the time this fruit was still relatively undiscovered, and the only place I could get it was at a farmers' market that only met once in two weeks about two hours away. I bit into it and was blown away. A bouquet of flavors flooded my mouth: sweet, tart, fruity, floral, tropical, earthy, juicy, smooth. I had to have more. I bought a whole box of them and ate them slowly over the next week. The combination of the taste, benefits, and exotic appeal was overwhelming. I knew I had something.

Personally, I had wanted to create a food product for a while, mainly to see what it took. Although I had some experience as a brand manager for a massively successful energy drink company, I didn't have any experience in creating or selling a product of my own. Although I considered myself reasonably successful within my own right, I did not have the volume of resources to throw at a project like developing a mass-consumed product.

However, that wasn't going to stop me. It isn't going to stop you either. I tested a ton of ways to create, develop, and ultimately launch a consumer product on a very tight budget, and through this book, we'll cover all of them. But first, let's figure out what your product is.

So What's It Going to Be?

On average, people spend 10 days researching for a washing machine purchase but only a few hours before investing the same amount in a company stock. I've seen people make nearly instant gut-level decisions about a product they want to create without really deconstructing the space first. This product could become your full-time business and your legacy—shouldn't you do some homework?

Before I get involved in a project, whether for myself or as an advisor, I want to know how the idea and the creator fit with what has been proven to work in the category. While of course there are often disruptive innovations from underdog founders, I think a good sanity check up front can help save months of effort that eventually conclude that the founders or the idea are fundamentally misfit from the category.

Some of this comes down to the personalities at the table. The mother-daughter team of Myers and Briggs created a test (based loosely on the theories of the psychologist Carl Jung) that helps people assess how they might behave in different situations. They

Who's Making Moves? Lefties or Righties?

We each have our own way to approach situations and make decisions. Myers and Briggs say there are 16 different personality types.

I'm an INTP. What are you?

Check out your personality type on myersbriggs.org/

used this during World War II to help place people in different factories. We're going to use it today to help you pick the right arena for your product. Certain types of people fit well in one industry better than in others. But there are 16 different Myers-Briggs personality types—and it would take a longer book than this one to review each of their pros and cons to every industry. I'm going to make this simpler for you—I think it is useful enough for now to think about two personality types: the Rational and the Creative. The Rational is a left-brained, analytical, calculating thinker. The Creative is a right-brained, emotional, gut-feeling decider. Most of us are one or the other, some us are both.

Now, take a look at some of the founders of both the large leaders and hot start-ups in the business category you think you would like to work within. Are they run by righties or lefties?

For now, don't worry as much about whether you fit the mold or not. I don't believe that any of us are held back by the way we happen to think. However, the way you think may say a lot about the kind of work you'll enjoy. Do we really want to get you involved in a project you won't enjoy?

Maybe. But only if everything else lines up, and with fully knowing that we're going to be uncomfortable for a while. The second step is to do some industry homework before getting too deep into the product you want to make.

The current trends in products like yours should be studied at least briefly, especially to see whether the bulk of successful new products tend to have technical or compositional innovations. What are some of the fun new products that you see succeeding in your category? If your inspiration came from fascination with an existing product, or perhaps the dollar signs of a big buyout, what did the company really do? Innovations are typically one of two kinds: technical or compositional.

Technical innovations often have to do with the scientific development of something new in the category. The innovator needs to be well versed and sometimes formally trained and immersed in the field to be able to understand these innovations, let alone come up with them. For example, better electronics are sometimes driven by the development of faster chips. New foods and beverages are driven by the chemistry behind new kinds of vitamins or sweeteners. New toys are sometimes (these days) driven by advances in production and software.

While not impossible, you will be at a disadvantage if you try to learn a whole new field for the sake of a product. Remember that as we speak, a thousand other people just had a similar idea. Many of them have deep industry experience, relevant academic training, and a high-powered network. You could swim upstream for a while, but are much better off acquiring a partner who can help you do some heavy lifting.

In other cases, innovations can be compositional: old components put together in new and interesting ways. In many ways, an insightful consumer can be better equipped for compositional innovation than the experts because they are more in touch with what they want. Also, the barriers are lower, since it will be easier to understand the concepts and components of something than it will to fully learn the underlying science.

For example, if you were creating a beverage, you might look at what's popular and say you wanted to create a cola. Or you could look at what the growing trend is and decide to create a fruit juice or an infused water. Both would sell for a similar price, and probably cost a similar amount to make. However, the cola is a product of fairly advanced food chemistry, while with a bit of research and

To Learn or to Recruit?

While it's up to you on how much learning you're willing take on before you think of yourself as an expert on a particular topic, it's probably somewhere between a week of research and an eight-year PhD. Our goal, however, is to launch a product now. So I'll pose it to you—if it's going to take more time and money to learn the art than it will to find a partner, I would probably look for a partner.

trial and error, you could probably create a juice or water product more cheaply.

As another example, if you were creating an electronic device, perhaps like a new kind of keyboard lamp for computers (something I'd like to do—I think there's space in the market here) you might need to learn enough about electricity to put a power source to a light bulb, but this would be different from trying to create an integrated circuit with everything on it. That takes special equipment, and more specialized knowledge than I could build in a week or so.

My point is while nothing is out of your reach, some things are closer than others, and with everything else being equal, it may make sense to grasp for the quick hits first.

Personal Predilection

At this point you should have an idea of the industry you want to play in and maybe even a mild idea of what kind of product to create. If you are choosing from a few different options as recommended in the last chapter, there are a few key things to consider: your personal network, your skills, and your interests as they pertain to market trends.

Your Personal Network

You would be surprised that your own personal network—the people you know—could be really helpful in getting your product out. If you initially think that you don't really have a special network, you're not alone. When I first got started launching my product, I didn't know anyone. I had a few close friends, none of whom were real experts in anything or who had beverage business connections. Then, one of my close friends gave me a nugget of great advice that sounds like common sense in retrospect. "It is nearly impossible not to have access to anyone," he said. "Even if you are not great friends with them, you could easily get in contact with the owners or managers of the stores you shop at, the restaurants you eat in, and other local businesses. Even an imperfect retailer will probably let you give away some free products to his customers if you wanted to get a reaction."

It turns out that he was right.

My network was better than I thought, and plenty of the people around me believed in me and wanted to help. All of the successful people around you got to where they are through the help of people who wanted to see them succeed. Be confident—you are just as likely to be doing a favor to someone you allow to experience your product as they are by allowing you to test them.

I had a few sources of people that nearly all of us have access to and I got started by putting my message out there in front of them. I reached back to my college alumni center, and polled them for alums either in my chosen industry or something close by. I asked all of my friends and acquaintances to check their circles for anyone who might be helpful, and I used the Web's social networks to blast out ideas and see what came back. I recommend you do the same—it will cost you nothing but an hour or so of your time.

Reach Out to Your Network

When reaching out to your network, you need to be prepared to trust your product. So, the first thing I did was capture my message in a quick, digestible bites. Feel free to recycle any portion of this:

> Hello, I am developing an innovative new _____(type of)_____ product. It is _____(adjective)_____, and _____(describe function)_____. I think people will really like it and I am willing to do what it takes to make it successful. However, before I walk down that path, I'm trying to reach out to everyone I know and learn a little bit more from experts in the industry so that I'm more likely to really get something valuable for everyone. Are you an expert? Do you know anyone who is? If so, I would like to take you or them out to lunch and ask a few quick questions. I would really appreciate any direction at all. Please reply with an e-mail to _____(e-mail address)_____.

While I don't think the exact wording is important, I tested a few different versions of that message, and it's what seemed to work best. It's written with the humility of a listening student, rather than the knowing arrogance of an ignoramus. It doesn't ask for anything for free (info in exchange for lunch!), and it has a specified next step (send me an e-mail!). Please note that I only used this message for blasting out. I wrote more personal e-mails to people I wanted to reach out to personally.

Even if you're not fully set on what your product is going to be, write an e-mail like the one I offer here (or copy mine) and send it out to everyone you know. You might feel like you're spamming your friends, but this isn't something we're going to do again. You might be surprised at how helpful and connected you really are when asking a specific question about something you are working on. Entrepreneurs love to see each other succeed, so if you do know anyone who might be able to help you even a little, it's more than likely that they will get back to you.

What is your existing skill set? What do you already know how to do? Whether you're a lifelong corporate stiff, a green college student or somewhere in between, you have real life experiences that you can reflect on in your pursuit to launch your perfect product. You may have a tactical skill, such as sales, marketing, or some kind of artisanship. You might have an operational skill like accounting, recruiting, and project management. You could have technical skills like coding or design. Any and all of these should be considered when creating your product. By harnessing your skills, not only will you feel more comfortable when facing difficulty, your product will be better for it.

My observation has been that there are four broad areas of skill that are needed to get a new product off the ground. You are going to need all of them so be honest with yourself about which ones you have, which ones you can build, and which probably need you to bring someone onto your team.

1. *Idea generation*: You might already have a sense for what your product is, and perhaps you have a skill in being creative, creating new ideas, free-thinking, or pulling ideas from people around you. No matter where inspiration comes from—one thing is for sure: you can't launch your product if you don't know what it is.

2. *Concept definition and product development*: Once we've got a small list of ideas, we've got to pick one to run with. We need to fill in some of the details that weren't thought through in the idea phase, and see how different features affect real considerations like cost and availability. Defining the concept is also going to include tracking down the different vendors you're going to need (don't worry, we cover that in more detail later) as well as making nitty-gritty decisions on things like design and color and detail. If you have skills in building new relationships, breaking ambiguous ideas down into concrete steps, and clear communication, you'll find all of them in use here.

3. *Sales and business development*: Once you've got your idea really nailed down, you need to shop it around and build the sales channels you'll use to get to market. You are either going to need skills in making cold calls (don't get nervous, we'll walk through that together) or in using your contacts to create warm calls. You are going to need to stay calm in the hot seat,

negotiate pricing for yourself, and understand a contract. I'll get you through the basics on all of these, but each deal is different, and here it will help to either have the skill or find the right people (like an attorney) to guide you through it.

4. *Project execution:* Finally, once all the talking is done, we're going to need to run the machine and create some product! This skill is mostly planning and project management. You will have to stay on top of aggressive time lines—your vendors won't do that for you—and keep all your participants on the same page.

Feeling daunted yet? Don't. Although it's true that there are a ton of different skills involved in creating a product, you're one step ahead of the game because you're holding this book. I've captured the lessons learned (often the hard way) by many people who have brought all different types of products to market. While there may be some areas in which you feel like you have a lot to learn or need someone to help you—you will at least know what to do.

Exercise: Talent Allocation

Write down your own top skill, one you want to learn, and one you want to give to a partner or employee. Don't worry yet if you don't know who they are. Knowing up front explicitly what parts of this product you're going to take on and which ones you're going to save will go a long way to helping you focus as we get further into your product.

Your Interests as They Pertain to Market Trends

Finally, sometimes what you like (your interests) and what is getting popular with your customers (trends) are more important than who or what you know. If you really love shoes, or if you sense that canned soup is about to take off—then by all means go for it, even if you don't initially know what you're doing. Sometimes the most interesting trends are hiding under something completely misleading—the guys who made the most reliable money in the 1849 gold rush were the guys selling the shovels—not the ones digging for gold.[1]

Ultimately, your product needs to be something you are excited and passionate about, or else you will be much more likely to drop it when you face resistance from friends, family, customers, and others. No matter how brilliant your idea, there is nearly always going to be someone who disagrees. So, just as with all things, before you embark on the journey of developing a product, take the care to invest emotionally in it.

Making It Happen

Before I started any of the ideas I've taken to market, I laid out and carefully considered my options. I had lots of ideas. In fact, to this day I keep a little notebook on me at all times just to capture the (sometimes great, sometimes harebrained) ideas that I come up with. I'm not some special ideator either—it's amazing how many ideas a normal guy like me can come up with when you always have a notebook on hand to write them down. My pocket Moleskine is never far away, and as a result, I can write down even fleeting thoughts for review later. However, having ideas, even lots of them, is not sufficient to create a product. I had to pick one and focus on it. So will you. After I gave myself a few days to think really hard about what I wanted to do, I collected my favorite prospects and sat down to cross all but one off my list.

My list of four ideas at the time.

1. A new kind of computer mouse: I had a crazy idea for a travel mouse that had an interesting way to always keep its battery charged.
2. An innovative clothing line: I had some designs for menswear and accessories that I'd never seen in stores near me.

Apply the Inspired Method

1. List
2. Test
3. Cull
4. Pick
5. Adapt

3. Some home aquarium decorations: I thought I had a solution to the extremely pressing problem of how to properly decorate a fish tank.
4. A new kind of exotic fruit juice: I had an interesting, new, and pretty compelling idea for a juice made 100 percent from starfruit.

Each one was innovative in an important way for its category, and solved a problem that I believed to be meaningful to the right customer.

So I set off to test and cull down my list. At the time, I had no assistant, no experts on hand, and certainly not this handbook. I had to do my own work, my own research and feel my way out—often during the hours of midnight and 2 A.M. because of the 80-hour-per-week job I held at the time. I hope to spare you the time, trouble, and uncertainty.

1. ~~A new kind of computer mouse~~: First, I knew no one who worked with mice and nothing about electronic hardware. Also, there were a ton of nearly identical products on the market, and every single one had a big company behind it. If no other entrepreneurs are coming to the party, did I really want to take the plunge into a field in which I would have a steep and immediate learning curve? Not so much.
2. ~~An innovative clothing line~~: I knew a few smaller fashion designers and fashion industry folks, but not in a way that I thought meaningful to starting a business. I had dabbled in garment construction, but was by no means an artisan. That was a skill that took years, and I learned that everyone in fashion thinks their stuff is innovative. Go figure. The worst part was—everything is different: design is an art after all, and resulting customer behavior is intensely subjective.
3. ~~Home aquarium hobby products~~: I used to manage a large and successful pet store, and knew a lot about underwater pet companies, publications, web communities, and unanswered issues. I was also an avid customer of my industry with a massive and well-populated fish tank that I am very proud of. (Yes—I'm a huge dork, but dorky businesses are often best able to corner a niche. What are you dorky about? We all are; don't be shy.) The industry was also growing as more urban

apartment dwellers turned to pet options other than cats and dogs. After a bit of exploration, I ultimately found that it would be too difficult to create, and for a market too small. In addition, I realized that I was much more passionate and prepared for a beverage product.

4. *Exotic new beverage:* I knew a bit about beverages because I had worked as a brand manager for a successful beverage company, and had consulted for some large retail and consumer products companies. I didn't know much about the start-up, but felt confident of my knowledge and network in the field generally.

I was down to an idea that I was pretty pumped about. You might be able to get right down to one or two, or you may realize that you've eliminated all your options. Either way, it's nothing to worry about. When I show you some of the ways to launch a product quickly, while running very lean, you might want to try to launch all your ideas (and you should) but I fully endorse a measured, calculated, fully committed approach your first few times around.

If you're really having trouble, go back to some of the ideas from the introduction—search the people around you for the problems that bother them, especially if they are all members of the same club or activity. What do they consume, and why isn't it good enough? Keep iterating here until you have one to three solid concepts that you are willing to test.

Lay Out the Idea . . . and Be Ready to Adapt It to Your Customer

Now it's time to get tactical about your product. After taking your ego out of the picture, your product is probably functionally one of the following:

- An existing product that is being fit to an innovative circumstance.
- Existing parts fit together in an innovative way.
- A mix of new and innovative parts that come together or something entirely new altogether.

An Existing Product in a New Circumstance

Most new bottled water products are an example of an existing product in a new market, package, or for a new customer. For many consumers, water is both ubiquitous and free, but each year, dozens of companies come out with bottled water products that each offers some sort of soft innovation—perhaps a superior water source, functional additives, funky packaging, or cause-based marketing. Some do none of those, and offer filtered municipal water in a bottle. These sorts of products are often the easiest for an aspiring product launcher to create; however, they will also face the steepest competition since barriers to entry and core intellectual property is low.

Parts of an Existing Product Put Together in a New Way

One step higher on the innovation chain is something like a granola product. While each of the ingredients is probably known, a new product could put them together in different ways to in an innovative assembly of existing parts. While it's true that oats, raisins, and a variety of other granola ingredients may already exist, it's possible that you could combine them in a new and interesting way. Perhaps in a blend that emphasizes a low fat, antioxidant, and great-tasting formula. This new product could have a meaningful differentiation from other similar products to the right customer. While anyone could do the same, your own formula is protected unless you disclose it to anyone.

Many ideas demand at least a few innovative parts—most new electronics products require at least a few, but the rest is an assembly of existing parts. Plenty of these come out each year, and are typically nuanced improvements or modification to an existing product, and remain compatible with the accessories of another. Most products that are inspired by another, already existing product tend to fall into this bucket. If your idea is, for example, to create a better, more interesting mobile phone, it is likely that you could use many of the components that went into it, rather than reinventing them all.

A Mix of New and Existing Parts

Finally, there are occasionally things that really are entirely new. Because of the nature of the problem being solved and the knowledge of the creator, these products have all new components or packaging. Any product that is building on a cutting edge technology or requires custom-molded, custom-made components falls in to this category.

When developing my juice, I found it very difficult to pinpoint exactly what my innovation was. I knew in my heart that I was bringing something genuinely different to my customers, but had trouble communicating exactly what that was. I reached out to my advisors and friends to get their thoughts, since I was so wrapped up in my project that I found it difficult to form an unbiased view myself.

One of my advisors was my old boss, and had a great mind for business and a great eye for a cool concept. He told me that my juice idea was really only a novel combination of existing parts. I was not going to invent any of the fruits or ingredients, and certainly not the bottle. I would only combine them in a way that I thought meaningfully innovative. It sounds really simple to write it down now and even simpler to read it—but at the time it was a breakthrough. When I thought I was creating something new, the steps to creating it seemed daunting. When I found that all my parts existed, all I needed to do was go get the pieces and put them together.

If your product is something you can assemble yourself, let's go out and buy the parts. If this is true, however, you should really ask yourself whether your product is truly a *product*. Unless there is something differentiated about your assembly technique or some other real barrier to entry, the door stays open for a potential copycat competitor. If you don't know yet how exactly to build your product, or what your barriers are, that's okay—we'll get there.

Product Basis

Why are you the right person to launch this product? It may seem like an odd or even intrusive question at first, but one that you will certainly be asked by big customers, investors, and (often most influentially) your friends. For example, if your product is a toy or contains electronics, or is a snack food or a piece of clothing—what skill, background, or interest of yours makes you more qualified than someone else in the world who may be mulling a similar idea? Out of the thousands of start-ups that are forming right now, why will you survive? The answer is typically one of four options: it is because you have the knowledge, experience, skill, or guts to make it happen.

If you studied the subject in school, or worked in the field, it is likely that you have more knowledge expertise than a layperson, especially with regard to technical skills that may be required to construct a more complex product. Knowledge about a field will come with some exposure to products that have succeeded in the past and what sorts of problems exist, as well as who some of the big names are.

Most products are part of a landscape of many closely knit categories, and it helps a lot to have a depth-of-industry expertise and understand how the major players work. For example, from an outsider's perspective, an item like a beverage might seem like a singular category; after all, a customer can go to a store and choose to buy whatever he wants from a collection of products that seems to be in all stores. However, there is a lot of difference between carbonated soft drinks, energy drinks, fruit juices, natural foods juices, flavored waters, and waters; and that is not a complete list and is only the nonalcoholic ones. It will be helpful to know firsthand how the product flows, specific companies that make it work, and how your own knowledge fits with the ins and outs of the nuances of this space. Compared to a layperson, an industry veteran will be much better positioned to launch a product.

Knowledge and experience alone won't ensure that we're able to work. They usually correlate, however, to functional capabilities. I personally believe that nearly any skill is transferable. If you've worked in sales or accounting or marketing or any function (if you've ever been employed, you've worked in some function), you should bring that with you to your product. An experienced salesperson should develop a product she can sell, and an experienced writer or artist can create great materials. No matter what your function, it enables you in some way, and articulating that will separate you from someone without those skills.

Last but not least, if you're even reading this book, chances are that you're thinking seriously about making something happen for yourself. While launching a product is not necessarily expensive or risky, there is certainly a sense of passion and faith needed to see past the gamble. While I show you some of the ways I stretched a dollar, and some of the ways I tried to make a safety net for myself, and how I automated a lot of the things I had to do, there are things that will cost money and problems that take time to solve. While some things can be expected, you will likely be faced with some surprise challenges while on your path. We'll face them together, and with some planning, be ready for what's around the corner. If you agree, this alone lifts you head and shoulders above the person who does not really wish to launch a product, as most people are more content to buy them. Hopefully, we can get you ready to launch a product that you are passionate about, and help you build a successful company that will pay immense personal, social, and yes, financial dividends.

While I firmly believe that we can successfully tackle the launch of any kind of product, I'll also acknowledge that each of us is better qualified for some than others. After all, if two people each start a similar project at the same time (as is often the case—nearly no idea is unique), the one with a better background for the project will spend less time learning through error, and ultimately execute better. The market is easily big enough for all of our projects, however. I think, therefore, that while we should first and foremost create a product that we are inspired by and can stand behind, we'll also be much better off if we do so in a domain where we are able to leverage knowledge, skills, and contacts that we already have.

Before I started creating my product, I took inventory of myself. I had some knowledge, but only from chemistry courses taken in college. However, I had not studied anything more directly applicable to this project. I had worked as a brand manager for massively successful energy drink—which left me with some insight into how the market worked, how customers connected with a brand, and what kinds of marketing techniques I might try. I had done work for several large consumer products companies as a management consultant, which gave me some perspective into global supply chain structure, but not nearly as hands-on as I would need. Lastly, I knew I wanted to see what it took to make this happen. However, I had no contacts, no real plan on how to get this done, and no access to testing channels.

At this point, I did not know yet exactly what my product was going to be—only that I wanted to create something interesting, new, and of some value to my customers. I wanted it to be a premium juice, but did not yet know exactly what went into it. I would recruit experts in my industry to do that.

What Is It?

After people hear your concept, and vet your personal credentials, they will probably want to hear more about what exactly it is that you've come up with. While you could try to explain further, it's far more professional, and often more effective to have a document that lucidly lays out the spec. Initially, this document will not be the tidiest, most perfectly formatted bit of art, but it should get the point across such that a customer understands what this is and why he needs it, and a manufacturer understands how she will help you make it.

A good product spec should have a visual and a written component to it: the visual can be drawings, digital renderings, or photographs, and the written component should lay out some pithy details about specific attributes. Ideally, you are able to fit this onto the front of a normal piece of paper, so that sharing it is easy. At the very least, your visuals should have a few angles, and if it's a complex assembly, an exploded view that shows all (or all the important) components that go into it. The description should have essential dimensions, and all the key descriptors of the product.

If you are not a great artist, that's okay. For now, it is more important to be able to get the idea across. The better you are able to do that, the easier it will be for a more talented artist to create a drawing or rendering for you. Your descriptions may not be perfect or in the right format for the industry, but if it is understandable, you can easily fix that as well. In fact, I often prefer to create a very minimal spec, and have the experts flesh it out for me, at no charge. How do I do that, you ask? We get to that in a moment.

The Factory: To Use or Not to Use?

Depending on what kind of product yours is (see the preceding), it may or may not make sense to find a manufacturer. In the long run, it nearly always makes sense—but a skilled entrepreneur can launch a product from his living room if he is driven and able.

Typically, products that are assemblies can be put together by a reasonably handy individual. If all the parts are available, you can get them. If any of them are not, you can have just those made. Putting it together yourself will take more time, but will save your wallet from some of the baggage that comes with a production facility or partner. However, if your product is either fully existing or fully new, it will often make sense to work with a factory. In the first case, you should find a factory that already produces this product, and simply pick some up. In the second, you will need a facility to partner with you so that your new item can be made at all. The exception is, of course, if you are an artisan and able to produce more complicated items on your own, or if you have the tenacity to attempt it and learn anyway.

For example, to take the bottled water story further, water exists, is freely available, and that's no secret. However, it's a massive industry because people continue to find ways to apply a nuance, create new packages, and sell it a bit better. In this case, you are probably better off buying bottled water wholesale, and putting your efforts on the differentiation. I'll tell you like my advisor told me: If you're spending time at the faucet filling bottles, you can't be putting together a good business at the same time.

Meanwhile, as part of an elite getaway camp, a snack food entrepreneur becomes a philanthropist. My buddy was on a college trip to Scotland, where he and a friend had the idea to create a self-sustaining charity. They chose paper as their product, with the rationale that it was a product that was essential to businesses. As they did their customer research, they learned more that most businesses would be willing to change their paper supplier if they knew that the proceeds were going to a good cause. Starting from scratch, they found a supplier who believed in their cause—using the proceeds to finance schools and education for poor communities. They put the same paper that their supplier had into a new package with their brand, and worked through their community in Scotland and through their network in London. In just a few months, they had built a thriving product business.

We used granola as an example of an innovative assembly of existing parts, but another great example here is bead jewelry. Anyone can get beads and wire, but sometimes, creations are different and interesting enough that people are compelled to buy them. The product here is differentiated through the artistic vision of the

What Makes People Successful?

People don't take action because they don't know what is achievable. Believing you can do it is most of the battle. You just need the confidence to know it. Not just think it—but really *know* it. Lots of entrepreneurs can serve a customer. Not all can break new ground.

Doing something truly genuine is the scariest thing in the world, because you can't follow in the comfortable footsteps of others, and you can't lean on anyone else for support.

The trade-off is not just success, but the personal satisfaction of having conquered the tallest mountain in the world—the human spirit itself.

creator, which is a great value when properly channeled. In small batches, you would be better off building something like this on your own, rather than giving that job to a producer. As particular styles gain popularity, you make seek the scale afforded by a producer, but that is a very good problem to have.

Most consumer packaged goods fall into the category of having one or two new things and having everything else as borrowed pieces. For example, a beverage concept could put a mix of existing fruit juices along with novel vitamin fortifications into a new product. Most of the inputs for this item can be simply purchased, except the one or two new parts that we can work with a producer to make for us. The initial product can still be made without a factory. But if your product is a hardgood, it also may fall into this category, and your new components may not be able to be fabricated by hand. In this case, you are going to need a production facility from the beginning.

One of my own products, Star Power starfruit juice, is an example of this. The full product includes a bottle and a fruit juice that already existed but my specific formula was brand new, as was the label and packaging. This kind of product is great for someone who wants to learn from the successes of existing products and leverage the infrastructure that they already have. I was able to create something new and interesting and use the factories that already bottle products seamlessly. Had I created something much more technically innovative, my start-up would have been both more difficult and more expensive.

If your product is in a niche or technical space, it's more likely that your innovations will themselves be more technical. For example, you could have a new kind of metal part that needs to be machined from scratch, or a bit of glasswork that needs to be blown or formed on its own. It is difficult to generalize about this kind of product because it really could be anything that requires fresh construction from raw materials because nothing about it can be purchased or proxied from existing parts. In these cases, unless you are equipped to produce it yourself, you are probably going to need a facility that makes somewhat similar items and can be fitted to produce what you need.

A young man in Scandinavia had a dream to create something entirely new that was both its own product as well as an enabler for the ideas of others. He wanted to create more than a product—a platform that others like him could use as a springboard as well. Cubis makes packages that are entirely innovative for the category. Each of their parts is made from scratch, from fresh molds in a factory that had never created such a thing before. Erik Nilsson's idea was born at a bar, as he imagined creating a product that would allow beverage companies to have a truly differentiated appearance—a bottle that looked like a cube instead of the more typical cylinder. After having a designer friend flesh out the concept, they tested the concept with potential customers, including some big manufacturers that they got to through their network and through cold calls. Even though they faced an uphill battle trying to make and launch the product, they found the perfect manufacturer and got to market.

In addition to the preceding, and often overlooked by aspiring product designers, is the value of your time. While you may not think it costs anything to produce your own items, the time you spend producing rather than developing business or marketing can often be far more costly to a business. Regardless of whether you think you should or should not seek production, I think it is a worthwhile exercise to see what the costs would be, so that you can make an informed decision.

The Friendly Supplier Review

Unless you're an expert, and even if you are, you probably don't know all your options when it comes to production. If you're like me, you don't even have a fleshed-out design at this stage. I prefer to harness the power of the market to make these decisions and work easier. I use a three-pronged approach when seeking suppliers and information for an industry I'm unfamiliar with: I try to speak to competitors, known experts, and supplier aggregators.

As part of talking to many different companies, we're going to build up a mountain of correspondence and build up an increasingly complex calendar of meeting times with everyone.

Speak to Competitors

First of all, nearly every established competitor in your industry is producing product somewhere, and you might be surprised to hear that not all of them own their facilities. If they are public companies, many will disclose their supply partners in annual or quarterly filings. Alternatively, the suppliers may be using the competitor's names as qualifications in their own quest for new customers. A bit of shrewd web research with this in mind should dig up some names.

While competitors are not going to want to give you information about their business and how to compete, nearly all of them will share their story with an aspiring entrepreneur like themselves. Put yourself in their position—if someone who reminded you of a younger or less-experienced version of yourself reached out to you, wouldn't you share your story? While some companies might be hesitant to share their secret sauce with you, most will readily share some of their big mistakes—arguably more valuable to you anyway.

Sample Note to Competitors   What follows is a letter that I've successfully used in the past to encourage a discussion with people I admire in an industry I am considering getting involved in. In addition to sending it to people you can think of, you should also send it to contacts and companies that you discover in your research. Even though I call it my "Dear Competitor" letter, keep in mind that we don't yet have a product, and so we are not yet competing with him. We're just looking for information. Be sure to replace the underlined terms with your own specifics.

> *Dear _Competitor_,*
>
> *I hope this message finds you well. Let me start by telling you that I'm a big fan of _your widget_. I've bought many of them and they rock.*
>
> *Right now, I do most of my work in _my industry_, but I am really very interested in _your industry_. Specifically, I'm curious about how your company got its start as well as where you think you're going. My thought is that _your industry_ is pointed up because of rising consumer awareness of _key selling point_.*
>
> *I would love to get a moment of your time so I could ask a question or two of you. Would you be available at _time 1, time 2, or time 3_ this week? I can call you at your convenience.*
>
> *Best regards,*
> *Vik*

Note that the point of this note is to be genuine, disarming, educated, and then to inspire action. You're more likely to get a response if the e-mail is pointed at a specific person, rather than a company black hole (info@, questions@, and other central e-mails). Also, I've found that these kinds of e-mails are best sent around 1:00 to 1:30 P.M., when people have just finished lunch and are in a generally good mood.

If you think this seems like a lot of effort, keep in mind that in this situation, we haven't offered any incentive for them to get back to us. I have tried offering gift cards to people who called me back or filled out a questionnaire, but realized that my hit rate was nearly as good if I just called them instead.

When you follow up your e-mail with a phone call, get to the point right away. What you really want to know is what they think the one to three things they do that make them successful, as well as the one to three things that they regret or mistakes they've made. Both of those are unlikely to be available through common web searches. After that, I'll get off the phone after asking if I could call back later if I had more questions. I won't announce myself as a competitor just yet—not to be sneaky, but until we know exactly what our product is, we don't yet know that we're a competitor. There's still time for that.

A little while later, perhaps in a week or two, I'll follow up with a message sharing some of what I've learned from all of these discussions, and ask for a chance to meet for lunch or for coffee, and in person, will share my story about how I'm planning a business that is not really directly competing with them. I've never had anyone get upset at this point—in fact, it is usually the opposite response: entrepreneurs love to help one another. I've done the same when approached this way by people doing the same thing. I'll freely share the source of my materials, the packaging firms I use, and anything else that is asked of me—since I know others did the same for me when I was just starting.

Speak to Known Experts

You also want to talk to the experts. Every industry has veterans, and many of those veterans choose to stick around in some way. Sometimes called brokers or consultants, these guys are a rich source of experience and contacts. Some are more tight-lipped than others, and some are more understanding of a bootstrapped start-up than others. One of my personal goals is to spend as few unnecessary dollars as necessary, and while I prefer not to take on a consultant, I have in the past and will likely do so again. However, I will always discuss my product concept with these experts because their gut reactions are often loaded with insight, and a bit of genuine conversation will often be rich with information, especially if you know nothing about the industry. Besides, the good experts know that you are more likely to contract their services if they appear credible and forthcoming.

I have many "Dear Expert" letters and they are often quite different. Although similar to suppliers in that you (often) represent a potential customer, I write these letters more like the dear competitor letters. I make them a little longer, and write a bit more about my concept. In my experience, the experts that you want to talk to are very busy already, and are more likely to respond to a note from someone who is really trying to do something, rather than someone who might be a dabbler or a spammer.

I'm not going to post a sample letter here because your letters to experts really should be tailored. After all, you might get the opportunity to speak with only three to five real experts. But here are some recommendations.

- Write each one separately: Introduce yourself and let them know that you're a fan of their work.
- Don't fill the e-mail with questions: These are busy people and may not get to them all, even if they wanted to.
- Briefly explain the merits of your product and the issue you're solving.
- Focus your message around two key questions:
  1. Top line bit of advice on an issue you're having or on their area of expertise.
  2. What it takes to get a moment of their time.

Although we're writing this letter in the pursuit of information, we really want to get to a live meeting. The broader goal here is to interview the experts to get the kind of advice they have after a lifetime of making the right calls, and to get them to join or affiliate with your team to have their guidance in the future. Sometimes all you have to do is ask—that's how I got my best sales advisor to join my team.

Speak to Supplier Aggregators

Finally, I'll use or talk to supplier aggregators. Depending on your product, there may be one or many places in which suppliers congregate and seek potential customers like yourself.

One of my best-kept secrets until this chapter was written, however, is that the consulates of supplier heavy countries are terrific sources of information and recommendations. I nearly never choose

Preparing for Your Interview with an Expert

Don't walk into your interview blind. Having a crisp agenda can make the difference between an insightful discussion and a waste of time. As a bonus, showing the expert that you are thoughtful and planned can make the difference in whether or not he elects to join your team. Even though you might walk in with a list of questions, remember that a good interview is much more about listening: you'll get a much better response by knowing your goals and listening to the answers than you will by checking off a list of prepared questions.

This agenda is one that I've adapted many times for different products. Depending on the interviewee, keep questions contextual—don't ask for manufacturing advice from a marketer. If they will let you, record the conversation as well. This will free you up from taking notes and allow you to focus on the discussion.

Agenda

Product synopsis—tell a bit about your product, the problem you're solving, and yourself.

You might not have a lot of their time, so make the best of it. We want to talk to them for their perspective on what makes a product successful, what makes for good products and marketing, as well as their perspective on the industry, macro trends, and any advice they may have.

I've broken down the following questions into categories, roughly prioritized so that if you are cut off during the discussion, you still get the best advice from your expert.

THINGS TO DO, THINGS NOT TO DO

- What do you think the success stories did really well?
- Where do you think entrepreneurs stumble?

PLACES TO SPEND, PLACES NOT TO SPEND, BEST PRACTICES

- What is the single best place for a budding product company to spend capital?
- What are the top one to three wastes of time and capital?

MOTIVES

- If you could give any advice to someone considering starting a products business, what would it be?
- What do you think differentiates a successful product entrepreneur? A successful product?
- What is your favorite product of any kind? Why?

HISTORY AND TRENDS

- Where do you see the future of consumer products going? What trends interest you the most?
- If you were to design a product today, what would it be?

A Note on Company Names

For better or worse, I've seen suppliers, especially those in other countries, respond much better to an inquiry from a company than an individual. At this point you might not have a company formed, or a name decided on—that's okay.

It might feel a bit disingenuous, so I'll leave it to you to decide whether you want to make up a company name for yourself or not. As long as you ultimately intend to work with your suppliers in a way that is mutually beneficial, I see no issue with a mild fib on the current name of your company if need be.

Like my mentor told me: Until you are, act as if.

a supplier without a call to the Taiwanese, Chinese, and Indian consulates. Take the time to meet your local delegate—they will be thrilled to help you later.

The white pages or business directory is good for finding typically domestic producers. Web sites like Alibaba and Tradekey are great for finding international producers online. In addition, nearly every industry has at least one trade show at which all the players get together and see what's new. If there is one in your area, it is nearly always worth the time and effort to go and meet some of these players live.

Sample Note 1: "Dear Supplier" One-Two Punch   The following is my "Dear Supplier" one-two punch. Its two letters—the first checks for a pulse, and the second probes for information. I'll send it directly to suppliers that I find either through an aggregator or through my embassy. Often, I won't address the letter at all, and will send it through the aggregator's web site or by e-mail blindly to as many suppliers in the same category as I can. In this situation, you're the customer. They have all the right incentives to get back to you. However, since you may find a lot of suppliers who are in the category, I advocate the two-step method to immediately eliminate any fake or outdated contact information that you may find. Don't worry about the extra work involved—we're going to set up an autoresponder to handle the response.

> *Dear Supplier,*
>
> *I'm writing to you on behalf of my company. I'm looking for the specific type of component that your company makes. Our business is small but growing, and we have the need to find new suppliers for this part.*

Do you make this item? Are you interested in taking on a new customer and a growing business?

If so, please send an e-mail to
autoresponseemail@yourdomain.com.

Best,
Vik

Sample Note 2: Sent by Autoresponder The second punch, as it were, has what I call my *sneaky designer* bit. I'll sometimes be looking to flesh out a product that I don't have fully designed, specifically so that I can be sure my suppliers can make it. How better to ensure that than have them design it themselves?

Hello,

Thank you for getting back to me and expressing your interest in working with us. Our company makes fine products for customers around the world. I am looking for item 1 and item 2 for use in our product. Item 1 is for this use. And item 2 is for that use. These items need to have:
- *Black paint*
- *Stainless steel construction*
- *Feature 3*
- *Feature 4*

[Alternative 1] I don't yet have an image of the item, so would appreciate it if you could provide a design drawing for me to approve.

[Alternative 2] I have attached an image of the item I am looking for—please confirm that this makes sense to you.

The ideal supplier will not only produce a product as specified here, but they will also be able to produce item 3 and item 4 that we may need in the future.

[Option, if you have it] It will also include an image of the attached logo.

Initially, I will need to order only a small volume, perhaps 1,000 units. We want to build a long-term relationship with a reliable supplier and grow this business together.

Please respond with your minimum order, price per unit, and lead time for this product. In addition, please send samples to my attention to:
- Company name
- Address

- <u>City, State, Zip</u>
- <u>Country</u>

Best regards,
<u>*Vik*</u>

There are several goals to this exercise of finding suppliers and writing the communications. The first is to sift through a potentially huge pool of suppliers for your proposed product, and implicitly test its feasibility. By demanding free samples, you test the hunger of suppliers in this category. If all of them scoff you away, then at least you will have an idea of what will work. Usually, for inexpensive items, or those that are popular enough to have multiple strong suppliers, you will be more likely to get samples.

Also, you are encouraging multiple skilled people to send you design drawings, suggestions, improvements, and more for a product that does not yet exist. In case you have some of this stuff already, feel free to tweak the alternate entries in the preceding e-mail.

While it may be a slight fib to pose as a company bigger than you are, I don't think any harm is being done. You aren't asking anyone to break any rules, and you aren't promising anything either. You only promise potential for growth, which, let's face it, is something you can only promise yourself, too.

Exercise: Set Up an Auto Response E-Mail to Deal with Messages That You're Going to Send a Lot of

If you have not yet set up your autoresponder, we should do that now. It takes only a six steps.

1. You will first need to either use a Gmail address or sign up for auto-responding software. I suggest Gmail because it is fast and free.
2. You're also going to need a dedicated e-mail address—I suggest supplier@yourdomain.com or some other address that you know is being used to test suppliers.
3. You then go into your Gmail settings and activate a feature called "Canned Responses."
4. Take my second note, or write one like it into a blank e-mail and save it as a canned response.

(continued)

Exercise: Set Up an Auto Response E-Mail to Deal with Messages That You're Going to Send a Lot of (continued)

5. Go back into settings and create a filter.
6. If any e-mail is addressed to that e-mail address, send back the canned response.

Keep in mind that you don't need to do this, and can write personalized messages or answer them all yourself if you would like. However, your time is better spent designing your product at this stage. Using technology like this well is a great way to multiply the number of apparent people on your team.

Now it's also possible that you will get some responses for which the auto-response might be out of context or not the right response. Given that all we are looking for is supplier feedback right now, and that the suppliers are naturally incented to work with you, I tend to let myself slide on this particular detail. More than 80 percent of the auto responses should be right on the money.

After I've got a decent list of suppliers, say 10 or so, I'll set off to have a friendly discussion with them. I call this discussion friendly because I am not actively negotiating anything from them, or even asking them for anything but their opinion on the feasibility and perhaps ballpark price for a product I have specified out. Since my specs will often be rough, they will ask exactly the kinds of clarifying questions I need to improve my spec, and diligent suppliers will often respond with sophisticated visuals that are much easier for them to produce. Not for no reason—even though this is an informational conversation, I know that they are thinking about a potential new customer, and I am writing down notes on how easy they are to communicate with (especially if they are in a non-English-speaking country). I want to know how responsive they are to my questions, how clear they are in their questions, and how interested they are in talking to me, often knowing that I'm working on a cautious entrepreneur's budget ($0). I look for hints on how sophisticated they are, and how big their business is.

Many of the companies you reach overseas may end up taking longer to get back to you than planned, and even when they do, you may often face a few days' delay simply because of the time difference in when they are available to answer your messages. It is in this meantime that I give my research assistant a few assignments to better prepare me for some upcoming decisions, but I'll get to that in a minute. . . .

Bringing It Back Together

If you've done all this properly, you should have at least a few discussions with suppliers, experts, and competitors under your belt. At the end of this round of discussions, which you may be able to squeeze into a single week, you will have:

- A vastly improved spec sheet
- A bit of feedback on your idea
- An understanding of different kinds of suppliers and the kinds of products they make
- A better idea of the products landscape and categories
- A glimpse into the difference between domestic and foreign suppliers
- A list of companies you like, and often a list of companies you have not yet spoken to

Finding an Assistant

In building your product, you will also need an assistant who can help you keep it straight. A good assistant not only keeps on top of a constantly changing calendar, but also can track correspondence, organize supplier information, and check for gaps as we move along. Remember that we need to keep our eye on the bigger concepts like what the product is and how our customer gets it (and often at this early stage, are trying to balance the demands of a day job).

Work Smarter—Delegate

Don't have an assistant? It's time for you to get one. Having an assistant is not only a great way to work more efficiently, but it is also a good experience in managing someone who is doing work for you. Having people report to you at your day job, the dynamic and the incentives are very different when an individual is employed directly by you, rather than when you both share an employer. Direct reports at your day job are actually your colleagues.

When it is your own money that is going into someone else's work, you are much more likely to want to keep an eye on him, demand results, and be particular about your needs. Besides, I am not talking about an unmanageable expense—my favorite assistants work for $5 to $7 an hour.

Delegating noncore work lets you focus on your product and the business without sacrificing the details.

When seeking an assistant for the first time (which I will often do, even though I have assistants whom I have worked with and can go to if I need them) I'll usually start by posting something like the following sample note on a web site like Elance or oDesk. Although there are a lot of "virtual assistant" sites that are available now, I like these two because their market economics keep prices low, quality high, and the process ergonomic. After I get some responses to the note I will refer back to it as a test assignment for up to three potential assistants so I can intelligently choose whom I like best.

If you feel like you're sending a lot of correspondence in this chapter—you are. Here is where we're laying the foundation for much of the work we do in the upcoming chapters. Your assistant is going to help with that work. On the surface, recruiting an assistant is analogous to any other type of recruiting you may have had experience with. Make them interview and pitch themselves to you—you will get a chance to interact with them, see what they are like, and ultimately make an informed decision.

Sample Note to Assistant

I use a note like this one, called my *successful assistant* note. Even in the title, I aim to inspire applicants to show themselves as successful.

> *To the successful assistant:*
>
> *I am starting a company to create and sell super-fun, awesome* <u>*widgets*</u>. *I am looking for an executive assistant primarily to help with:*
> * *Web research*
> * *Contact lookups*
> * *Meeting scheduling*
> *The superior applicant will also have the ability to make phone calls, have excellent spoken English, and a good amount of project management expertise.*
>
> *Workload will vary, but should be limited to a few hours each week. I will always provide all the information that I have for a task, as well as specifically what I need to consider it successfully completed.*
>
> *The ideal applicant will be able to work at a competitive hourly rate, have the experience to work efficiently at tasks like those listed in this letter, and truly enjoy interacting with people and playing an important role for an aspiring product creator.*

If successful, the ideal applicant will have the chance to take on more work over time, and grow this into a long-term, stable working relationship.

The first tasks that I will have for you are:

1. *Researching the industry—who are the major players, what are their annual sales or estimates, and how long have they been around?*

2. *Researching competitors—of the major players, which ones compete most closely with my widget? Collect contact information of the most senior person possible at these companies.*

3. *Researching experts—What are some of the top blogs or sources of information for this industry? Who seems to be selling their consulting or other leadership service in this space?*

If you can, please include an answer to these items in your response.

Best,

Vik

The goal of this document is not only to get people to apply, but to get people with an interest in your subject to sell themselves to you after doing a bit of work for free. Depending on the country of origin of your favorite assistants, their rates could range from $4 to $10 an hour. If it is much higher, I would make sure they are not misunderstanding your task. Also, the country in which they live might have a limiting factor on whether they are able to place calls for you or not—you can decide later whether this is a deal breaker.

The Quiet Before the Storm

Now that you've had a chance to learn about the industry, flesh out your concept, test the market, and consider the supply chain, you should have both a well-grounded understanding of your product as well as a host of second guesses. Deciding to push forward will come with all the excitement, responsibility, and chaos of launching your product, but shutting it down now might save you a year of turmoil with a poor product. I take a moment during this quiet before the storm to reflect on some of the pressing questions at hand:

- *Is my idea a good idea?* At this point you've gotten a taste for what some industry experts and suppliers think of the idea. There is a bias here, as nearly all of these people see us as a potential customer, and are incentivized to feed us honey. In this case, if a supplier says he cannot make the product, and if an expert says there are some fundamental flaws with my design or my assumptions, I'll often put a bit more thought into this. We haven't tested the product with customers yet, but we based the product itself on what we thought was demand. The experts are not always right (that's why people like you and I exist!) but are almost always educated in their opinions.

- *Do I need a manufacturer?* I like to collect ballpark pricing and minimum order requirements from suppliers as part of the conversation. This way you know what you are saving per unit by bringing them on—after all, they are going to have greater economies of scale than you are initially. I also know what my initial investment is going to look like. A supplier that needs 100 units to be purchased is far preferable to one that needs 1,000, even if his price is a little worse. Alternatively, if the price differential is not that big, their minimum volumes are sky high, or I have the time to make the product myself, I can decide that I do not need them yet. Don't let minimum volumes scare you—we aren't going to buy anything without a solid plan first.

- *What rules do I need to follow?* Nearly every industry has regulations to follow, and it is unlikely that you will know about these at first. However, when your suppliers brag about their FDA/USDA certifications, their ISO or FCC certifications, the size of their insurance policies and more, you will start to get a feel for what people think is needed and where you need to look to learn more. The last thing you want to do is design a spectacular product and be excluded from the biggest channels because of regulations. For example, in food and beverage, if a product contains ingredients that are not FDA/USDA approved, it can only be sold as a supplement through supplement channels, rather than through mass or grocery channels. If certain hardgoods are produced in facilities that lack ISO certification, it could make a material difference in your insurance premium, and compensating by getting less insurance will similarly lock you out of the bigger channels.

- *How will I get to market?* The experts and suppliers that you speak to are more than likely to spill a bit on next steps, likely getting your product to distribution and sales channels. We're going to get to that in Chapter 6, but I like to get the gears turning early anyway.

V-Zero Prototype

It is critically important both to have skepticism about your product as well as to get over it. After tackling your fears, we're blazing a confident trail from concept to shelf. The first major milestone to nailing your concept is to actually physically make your product. Even if imperfect, a prototype will help you understand your own idea and sell it to customers. The first prototype is not really a *prototype*, as I typically reserve that word for a production version of a product. It's more of a conversational prop. If your product is a food, your V-Zero is a kitchen-produced version of the snack with whatever packaging you happened to have. If your product is a hardgood, it is whatever you can make with the materials you have—nuts, bolts, paper, tape—it doesn't matter. With a descriptive spec sheet, and a product mockup, you will have enough to further develop your idea.

With prototype in hand, talk to people. I start by talking to friends, family, and colleagues to see what they have to say. Does my product solve a problem they have? If so, how much would they imagine paying for this? If not, how can I adapt it to do so? Have they seen anything else like this?

I'll try to have such a conversation with nearly anyone whose opinion I trust, or anyone I think is a potential customer of the product. I'll show them the mockup, describe the benefits, and gauge their reaction.

Key Feature Identification

One of the main goals of talking to third parties about your product is to crystallize the things people latch on to. These are probably some of

A Note on Naysayers

Not everyone will like your product—don't take it personally. Not everyone will think you're capable of doing this—forget them. Some people might even be jealous or thrown off by your sheer audacity—Let's see how jealous we can make them through success.

On occasion, you will get a sound, constructive argument against your idea, by someone who really wants to see you succeed. Take note—you will want to address the shortcomings and talk to these people again.

the keywords, selling points, or main ingredients that customers find important or valuable in your product. Add this to what you learned from suppliers about what is most difficult or easy for them and you can start to build one of my best-kept secrets in product development—the matrix.

What is the matrix? It's a way to compare the impact of various key features and lay the groundwork for product testing. While you won't use this yet, it is something I like to have in mind before going through some of the exercises in the next few chapters.

Once I have figured out what my key features and selling points are, I compare the options two at a time to see what effect a few different options have on my selling points. The point of this exercise is not only to guide decisions we might make on the product, but also to better understand the interplay between what customers have told us they want, and what we think we want to sell.

In Table 2.1, I compare what percentage of the product could be juice (the rest water) as well as how to sweeten it. I then try to fit back what customers have told me they like about products, what their favorite products are, and what they pay for them. In my case, I had the ingredients, so I was able to mix them to see how I liked

Table 2.1: Sample Key Features Matrix

Percent Juice versus Product Sweetening	No Sweetener	Apple or Pineapple Juice Mix	Sugar or Agave Sweetener
100% juice	Cost: 7 Price: 8 Personal Taste: 8 "No added sweetener" "100% Juice"	Cost: 8 Price: 7 Personal Taste: 9 "No added sweetener" "100% Juice"	Cost: 9 Price: 9 Personal Taste: 7 "Naturally sweetened" "100% Juice"
50% juice	Cost: 4 Price: 4 Personal Taste: 4 "No added sweetener" "Contains real juice"	Cost: 5 Price: 5 Personal Taste: 6 "No added sweetener" "Contains real juice"	Cost: 6 Price: 6 Personal Taste: 5 "Naturally sweetened" "Contains real juice"
25% juice	Cost: 1 Price: 1 Personal Taste: 1 "No added sweetener" "Contains real juice"	Cost: 2 Price: 2 Personal Taste: 3 "No added sweetener" "Contains real juice"	Cost: 3 Price: 3 Personal Taste: 2 "Naturally sweetened" "Contains real juice"

them myself. I then applied rankings (1 to 9) on each variable and collected potential selling points for each product.

I did similar matrices for domestic production versus international, size of the bottle versus number in the case. Unless your idea involves a very similar product to mine, you won't be able to use any of the preceding as-is. What you should do is walk through the aisles of your favorite retailer and check out the products that look like they are doing really well. What do they have in common? Often even when products themselves claim to be quite different, they will share selling points that indicate a common consumer need. For example—foods recently started emphasizing *organic, natural,* and some other keywords that all point back toward food that is indicated to be healthier than those without the keywords. Find out what your category's killer buzzwords are and create a matrix like the one I created here that maximizes them.

Joey Allen is a guy who knows a thing or two about developing a killer product. His name is practically a buzzword itself in beverage industry circles. He works with product launchers who have a vision for a product and makes sure all the details work out. While his actual client list is a closely kept secret—part of a product developer's value is appearing as if the brand came up with the product—he and his company have had their fingers in dozens of successful products. The best part is—many product development companies do it practically free of charge.

His advice is simple: identify a large market and give them what they want. "Good product launchers don't have an opinion on the product—they just test it out and do what works." Joey emphasizes that testing is more important than surveying, since people often behave differently from the way they think they do. For example, people consistently indicate that they *want* healthy foods, but then turn around and buy soda and French fries because they like the taste.

Most categories have many companies set up to help people with vision but without technical skills to create something great. Joey says that a good product developer will follow a pretty set pattern, and should be easy to reach and easy to work with.

First and foremost (and this is the dealmaker) a good product developer will not charge money up front. This is because a good product developer knows that he can make a good product. They see themselves more like investors in the company, because over the long term, they make their money on the parts and supplies that go into the products they design. Typically, after they are done developing your product for no charge, they will want to sell you the raw materials that go into it—you shouldn't mind: this means that not only do you get your product made for no upfront cost, you don't need to worry about some of your suppliers afterward.

Full disclosure: I did not use a product company to create my product—I did it myself. Then again, I'm an outlier. If I had to do it again, I would absolutely work with a guy like Joey to make it happen. Creating a good product is possible by any of us. Creating a terrific product is in the domain of experts, and it took me a long time and much iteration to get my product right. Joey told me: "If you have a toothache—go to a dentist. If you need a product made, go to a specialist." To these guys, developing a product is easy—it's selling it that is tough.

Summary

In this chapter, we tried to get into some of the details of the product you want to create. We thought about all the opportunities in front of you, and which ones you are best suited to pursue. We reached out to a ton of people, including potential customers and an assistant. Finally, we stepped in to some of the key features of your product and sat down to create a prototype.

There is not yet a need to make firm decisions about what your product's details are going to be, but you should get an idea about how your costs and price points change with the addition or subtraction of some key features. Before you can really get your product straight, we are going to do a bit of exploration into how the channels work.

I knew I would find a way to take my product to market. With a prototype and a few suppliers in hand, step in to this adventure with the same confidence. You're going to make your concept real and put it on shelves all around you.

❗ Challenge: Seize Opportunity

While we strive to create win-win situations in our dealings, there are times when you should know to take advantages of windows of opportunities that present themselves. Try this little game to see how comfortable you are in competing for space and progress with those around you.

Go at rush hour to the commuters' hub in your area. In some places, this might be your local train station; in other places, the entrance to the highway. (Be much more cautious if you are doing this in a car). When the most people are rushing in and out of the building or the most cars getting into or out of the highway, squeeze your way in and try to make it through the crowd just a little faster than those around you. If you don't have this kind of thing nearby, a crowded bar could work as well too.

You might start to see that the natural flow of people leaves tiny, transient gaps that you can use to weave your way through the crowd. They don't last forever, so you can't think too much about whether to take them or not—just like in real life.

If this is easy for you, great. If it makes you uncomfortable, that's natural too. In launching your product, just like at rush hour, not everyone gets where they are going the fastest. People can learn to adapt to their surroundings, be courteous yet shrewd with their moves, and seize opportunities that present themselves.

3

Brand Marketing

Manufacturers have market power because they have information about a product . . . that the customer does not and cannot have, and does not need if he can trust the brand. This explains the profitability of brands.

—Peter Drucker

In the preceding chapter, we thought through our concept and started thinking about how we were going to make it. In this chapter we think less about the actual product itself, and more about the ideological package that surrounds it. Your product's brand is important because it holds the potential to communicate a lot. Tightly packed with the brand are ideas like quality, premium, exclusivity, and use. We get into these details, and discuss how a well-defined brand actually makes your product easier to develop, and conclude with some of the tools and techniques at your fingertips to create a brand-marketing strategy and share your concept.

The idea of your product is just as important as your product itself, and getting it straight will go a long way toward helping you keep your product true to vision and in selling it to your customers.

In 1997, a young man named Sidney was facing an uphill struggle. He had no one to blame, as the struggle was due to a challenge he himself had taken on. He, like you, wanted to build a successful product where there was none, and to sell a premium brand where it was believed one could not exist. His sector of the industry had been plagued with boringness since its inception. While customers expressed a need for a better product, none yet had appropriately risen to the challenge. Sidney decided to rise up, and found great success waiting for him. As you build your product, will it be casual and me-too, or remarkable and category defining?

From Cattle Brands to Car Brands

It used to be that a businessman would put his own name on a product (or literally brand his cattle with a red-hot iron) as an indication that it met his quality standards and that he stood behind it. Brands today have taken on a life of their own, and the expertise and sophistication behind the most successful brands have raised the bar for new companies just getting started. Many entrepreneurs are so seduced by the concept of their brand that they lose their product in the shuffle. History teaches us that for the most part, great brands are built by great companies selling a valuable product—it does not stand alone.

People can get carried away in the mysticism of brand equity and brand-building that they often forget the premise of a brand. At its core, it is a mark of consistency and a level of quality to simplify the decision-making process of the consumer, and drive sales for you. Indeed, luxury automakers rely on their brands to drive cars out of their dealers' lots!

A great product needs a consistent, appealing brand to carry it. While a brand is being built, it often floats on the aspirations of its founder; once built well, can provide a cushion for the aspirations of its customer, not to mention benefits to margin and customer loyalty. For me, a brand is a deep concept that concerns three major areas:

1. The product itself.
2. The representation of the company.
3. My interpretation of the company's other customers.

The Product

The brand of the product starts with all the tactical elements of the product line: things like the name of the product, the colors used,

> ### Build Platforms, Not Products
>
> When thinking about your brand, think bigger than just the product you have in your mind or in your hands right now. When the time comes, your brand should provide guidelines you can use to create your next products.

the styles of photography, design elements, fonts, packaging, and other tangible elements of presentation. If it is a food, is it for breakfast or nightlife, for work or for play, luxury or necessity?

The Representation of the Company

Second, the representation and connotation of the company matters a lot. What does your customer think when they hear your name or see the product? This is affected by elements of your marketing strategy—publicity, sponsorships, brand events, charity. It is also influenced by nuances of your messaging—what kind of language and vocabulary is used in materials, what kind of people appear in photographs, what tone, style, and interaction is had between company agents and the external world?

The Interpretation of the Company's Other Customers

Finally, the customer becomes included in the brand. Although you will initially play a big role in choosing the customers you serve, they will ultimately define your brand for you. Demographic indicators on your customer segments like their age, gender, and how urban they are will indirectly speak volumes about your product. Depending on these, the brand creator will need to make some decisions about what is important to them, their customer, and their product. Who do you want your brand to be?

Brand Pillars

When starting work on a new product, I've realized that an interesting product is helpful, but an interesting brand is *essential.* Developing a brand can be challenging regardless of what the product is. Whether your product has an innovation in chemistry, mechanics, or just plain appearance, it is going to need a message that captures what it is, why people need it, and why it is better than other items out there.

It needs to express the motivations of the company and the founder through its imagery, associations, and events that go along with it. Broadly speaking, that is your brand, and it can be a great asset for helping you sell.

Before you're selling, however, a solid brand can help guide otherwise ambiguous decisions. For example, if you were creating a series of snack bars for a brand built on value pricing, bold packaging, and community service, are you going to decide on the common ingredient, or the more expensive exotic one? On a white package or a red package? On a snowboarding trip or an afternoon at the soup kitchen for your teammates?

Designing and launching a brand is a bit like sculpture. It's an art with multiple dimensions, where decisions like appearance and price are often impossible to undo. Fortunately, however, there are some great models out there that can provide a framework on what works.

When I was building a brand for my beverage product, I wanted not only to capture the core qualities of my product—all natural, exotic, health, but also to capture my own values—social awareness, edgy events, and fun. What is your brand about? While that may seem at first like a rhetorical question, having a firm, explicit (written) brand identity is extremely helpful in making difficult decisions. It will also go a long way toward ensuring the consistency of your appearance, approach, and other specifics.

Let's take a look at some pillars of brand identity:

- Quality
- Appearance
- Availability
- Price

Quality

First, any product needs to be of suitable quality to be used by a customer. Those are the table stakes. However, a brand may require that certain aspects of quality hold up to more rigorous tests, so it can support claims it wishes to make in its marketing (or because quality in and of itself are of commensurate value to the founder or the customer). While it may sound anathema to some entrepreneurs to think they can compromise on quality, keep in mind that quality often comes at a greater cost of production. In clothing, for example, a single seam will hold two pieces of fabric together. However, many brands will double- or triple-stitch its seams to reinforce them from longer-term wear and tear in an effort to increase the build quality of their product. This makes the product more expensive to make (and hence to buy) without any real immediate benefit to the company or consumer. However, over the longer term, issues or accolades with build quality can have a tremendous impact.

While your gut response might be that your product needs to of course be of great quality, remember that quality itself is a subjective idea. If quality means that your product will last much longer than your customer is expected to use it, this *could* be considered a waste of resources, especially if this came at a higher cost. Your customer's segment will often dictate a perception of quality, since an affluent metropolitan professional is likely going to have a very different opinion on what makes a quality product and what it's worth than a less affluent, rural, blue collar worker. It isn't a matter of who is correct—they both are. The quality of a product is subject to the approval of its customers, and is often on a sliding scale with price.

Appearance

By far, however, customers have a gut reaction about your product. In the blink of an eye, long before they've heard your sales pitch. Your product needs to look *good* to succeed.

The outward appearance of the package or product is what often creates the first impression on a customer. The selection of materials, size and shape, colors, and messaging are what will shape the image of your brand in your consumer's mind. The moment they first pick up a product, a gut-level decision is made on whether they like it or not, regardless of all the marketing they may have seen. As with most brand decisions, the appearance of your product will be judged only by your customers, and with their wallets. Certain customers like a lot of education on a package, and some prefer simplicity and white space. Certain fonts or other elements may mean one thing to you, but inspire a different emotion in your customers.

The next time you're in your favorite electronics store, take a look at the difference between the appearance of products from Apple and from Microsoft. Both are massively successful, but with a very different appearance. There are years of schooling and whole companies devoted to the art and science of making products look good, but I will try to cover the basics in this book.

Availability

The next and most critical question for the entrepreneur is where the product will be available. The choice of sales channels each come with potential revenues but often hidden costs as well. Consumers can buy more of your product if it is in more of their stores—but each of those stores will look to you for support afterward. It is always the brand's job to drive customers to its channels. Also, the product's brand needs to be compatible with the retailer's and the distributor's brands as well. An upscale product may suffer in a budget retailer, and vice versa.

Over the longer term, the relative ubiquity or exclusivity of sales channels can prove to be an asset to a brand as well. Be consistent. If exclusivity is truly important to your brand, be exclusive. That means actually turning away customers or even hiding from them. Faking exclusivity will only shatter your house of mirrors. On the other hand, if you mean to be available, do your best to be in all the right places. Whatever your decision, as long as it is consistent with your brand, customers will understand.

Price

Price has unique power to dictate the perception of a brand—sometimes more than most other factors. For better or for worse, shoppers often perceive a more expensive product as better given the often-mentioned axiom that "you get what you pay for." Over time, price has become a lever that a brand can pull to test demand and perception. The intended customer plays a huge role in this decision: certain customers may often prefer a more expensive product, and certain others may often opt for a lower-priced product. Further complicating pricing is that most product businesses rely on multiple steps to market: brand sells to a distributor, who sells to a retailer, who sells finally to a consumer, each of whom needs to make a margin and have significant sway over pricing.

If all else were equal, it is simple law of economics that the product with a lower price will sell more. However, the ramifications of price point selection include your margin and the perception of your brand. While it is usually simple to decrease price, it can be complicated to increase it. How does a product launcher balance the need to maintain a margin with the need to get a new product launched? Either by pricing high and slowly lowering price while testing price points or starting low and increasing it. Both of these methods can be effective, but have their cons as well. A steadily falling price could make potential customers "wait and see" if your price is going to decrease further rather than purchasing immediately. On the other hand, if your price keeps increasing without a reasonable explanation, your customers may be left wondering what the value of your product is, if the price seems to increase unprovoked.

My preferred approach to pricing, and one that I've seen agree with many retailers (because of consumers), is to set a price point according to the market, not according to my costs. Initially, take this to mean an average price for a similar product from your competitors. I will then layer on top of this a first-time discount to allow accounts and customers a low-risk way to try me, along with a long-term pricing incentive for loyal customers. For example, when designing an entrance for Star Power, I ran a program in which an account's initial order is a buy one–get one free deal, and after that, they get a free case for every 10 cases. In this way, customers are incented to try (50 percent off the suggested price) and incented to be long-term customers (10 percent off the suggested price) while

Consumer and Retailer Incentives

Price is sometimes the quickest way to get someone to adopt a new product—and that means having promotional sales. Each time, the cost of the sale comes out of your pocket—which means each one is an investment. A discount to the consumer must be paid by us to the retailer (at retail prices), and a discount to the retailer must be paid to the distributor (at wholesale prices).

While it may sound like the two are very similar, the way they are run makes a huge difference. Incentives of any sort have an associated cost—if you want the retailer to offer a sale to customers to get them to try your product, they will want you to pay the difference at their rate. If you want the distributor to give the retailer an incentive, they will want you to pay the difference at their rate. Your customers will not want to take a hit just because you ask them to.

Given that the cost of your incentives increase the closer you get to the consumer, it may make initial sense to incent your distributor to get the product out there, while working on marketing for your consumers to buy your product off the shelves. This way, you will make the most of your dollars in terms of cost per unit.

While you could also choose not to run any discounts or incentives, you will then have a more challenging sales task before you.

still allowing me to test price sensitivity (using different sets of initial and ongoing discounts).

Brand Design: Premium and Utility

While there are many ways to break down the products and services available in the market, we choose a simple framework to help guide this chapter. While quality, design, product availability, and other metrics do differentiate a wide variety of products, these are subjective: easily disagreed upon, and not easily proven. After deciding what brand pillars your own brand is built on, we will design a brand that suits you and your product and helps you stand out from the crowd.

Price is an immediate differentiator—two similar products on the shelf can be compared penny for penny. In many cases, this is sufficient. With all else being equal, the lower-priced product will be purchased. In most categories though, all else is not equal. A product might be more expensive because it is more durable, and not just more expensive. For example: an incandescent light bulb and a fluorescent light bulb will both light up your room, and could both be just as nice, but the fluorescent will cost more because it lasts much longer. There are two key differentiators to think through about your business before designing its brand:

1. How you want your price point to compare to competitors in your category.
2. How often your product needs to be purchased by your ideal customer.

For the nature of this discussion, we have chosen durable versus consumable to help understand the differences between brands as shown in Table 3.1. Ultimately, the choice of categories is not as important to the outcome of this chapter as it is for you to understand where your product falls and what decisions you need to make as the brand's creator.

Roughly speaking, if your price is above the median price for your category, let's call it *premium;* if it is at or below, let's call it *budget.* If your product is destroyed or depleted with use, we'll call it *consumable;* if it lasts awhile longer, we'll call it *durable.*

Table 3.1: Product Categories

	Durable	Consumable
Premium	Infrequent purchase, but potentially frequent use. Relative product quality paramount. Example: Apple computers	Potentially frequent purchase. Marketing and merchandising paramount. Example: Glaceau SmartWater
Budget	Same as above with pricing paramount. Example: Vizio Electronics	Same as above with pricing paramount. Mindshare and ubiquity important as well. Example: Poland Spring Water

Consumable products could also be called consumer goods, or consumer packaged goods. Products like snacks and beverages, batteries, and soap are consumed, destroyed, or otherwise lost in the process of use. At that point, the customer needs to think about his experience with the brand and make a purchase decision on whether to get another or not. He may need to make a purchase decision multiple times over a given period. While the threshold for such a period will always be arbitrary, we'll call it one month for the purpose of this discussion. A great example is bottled water, which someone might buy daily or multiple times per day. Also, frequent purchases are made across food categories, and consumable goods of all kinds like candles (if you use them), golf balls (if you lose them), and razor blades.

Given that a customer of a frequently consumed product must make frequent purchase decisions, the brands in this space will potentially need to compete for each of these purchase decisions. Along with the fact that competitors can typically easily find each others' products, successful firms often converge on similar products as driven by demand. They also tend to be the companies that flood the ether with marketing, as purchase decisions can happen almost anywhere and at any time. Think about the number of times someone marketed a soda, beer, a bag of chips, or batteries to you, and how similar the leading products in these categories are to each other.

Durable products are often purchased for a longer term, and thus any particular product is purchased less frequently. Electronics are a good example, as are clothes, furniture, cars, and power tools.

Of course, purchase frequency ranges and can be subjective—one consumer may buy clothes once a month, another may buy nearly daily. For the purpose of our discussion here, let's consider the purchase frequency within the category, for a single stock-keeping unit (SKU), rather than your (or anyone's) personal behavior as a consumer. While you personally may buy milk only once a month, it is a fast moving, daily purchase category. In contrast, while you may buy a new phone or laptop each month, brands in those categories are typically dealing with a slower customer who only needs a new product perhaps every year.

The real decision that the entrepreneur makes is how much he wants to charge customers for the fruits of his labor. Price point comes with brand implications that make it difficult to change once it has been established.

■ ■ ■

Remember Sidney, the young man from the beginning of this chapter? He had some decisions to make about his brand, too. He wanted to break the rules of his category, and differentiate his product from so many others out there that seemed like perfect substitutes. He was trying to build success in a competitive, price-sensitive, frequently purchased category.

He decided that imported product seemed to carry more credibility in his category than the domestic stuff, so he set up a relationship with a distillery in France, and became an importer. He studied the other products on the shelf, and leveraged best practices from the wine industry—a tall, sleek glass bottle, an elegant cork, a premium look. He would make a product so refined and gorgeous that no customer would dare to compare it to the otherwise similar products next to him.

He was selling vodka. Although experts opined on the differences between vodkas, it was by its nature colorless and flavorless, and so laypeople could not usually differentiate it by taste. It was also seen as common, and participated in a strict regulatory environment that made advertising tricky. This means that not only would people not immediately believe his claims, but the wrong claim could end up costing him his company. He was stuck.

Premium Pricing

For both durable and consumable items, premium products carry a price point slightly higher or considerably higher than others in their category. They tend to support this price point by delivering value that over and above what is delivered by their competitors or separate from what is expected in their category. For example, a car could carry a premium price by having a more powerful engine and construction (by being a *better* car) or by having comfortable seats, the latest technology, and appealing design (strictly speaking, attributes external to the core function of the product).

Innovations in business model can affect premium pricing as well—recurring purchases or subscriptions are growing in popularity. Products like FRS and Mona Vie (both beverage products) have built subscription models with margins that should dwarf traditional distribution (this isn't disclosed, only my deduction based on their business). These brands use a mix of web sales, subscriptions, and multilevel interpersonal marketing to move a product. The customer makes an active decision to start a subscription, and afterward, can keep buying until they decide to cancel. A recurring purchase needs to have a brand with a recurring promise.

Pricing Consumable Premium Items The brand of a frequently purchased, premium consumable product has considerably different demands from the occasional purchase. Because of the nature of consumption, food products appear most often in this category. A consumer needs to think of your brand more often, so mindshare through the strength of your impression becomes more important. The strength of your claim as it relates to the issue being solved is most important for this group. You need to persuade your customer at every decision point—"Buy me at a higher price than those next to me. Even though they might be similar, I am delivering more value to you." One of my favorite examples in this category is Emerald Nuts, and their use of packaging, product, and clever marketing to demand an extra dollar (or more!) at the shelf.

As another example, *The Economist* is a publication that is notoriously more expensive than its weekly newsmagazine peers, and almost never offers promotional pricing. Their promise "[The] authoritative weekly newspaper focusing on international politics and business news and opinion" keeps it simple and humble (it's really closer in format to a magazine) and their content delivers on their promise to their readers.

Pricing Durable Premium Items   Durable, premium products have a slightly different angle. It can be challenging and capital intensive to build a brand for the occasional purchase, but since they tend to be more expensive, long-lasting goods, a high-quality product will reinforce your brand values throughout its life. An Alienware laptop, Bose home theater system, and a Hermes belt are all items you may buy only once every few years. However, if the consumer feels that the product is worth the premium paid, then its value is built and reinforced through each interaction.

Think about your favorite toys, electronics, and furniture—don't you like them more each time you use them? Don't you refer them to your friends and assure them that they're worth the price?

Budget Pricing

The polar opposite of premium products, budget products are typically priced below average for their category and their price point tends to be a key selling point. They will often have product features that are the most demanded, and be otherwise barebones. Don't let the name fool you—there is tremendous value locked in the budget space. In addition to many of the great private labels kept by retailers, examples include Old Spice cologne, and many products from retailers IKEA and Wal-Mart.

These businesses make reasonable promises and deliver on reasonable expectation. Their brands often emphasize values that are taken for granted in their categories, and they will often compete with each other on (apparently) nominal claims or nuances of price. They may often be the leaders of their category, or the standard. Great examples include Gap clothes, Budweiser beer, and Mars candies.

Pricing Consumable Budget Items   Budget-friendly consumer brands get the vast majority of dollars spent in the market. Your morning cereal, daily soda or bottled water, the disposable pen you write with on your sticky notes. The condiments you put on your lunch, your evening beer and the party cup you drink it in. Before you sleep, it's the toothpaste you brush with, the floss you clean with and meds you take for your muscle pain.

This is the mass market. It is full of large, experienced players who use massive economies of scale to enforce their position. While many products aspire to this, not many can start here.

Pricing Durable Budget Items Perhaps more challenging is to create an inexpensive product that is meant to last. Until recently, few companies were eager to design brands that could compete on budget prices and be hardgoods of reasonable quality. Given that durables tend to last longer, their design and construction process are more important, and the added cost tends to demand higher prices. However, given the recent advances in digital designs and globalized production, shrewd companies like Coby and Vizio have been able to sell electronics at budget prices.

Once you've decided what tier and type your product is, you need to make sure your message is clear, concise, and easily understood by your target customer. Crafting a brand is more art than science, and by making sure you have thought through the uses of your product and the customer who needs it, you should be well on your way to creating a great platform for your product.

It's All in the Name

If you've been following the chapters of this book, at this point you might have good idea of what your product is. Now it needs a name.

Sidney, our budding vodka tycoon faced this challenge as well. What could he name his company to stand out from his competitors, exude class, and validate the price point he wanted to reach? He was stumped. He wanted something that sounded refined, imported, and European. He eventually managed to come across a great name—one that would make him a billionaire.

The best names are descriptive, memorable, novel combinations of real words or novel words on their own. Inc. magazine and AOL Small Business did a quick and enlightening study of company names that came to some conclusions that are commonsensical in retrospect.[1] The best names are not only easily spelled and pronounced, but also contain an evocative quality to them that is significant for the company's mission.

Some of my favorites include:

- Amazon—a retailer so massive and diverse it's like the rainforest
- Travelocity—a travel agent that promises to be fast
- Honest Tea—a beverage that promises not to cheat you

Choose a name that is descriptive without being boring, and ideally one that does not require an explanation to get to your product. For example, you might not know what Pringles are, but you might know what PopChips are (they're popped chips).

Your name should leave room for growth too. Suppose your business is in T-shirts, and is located in Massachusetts. You could decide to name it MA shirts. This would be descriptive and concise, but what happens when you decide you want to sell sweatshirts and pants? What happens when you want to expand outside of Massachusetts, to perhaps California or the rest of the country? A better name for the company might be American Apparel (even if the founder is Canadian).

But the most important thing to remember is not to make this crucial decision yourself. The name of your product is one of the most important decisions you will make, and its effect will echo through all the rest of your branding work. It will likely play an important role in the success of your company.

Tap your customer's help in naming your product. After we figure out who your customers are, we will ask their help through surveys and tests to gauge the appeal of each of your top 10 names.

Create the Name

Shakespeare may have suggested that a rose by any other name would still smell as sweet. Your product is not a rose, though. It's something new, and the name is the first thing your new customers will read on the package. The name of the product can inspire a gut-craving or repulsion that closes or ruins the sale long before the customer has a chance to try it. Here are five steps on how to develop the name.

1. *Top 10 names:* Write down the top 10 names you would have for your product. They could be descriptive, fun, personal, and hopefully, memorable. Even if you have a name you really like, challenge yourself to come up with more. Ask friends, family, and advisors—just write them all down, and then distill the top 10.

2. *Check for trademarks:* You did hire an assistant from the previous chapter, right? Check for trademarks on all of your names on the U.S. government Patent and Trademark Office web site. You don't want to spend the time and resources building up a name only to find out you can't own it.

3. *Check for and buy web domains:* While doing Items 1 and 2, check for the availability of web domains at a registrar like godaddy.com. Keep the domain as simple as possible—it needs to be memorable, and short enough to go at the end of your email address. Just like trademarks, you don't want to prepare a product only to find that your perfect name has already been taken by a family blog or an audio-video retailer.
   a. This was a lesson I learned the hard way with one of my companies. After registering the name "Star Power," I discovered that a band by the same name had the domain name. I ended up having to take drinkstarpower.com. It worked out for me, but I learned to always secure the web domain first.

4. *Test the name:* Once you've got a few names that you like, we'll need to test them.

   In many service businesses, like consulting or law, the partners names are the firm's name. For your product, however, your company's name is also your first line of marketing. This is why we are going to test it as rigorously as we can before we settle on it.

   The first test is to get the reactions of those around you. While you may already have done this to come up with your name in the first place, we're going to get a standardized set of responses from as many of your contacts as we can to see what the prevailing thought is.

   You can do so through surveys, social networks, pay-per-click ads, and key customer interactions, but my preference is to do this through e-mail and social network platforms. Use a centralized method like Google Docs Forms. If you don't yet have an account, go to google.com/docs and sign up. It's free, and very useful.

5. *Register the name:* Incorporating a business used to be a huge hassle. Now, you can have it done in five minutes on legalzoom.com. The two major questions here are the type of business to choose and the place to incorporate it. If you think you are going to need to raise money, you should consider incorporating in Delaware, primarily because it has lenient business laws, and as a result, is a popular place to incorporate and the rules are well understood by investors. You also want a C-corp or S-corp that allows the company to issue preferred classes of shares.

Survey: Test the Name

Create a new form with a few questions that you can then blast out and hope for good responses. I like to ask a few discreet questions as well as some more open-ended ones, but never more than four or five. I've seen a good correlation between the length of a survey and how unlikely someone is to fill it out. Also, people are more likely to answer your first few questions than your later ones, so we'll prioritize the way we ask them too.

1. Would you buy a (type) product named (name)?
2. Can you tell that (name) is a kind of (product)?
3. When you see the name (name), what is the first image that comes to mind?
4. Can you suggest a better name?

I would make the first two yes-or-no questions, and the next two open-ended.

For your reference, I have included my survey here. It's brief and to the point—it got a high response rate and priceless feedback. Feel free to replace the underlined terms with your own.

1. Would you buy a fruit juice named Star Power?
2. Can you tell that Star Power is a juice or beverage?
3. When you see the name Star Power, what is the first image that comes to mind?
4. Can you suggest a better name?

If you have three names left on your list, make three versions of the survey and send them all randomly to different people. E-mail everyone in your address book, and message all of your Facebook friends. After all—what are friends for?

However, if you plan on staying local and private, the LLC structure in your home state will make filing taxes easier. Whatever you choose, I am not a business lawyer. Talk to one if you have doubts (most will let you consult with them on this at no charge).

Matching Your Product to Its Personality

Many marketers turn to the personality of the brand as an easy way to communicate its key points, and as a model to make brand decisions. A clear brand personality can save you headaches when auditing the decisions of potential partners or staff. If your brand were a person, what would he look like? Long hair or short? Clean or unkempt? Suit, T-shirt, or pants? Is he outgoing and bold, or does he attempt to fit in? Is he a rebel? Does he make friends or make fun?

It may sound silly at first to anthropomorphize your brand concept, but it will go a long way toward standardizing the decisions that ultimately add up to the idea that is your brand.

Ultimately, a brand helps a customer predict the experience he will have. Arguably more important than every other aspect of a brand is how consistently they remain across products, and even within a batch. When properly defined, a brand simplifies a purchase decision for a customer—if a brand that promises quality, design, and utility of certain levels consistently delivers to a customer and even across customers, they will come to place those attributes on the brand itself, enabling easier decisions and brand loyalty.

If appearance and quality deviate from one product to another, however, the brand's promise is diluted, and will not be built as reliably.

How well the experience fits together depends a lot on your customers and how well you understand them. Is your customer a young, outgoing, early adopter? Is he an older professional who is into health and fitness? Is he a middle-aged dad, whose main concern is his kids?

Knowing your customer, the places they shop, and the mechanics of their decisions will go a long way toward making sure your brand is relevant and effective. You otherwise risk knowing only what you get in sales reports from your distributors—that your consumer bought your item—and not know anything about why. While true clarity is tough to get over an extended supply chain, knowing that you have a clear brand and understanding your customer helps.

If that channel is convenience stores, your product needs a brief and convenient brand that makes the most of its format. If they are more likely to pick up your product in a larger shop, like a department store or a supermarket, it is more important for your brand to be loud and visible, so that customers seeking it can find it easily. Or, your customer might go mostly into niche shops like high-end fitness retailers or natural foods grocers. Authenticity will be your best friend here, and your brand needs to be sure to fit in and do so with integrity.

> ### How to Take the Biggest Brand in the World by Surprise
>
> If you're intimidated about the idea of going up against the big guys, you're not alone. They have track record, infrastructure, and capital that you probably don't have, as well as tons of people, contacts, and experience. However, when something is working well, successful companies, especially big ones, can get blindsided.
>
> When Asa Candler bought John Stith Pemberton's little beverage base chemicals company in 1888, he could not have known that a chain of events would create the biggest brand in the world. To this day, Coca-Cola makes nearly $30 billion selling nearly 400 brands around the world.
>
> In 1936, however, a smaller shop that had been operating quietly for several years considered its options, studied consumer demand, and decided on its innovation—it would sell twice as much product as the leader for the same price. At the time, it was unheard of to have a 12-ounce bottle, though we now take that for granted. Coke built a following with fountain drinks and a 6-ounce bottle. The 12-ounce bottle had a strong appeal and put Pepsi on the map.
>
> The lesson there is that a simple innovation that cost them nearly nothing (it's a tiny bit of concentrated syrup mixed with water and bubbles, after all) put them on par with a market leader and allowed the opportunity to build a sustainable advantage.

While the preceding example walked through the merchandised experience in a retail store setting, there are other channels available for a product to flow through. Since this book is about getting on the shelf, and not building broader sales, I will touch on them only briefly.

Your brand will be different if designed to be sold directly through the Web: your partnerships and web design are much more critical. Your brand will also be different if intended to be sold person-to-person in an extended distribution model. Then your brand needs to be both for a product and a business opportunity. We won't touch much on either in this book. While these methods can certainly build sales, the mass market and its retailers represent great opportunity.

And by the way, our entrepreneur, struggling to compete, was Sidney Frank, and his company was Grey Goose. And, according to *New York* magazine, he sold it to Bacardi in 2004 for $2.2 billion.[2]

Exercise: Design Your Brand

The following exercise may look like a lot to do, but I assure you that it's possible to design your brand in one day.

Why do "American Idols" always sell records? They were chosen by their fans *before* their record deal. Whenever possible, you should have your customer help you make decisions.

In this exercise, we're going to continue working on our brand. You should be close to deciding on a name, and here, we think harder about what differentiates your brand and what sort of personality you and your customers think it should have. In this exercise, we will also touch on your logo—what may be the single most important graphic for your brand, as well as your tagline, which may be your most frequently used words outside of the company name itself.

While this won't be easy up front, committing now to your brand, your image, and your presentation (through logo, name, and tagline) will go a long way toward simplifying future decisions and keeping them consistent with your goals.

- *Product type and category:* You should have this from a previous exercise.
- *Competition and competitive edge:* What are other companies, especially the market leaders, doing well? Successful competitors are a great display for customer preferences. Are your market leaders premium or budget? Selling image or benefits? What can you offer customers that is better than what the market leaders are offering?
- *Give your brand a personality:* If it were a person, what would he look like, and how would he act? If it were a product in another category, what brands would it be?
- *Mock-up logo:* Just as important as the name of your product is the logo of your company. This image will go on all your marketing, your web site, and your product. A memorable, likable logo will only help you develop the association you need to your product to help you get your message out.

  There are three broad categories that your logo could fall into: simply your company or product name, a non-text image, or a combination.

  For example: Coca-Cola has its name in a stylized script as their main logo, while Pepsi has their signature red, white, and blue globe as theirs. McDonald's has a logo that includes the signature golden arches atop a box labeled with their name.

  Without sufficient polish, your logo can detract, rather than add, legitimacy to your project, which is why I will recommend having one made by a graphic designer, if you happen not to be one. Fortunately, that is not expensive at all, as long as you have a fair idea of what you want.

(continued)

Exercise: Design Your Brand *(continued)*

At web sites like 99designs.com, talented designers dedicated to their craft can compete for your project. This means you will get to post your description and your own drawing if you have one, and see responses from multiple designers before choosing whether or not you like them.

As my advisor told me, "Having options makes for better decisions."

Go to 99designs.com now and post your project, give it a few days, and see the volume and quality of the responses you receive. It won't cost you anything unless you find one you like, in which case, you will also find a designer you can work with on the rest of the graphics you're going to need. It's win-win, really—and totally worth a few bucks.

- *Write a tagline:* Just as important as your logo is a quick description of your company and goals, often called a tagline. Perhaps the most famous example is Nike's "Just do it," but nearly every company will have a tagline that succinctly and perhaps poetically describes what they are up to. If you only had two words, how would you describe your product? Your mission?

There are probably many options and each of them is going to sound equally good. When I was creating my tagline for Star Power, I went through dozens of options before I got to my top four: Live Healthy, Live Happy, Live Better, Live Longer. When writing a tagline for my clothing company, V Bespoke, we came up with just one: "Custom clothes at rack rates." How do you select just one (and you have to choose just one) from a list of otherwise identical options?

We'll enlist the help of our customers, even if they don't know it yet. Google Adwords is a service offered by Google to serve pay-per-click (PPC) advertisements to people surfing their site. What we're going to do is create a series of PPC ads that simultaneously test the company name, domain, and tagline to help you finalize these decisions. By showing millions of web surfers different combinations of your company names, taglines, and domains, we will see which the most appealing are based on what people click on. It doesn't matter if your web site is not yet built—we really are testing customers before they even get there.

Go to google.com/adwords and sign in to your account. Create a new campaign, and then a new "Ad Group." Here, write up all the variations you have. If you have three possible names, four taglines, and two domains, you should write 24 ads.

Let them rip and forget about this for a month. Depending on the type of product this is about, this month-long experiment should cost less than $100 and leave you with results based on millions of impressions. At the end of the month, see which names, taglines, and domains performed best and make a decision.

In 2008, three young guys, David, Fabian, and Michael, decided to invest their lives, time, and savings to build the company of their dreams. They wanted to make a new kind of T-shirt, with a pocket more usable than the typical chest pocket. They wanted to do it in a socially beneficial way, using recycled materials, and giving all profits to microlending businesses that multiply the positive social impact around the world. They wanted to build a brand that combined fashion with social responsibility.

To them, the mission was more important than the product, and is a defining piece of their brand. Its not all hand-waving either: having a strong mission has helped them get clients, recruit better talent, and keep the partners honest in the face of new opportunities. Because they have a strong, well-articulated mission, they can check any pending decisions. Does the new product use all recycled materials? Does the potential partner have any positive social impact? Simple questions and simple answers help guide a budding brand toward the light.

Exercise: Write the Mission

The final piece of the puzzle is to capture your vision in a few sentences that concisely explain your proposition to customers, partners, suppliers, and potential investors. A good mission should do more than decorate your web site—it should keep you on track, focus your activity, and explain to anyone what your vision is.

When properly captured, a mission forces difficult decisions, inspires activity, and differentiates you as a company. What you do every day should work toward your mission. Too many companies these days have broad, general missions that mean nothing. Don't be one of them, please.

Brand Marketing

Now that we've named the brand, developed its pillars, created a personality, and decided on a mission, we've got to lay out a brand-consistent plan to get the word out. In doing so, we're going to review all the tools at your fingertips: brand elements, point of sale, events, incentives, and more.

The tactical elements of your brand (the colors, the fonts, the images) are very important as elements that shape the experience your customer will have. However, they are effectively sterile without solid, interesting brand marketing to bring customers to your door. After you design your brand, you have to tell people about it.

While we will focus on the actual execution of many of these components later in the book, you should be thinking about them as you design your product and your brand. Brand marketing comes in several flavors: there is signage and point-of-sale materials that silently speak to your customer, experiential elements like discussions with your staff, authority figures who put their voice behind your product, social media dialogues with your consumers, special events, sponsorships, and traditional advertising.

Create a Point-of-Sale Program

A well-thought-through point-of-sale program with clean, compelling creative can properly shape consumer experience in a retail environment without me there. If I am in the store, I can greet them as they walk in, talk to them about the benefits of my product, and if they like it, I can put one in their basket before they check out. Without me there, however, I need a strategy at the point of sale (POS) to help make this happen without me.

In a perfect world, your customer has already heard of your brand and wants to purchase it because he already knows where it is and why he wants it. Short of that however, we need to help him.

In my mind, there are three distinct steps to effective in-store POS: Creating awareness, communicating benefits, and auctioning through incentive.

You first need to tell a customer that you exist. External signage, like a sign on the door that says something witty along with the idea that you exist is a good first step. Have you ever walked into a store and the Push sign on the door is actually from Coke or American Express? It isn't by accident.

Good placement is also essential for great awareness. If you can get your product on a bunch of shelves in a prominent spot in the store (often through a great relationship or a good chunk of change) it's likely that people will see it.

Lastly, some retailers will let you put up internal signage as well, like a banner or poster or little stickers near the shelf to let customers know you exist.

Managing the Seasonal Sale Cycle

After awareness, you'll need to communicate why your product is special. Most products have a seasonal nature to them. In-season, this is most often done in terms of the problem you are solving, rather than as a descriptor of your product itself. For example, a brand selling coats in the winter might be better off describing how warm and dry they'll keep the shopper in a blizzard rather than an attribute of the coat itself. In the off-season, though, when the issue is not as important, descriptions of the product itself can help to differentiate it against otherwise similar competitors.

Many product categories have very seasonal sales cycles. Keep an eye out next summer for beverage benefits like refreshment and hydration that switch to benefits like taste and functional benefits in the fall and spring, and may disappear entirely over the winter, or hold on to a strategic winter partner to maintain relevance.

A lot of durable products have seasonalities that are based on the activity they correspond to—a football-related product will probably do best during football season. They could also vary based on their customer—a product aimed at college students will do best during the school year.

What kind of seasonal effect are you expecting for your product? Are there fluctuations in timing that you may not have thought of? Are there gift-giving holidays like Father's Day, Valentine's Day, or any of the December holidays that could affect you?

Incentivize Your Customer

Finally, when visibility and benefits aren't enough, you should have a clever way to get customers over the hump of trying to purchase a product from a new company. An easy way to do this is by discounting. Whether you choose to do coupons in the newspaper, by e-mail, text message, or from a live person, you should make sure your retailer is willing to participate. They most often are, since it doesn't cost them anything—the brand bears the cost of the offer (that's you). However, if they don't know that you want to run coupons, they may not be expecting them, and customers who are expecting a discount will be surprised and frustrated to hear that they don't work. I have seen this happen to many different brands that are well-intentioned in their promotions but fail to connect the dots with the retailers, myself included.

I once ran a campaign in which customers who filled out a survey telling me a little bit about themselves and what they thought of my product got a dollar off of their purchase. The customer loved it, and for the most part, retailers were okay with it. After all, I made it easier for customers to try this product, helped the retailers turn my inventory over, and I reimbursed them for the coupons they sent back to me. (As a silent bonus, less than 100 percent of retailers sent back the coupons.) However, from time to time, I, or one of my staff, would run the survey-and-coupon deal without the express approval of the retailer—the cashiers refused the coupons, and many customers were angry with the company, me, and the retailer for a simple mix-up over just a dollar. I must have lost hundreds of dollars in sales this way. Don't let that happen to you— make sure your retail partners know about your coupons.

That said, cash discounts are not the only incentive that works. Status, social relevance, and rewards programs have also been shown to work just as well. Pop culture tie-ins through celebrities or communities have done great things for brands. Crystal Champagne had a great run when they won favor with hip-hop royalty, and Adidas sneakers became very well respected among breakdancers, while Coke rewards gave people a reason to keep their caps.

No matter how excellent your POS scheme is, experiential components to your brand are likely to be more memorable, even if less scalable. If your product has any tactical usefulness, you should try to find ways to let your consumers try before they buy. Have you ever seen people giving out samples in your local supermarket? Have you seen electronics on display at your local big box store? Have you ever seen people trying on clothes in a clothing store? Experiencing your product is potentially the best way to a sale with no surprises. There are two primary places to do this: at the retailer's or anywhere else the customer can make a purchase decision immediately, or else at another location when a purchase decision cannot be made right then.

There are pros and cons to both approaches. Onsite at your retailer, besides the fact that you could be on the shelf and ready to purchase, there's an added sense of legitimacy that can be missing somewhere else. When I'm in Whole Foods, trying a new brand I've never heard of, I'm reasonably sure that it's a decent product. On the street—not so much. Also, I'm more comfortable trying a product in a store that would sell it, because if I'm in the store already,

I am obviously here to buy something in that category or close to it. If I am already inside Nordstrom's, I could try on a sweater even if I only went there to get a T-shirt. It would be trickier to get me to try a new kind of candy bar there, since I am not expecting to get food in a clothing store. Finally, inside the retailer, you don't need to worry about venue or permit—there's no overhead. The downside is that the retailer controls the experience, and holds the power since they own the customer. They are going to tell you when you can or can't use their store, they are going to tell you how much space you get, what you're allowed to say, and some will even try to have their staff run the event and charge you for it.

Offsite, the rules ease up a bit. With no shop, it's up to you to define the venue. You can either rent or use an existing space or use the street. In either case, you might need to think of any regulations you would need to follow (most municipalities will not let you distribute food or alcohol out in the open, for example). You will need to make sure you have materials to fill the space with, unless that isn't your style, and will also need to make sure you proactively breach the question of legitimacy and prove to your consumer that you're not just operating out of a suitcase (even if you are). Most of these are double-edged, with the downside being the related expenses are on all of the preceding options.

A third option, which could be effective, is to have consumers come to a place that you control, like your house or apartment— where the customers are able to make a purchase decision. While this could work initially, and while some companies have made great progress with the in-home, person-to-person sales approach, there are also many compromises in scalability, in my opinion, to build a high margin business. Although Tupperware was able to start this way, you can still buy them in any supermarket. These days, it seems that everyone has a customer-driven or multilevel marketing program that tries to build out its own distribution channel. In general, I think the purported success of these programs is engineered to be far greater than their actual success—my observation has been that successful multilevel salespeople dedicate a lot of time to it, and are still not always very profitable after the costs of running their little business.

My recommendation is to make use of your best retailers after you get them and personally get in front of your customers to tell them why your product is hot. This is something you can do pretty effectively on your own, and at a very low cost.

Work the Streets

Sometimes, you're going to want to get out of a retail setting to market and share your product with the populace where they are— in the streets. Guerilla marketing is itself explosive and creative and tough to categorize, but there are three primary goals, and campaigns can often mix them together.

For awareness, you could do a campaign that ranges from anything as simple as wild posters in the streets, to chalk on the sidewalks, to people walking around wearing signs and screens. For product exposure, you can easily approach people as they walk around popular areas and show them your product, let them have samples if that makes sense, and get their thoughts. If the goal is promotion, you can have people give out coupons in well-trafficked areas. While the impact is sometimes debatable, guerilla marketing often performs far better than traditional advertising in regard to total cost and pure cost per impressions.

According to Andrew Loos and Christian Jurinka, founders of Attack Marketing, "Too many brands get caught up in traditional media. The world of experiential marketing is getting savvier. There are newer and better forms of ROI [return on investment]: e-mails, fans, and other real-time metrics, instead of just clicks or impressions."

They see the larger trend that traditional marketing is less memorable, whereas an experiential or guerilla event is designed to connect and be memorable. Think about it—what are you most likely to remember: a full-page magazine ad, or a two-minute conversation with a interesting guy in a crazy outfit on the street corner who gave you a free product sample. They both could cost around the same amount.

The guys at Attack recount a three-part plan to a successful guerilla event:

1. Start before the event by reaching out to your demos and telling them it's coming.
2. Have the event, and make it different and memorable.
3. Keep the conversation going afterward, and capture data, feedback, and comments.

"Every event needs the longest tail it can get. The longer you can keep a conversation going about an event, the stronger your impact."

Andrew's and Christian's Advice to Entrepreneurs

- Get your feelings hurt: Ask enough questions of different types of people the right way until you're sure of an honest response. Get some tough criticism.
- Don't think your product is the best ever: Listen to customers, be open to new ideas and feedback, and don't be arrogant.
- Use the Internet to access critics: Find people to give you feedback by building a genuine online relationship with customers and critics (for example, yelp.com). Through the Web, consumers are empowered and experts are accessible.

Align with Local Authority Figures

Authority figures on the local or national level can go a long way toward establishing credibility, especially those about which the core product is less differentiated. While a celebrity endorsement may be expensive (but not inaccessible) for us normal folks, local authority figures are often pretty available.

Is there a good reason not to approach the local superstar college quarterback with your sports drink? Or your town's mayor with your productivity tool? The head of your biggest gym with your snack bar? The town physician with your supplement? You should do all of those. What local authority figures could help you and your product?

Of course, there will be some exchange for their support, but in many cases, you could slide on a good product, and a genuine appeal for their help. If they think they are doing some good by mild promotion of your product you're already halfway there.

Seth Tropper, the founder of Switch2Health has had some experience with getting high-profile individuals for his company. It can be an uphill battle persuading just anyone to work with you, though most people will for the right price. Seth has found that the best partnerships are forged with icons who have similar goals and passions to you and your brand. Seth's company, Switch2Health, is about encouraging people to be active. They created a partnership with an NBA star who himself had a passion for fitness.

Not all icons and authority figures are going to be right for your company, and not all the ones who are right will want to work with you.

Through diligence and a bit of luck, though, you can find the kind of advocate who will take your business to the next level.

Communicate with Your Customer through Social Media and Events

Another low cost and fairly experiential marketing method involves the use of social media channels to get your message out. There are many opinions out there on what the right ways to use social media are. I don't claim to have all the answers but I have seen some techniques work, and there are some baseline elements of good marketing that apply double to this medium.

I see mainly two kinds of social media marketing: Personal and impersonal communication. Personal communication is usually used for answering customer questions directly, or reaching out directly to prospective customers. Since all of the media are about conversation, you can find groups or conversational topics relevant to your product and add something meaningful. Impersonal marketing is like broadcasting. You blast out a message and hope people read it. If it lends itself well to sharing, and is interesting, it can spread through a network like a virus (hence *viral*).

If you don't already have thousands of friends, fans, or followers (take your pick) you will need to build them by being genuine and involving yourself in the discussion. Social media is not just about creating a Facebook page, a Twitter account, or a blog. It's about real interaction with people, which will backfire if you aren't active on all your channels. Because the interaction is genuine, that does mean you run a risk of getting some constructive (or just plain negative) feedback if people don't like what you're slingin'. Ultimately, social media represent a way to make a real connection with your customers—difficult to do when your product flows through an extended supply chain and your customers never really meet you. While it can be a lot of work (read: skillful delegation to your assistant) it can also lend itself to great loyalty when executed well.

An active and relevant events strategy goes a long way for products that can do them cost effectively. For example, while Red Bull may be best known for their energy drink, each of their events (and there are many of them) are held in the highest esteem within their niche communities. And they didn't wait until they were big to start this. Red Bull's Icebreak (now discontinued), BC1, and Flugtag events each displayed something key to an underserved customer.

Surfing in the Northeast, large-scale breakdancing competitions, and just fun silliness broadcast on TV brought people together in a way that happy hour at a bar just doesn't cut.

If your target customer segment has a special activity that you can make more special—in a heartfelt and genuine way, of course—try it. You might even make money on the event, which totally beats spending money on marketing. A successful event is like having your customers pay you to be marketed to and then loving you for a good event.

For example: there were two events I was working on for my Star Power customers. Unfortunately, I ended up having to cancel both of them—I challenge you to create something similar (or better!) for your customers. Or go ahead and copy me—I only ask that you send me tickets!

Star Power Yogalympics: A competition in which different yoga studios can send teams to compete in events that are different poses. The event was filmed for local or national TV, and was genuine to the existing community. Several prominent yoga studios were engaged. We were getting teams to sign up, and working on finding a venue, especially a publicly visible outdoor one, all the while keeping the focus on the competitors and staying true to the art.

Star Power MotoPolo: A polo tournament on motorcycles. A spectacular event for the sport bike community. If that sounds dangerous, that's because it is. But to guys who play obstacle course on the highway at 90 miles per hour, the excitement bar is set a bit higher. Anyone could register a team and play in the tournament. If possible, we could use a local park and dirt bikes to make it a bit safer.

A Note about These Two Events

Neither of these events happened even though we had a lot of community interest and support. At the time, however, we couldn't afford to pay a coordinator to stay on top of it while I was busy focusing on the core business. No regrets, though—I might use them again soon, or I welcome you to use them for your product if it makes sense.

Sponsorship of events important to the brand's customers is one of my favorite ways to get involved in existing events. This usually involves going to a great event as a VIP too. This doesn't need to be expensive—most of the time, you can sponsor an event in product. Not only does this actually cost you half as much (or whatever your margin is) in real dollars, but it helps keep product moving and into the hands of customers. Because my product was a beverage, I designed some cocktails (it helps to have been a bartender) and would always allow charities or other special events to take free product.

There are other cases in which sponsorship can come with a heftier price tag and will not accept product. This is a business decision that you should not weight too heavily on the event for. Do the math—if you are paying more than twenty dollars for a thousand impressions ($20 CPM) I would stay away. Cash is too valuable to throw at random events for minimal impact.

Finally, you can always buy advertisements. Traditional ads run the gamut from print ads in magazines, display ads on the Web, highway billboards, to TV. Each year, customers indicate in surveys more and more that they are moving away from TV and toward the Web. They still read magazines, though, and often with intense loyalty and subscriptions. However, advertising is expensive at face value. Get away from sticker-price ads by using a broker or by negotiating yourself. Magazines have to sell their ads before they go to print, so a week or so before the release date is a great time to call the ad department of a magazine your customers read. I've gotten as good as 90 percent off the rack rate. Using a broker, I've gotten only as good as 80 percent off, but this doesn't require any negotiating work on my end. Keep in mind that it still isn't cheap—a decent publication with over 100,000 copies in circulation will still cost a couple of thousand dollars for a full-page ad (which is the only kind you should get).

Web display ads are different in that you can track conversions from people clicking on them, and may make sense depending on whether you plan on selling your stuff on your web site or not. There's a place for billboards and radio and TV ads too, but it really depends on your goals, your budget, your product, and your customer. If you're thinking of running TV advertisements, chances are that your budget allows for a much less bootstrapped approach than the one I'm advocating anyway.

Summary

We spent this chapter designing a brand based on your product, its mission, and your customers' needs and likes. We registered your name and your web domain. We got into a few of the challenges you'll face as well as some of the channels and techniques you can use to get the word out about what you're doing. This can be difficult work, but also extremely rewarding as you see your creation come to life.

> ### ❗ Challenge: Fortitude
>
> When putting a new product on shelves, developing a brand or even sharing a new idea, you are bound to face challenging questions, pushback from friends and family, and moments of weakness when you aren't sure you're up to the task. No matter how simply and honestly this book presents the facts, you will need to rely on your own inner strength and willingness to swim against the current to truly make your product dream happen. If you're like me, this challenge will take you way out of your comfort zone the first time you do it.
>
> First, head over to your local shopping mall. We need a place that is somewhat crowded, popular, and has an escalator. Go to the bottom of the down escalator and start climbing up. After you get up to the middle of it or so, match your pace to the escalators so that you are staying in place, as if you were on a Stairmaster.
>
> As other people come down the escalator, greet them if you would like, avoid them if you would like, but stay on! The goal of this challenge is to get you comfortable with the curious eyes and skeptical questioning of others. I started out by simply telling people that I was doing an experiment, and would even apologize for being in their way. After I grew bolder, I offered wittier responses like "This is the cheapest gym in town!" or "I can't figure out why I can't get up the stairs!" and usually got a giggle or two.
>
> Make no mistake—the subtext of this mission includes challenging the system around you and sticking to a job that seems arbitrary and monotonous because the job has to get done. Bonus points from me for catching this on video and showing it off.

CHAPTER 4

Design the Process

The ladder of success is best climbed by stepping on the rungs of opportunity.

—Ayn Rand

I was working on the whiteboard when the doorbell rang. I had been expecting this for hours now. Earlier this week, I had finished discussions with my packaging supplier, label designer, raw materials broker, and bottle filler. We were going to pull the trigger and create a test batch of products for my approval.

I signed for a small, heavy box and gingerly cut the tape that held it together.

I held my prototype in my hands with cautious excitement. It had standardized product (read: not from my kitchen) made in a beverage factory, was in a spectacular frosted glass bottle, and had a coolness to the touch. I immediately took photographs that I shared online to all the people I had met so far in the industry. Before long, I was getting questions from industry big shots and potential customers. I was a *made* guy.

Or so I thought. I didn't know that I had overlooked some of my biggest upcoming challenges, and had grossly miscalculated my business model. In fact, when I had my product in hand, I couldn't say I even knew about a viable business model. I had always been told that a good product would sell itself, and in my naïveté, thought I had a good product.

When I first started creating Star Power, I had no real prior experience except my work as a brand manager and as a bartender—not exactly the sort of expertise needed to create something new from scratch. My first batch of products was made in my kitchen, using a juicer, some fruits from the supermarket, and my oven for a pasteurizer. I was very intimidated by the idea of mass producing anything. Besides being a daunting task, it also felt like a risky investment with unclear goals. I didn't really have anyone to ask either, so I did what any respectable geek would do—I googled my random questions ("How do you create a beverage?") and read up on industry trade magazines, and sent out feelers until people started responding to me.

The first people to get back to me were the brokers and consultants that seem to pop up like weeds in the consumer products space. These guys tend to have a decade or two at a recognizable major company, and want to feed you just enough information to sign you up for a lucrative monthly retainer. Because most product entrepreneurs are inexperienced, these guys have an easy sell. In exchange for only three to ten thousand dollars a month (and more, I'm certain) they will offer their advice and sometimes put you in front of customers. Their contracts nearly always have a buyout clause that makes them difficult to get out of.

However, not knowing that at the time, I thought I needed one. Using the Inspired Method, I spoke to a whole bunch of them, thinned the list down to people who seemed the most reliable and chose a partnership of two guys who had great reputations and great resumes. They were energetic, optimistic, and full of ideas—until it came to action time. I felt like a sucker. For two entire months, these two guys did nearly nothing. They called another broker one week, were traveling the next, and on vacation the week after. When I suggested that they weren't really working hard for me, they said they're sorry, but busy with other clients. I tried to be both persistent and patient, but finally, after six weeks and no result, I decided to terminate the relationship—this is when things get even more exciting.

"We've been working really hard for you," they said. "We made a call, set up a meeting—and continue to try."

"If you went after customers as hard as you come after me for the weekly check, we might have something here," I responded.

I then read back to them the list of actions I had been keeping on them. They literally had done three things in six weeks. This was complicated by the contract including a six-month trial period during which I was not supposed to terminate the relationship. However, knowing that these vampires were just going to bleed me slowly for six months, I pulled a difficult move.

"I can't afford to pay you guys without results, goals, or milestones for the next six months, guys. Throw me a bone here—what will you deliver?"

Silence. Awkward looks.

"Then I guess that's that. I'll be sure to get back to you when I can afford your services, and until then, I only wish you well." After that, I stopped paying them, and never heard from or spoke to them again. While it is possible you'll need help, I've heard very few stories of a magic consultant being able to make your company a success without you. More often, I hear stories like mine, where really high expectations are met with dismal results, heartbreak, and wastes of time and capital. The lesson learned? Treat contractors like employees: with a lot of diligence, a slow ramp, firm goals, and a clear exit if it isn't working.

I also got contacted by salespeople at packaging firms. At the time, I did not know that such a thing existed—my assumption was that all bottling plants already existed at the behest of a monstrous company like Coca-Cola, and could make exclusively their products. There's an entirely different flavor of packaging firm—one that will contract out to anyone who wishes to use their facility. Contract packagers, or co-packers for short, make the difference between a guy who looks like he's running his business out of a garage and one who looks like he means business. Chances are, many of the products you've bought are put together by co-packers, and run by people like you who are living the dream.

Co-packers bring all the hallmarks of legitimacy within your reach—industrial techniques like flash pasteurization, encapsulization, clamshell packing, injection molding, printed cases, labeling, and all the other details that consumers associate with a real product. However, as big as some of these companies are, they can be tough to find. Part of the deal is that the *brand* gets to look like the *manufacturer*, which makes finding these firms difficult for an entrepreneur. The stealth isn't an accident—I couldn't find one that wanted to be named in this book.

I made friends through a mutual acquaintance with a guy I'll call Mark, at a company whose name I can't print. Mark walked me through his facility and gave me the low-down on how it works: I could tell him and his team of chemists and product designers what I wanted to make, and they would make it for me. If I had a graphic designer, they would work with them on the label and graphics, but if not, they had some of those in house too. If I had a packaging supplier, they would work with them, but if not, they had direct access to tons of packaging or could make me something custom. I was like a kid in a candy store (ironically, I could even have chosen to make candy there). Mark told me that his guys could make nearly any product and then even help me sell it. All I needed to do was to tell him what it was.

Co-packers are a well-kept secret for good reason. As a consumer, are you just as likely to buy a product if you knew that a single person was behind it as if a massive public company were behind it? Co-packers work by bypassing the natural skepticism of the consumer with psychological jiu-jitsu. Their products look professionally made because they are, and because of them, you, the creator, don't need to own the factory.

Once I knew how I was going to do it, I needed to construct my product. During my exploration, I got in touch with several packaging vendors. These companies are those that literally take plastic, glass, aluminum, and paper and turn them into bottles, clamshells, cans, and boxes. Packaging is important, because it is sometimes the only chance you get to speak to your consumer and tell them why to buy your product. Packaging carries that messaging, and also is a showcase for your product. Packaging is the difference between the flea market and the shopping mall: people tend to pay more respect and more money for a product in a package.

I had the good fortune to meet a man I'll call David—a veteran package salesman whose name and company I can't print—over a glass of scotch one day early in my search. His company is a leader in sourcing and producing packaging in the beauty industry—if you've ever seen a vial of nail polish or a bottle of perfume, there's a good chance he had his fingers in the sale or design of that bottle.

Experts like David can help you fine-tune and reality-check your packaging to be cost effective, producible, and compatible with your packing process. While you could try to create a design without their help, they can help keep you grounded with what is and isn't possible, as well as simple features that meet your goals while keeping costs as low as possible. When they are done building your dream, they'll keep it running from the background to make it look like you're running the show on your own.

Guys like David and Mark are not the consultants I mentioned earlier. These guys are executives at the supplier and co-packing firms and have the direct ability to create your product and get you closer to your customer. Any products business that's looking for real scale has many customers. While we might start by selling to a few consumers from your web site, ultimately, the dream is realized by putting your baby on store shelves everywhere so that your consumers can get to it. For that to happen, a consumer needs to want it, a retailer needs to buy it, and a distributor needs to deliver it. All of them are customers for your product.

A well-planned supply chain can go a long way toward keeping costs down, time lines reliable, and headaches low for an entrepreneur building a fledgling product. The more rigorous and meticulous your process design, the better your company will be able to cope with the numerous unplanned obstacles that are sure to arise in your path.

The supply chain includes every player and every decision that needs to be made from raw material to a consumer's hands. Each step of the supply chain has an implication on cost and control for the entrepreneur, so it is important to know the decisions made at each step.

In this chapter, we get you thinking about the key players for your product at a conceptual level, and then give you the tools and guidance needed to meet them in real life. While it is true that each and every product is different, it is also true that product supply chains tend to follow predictable paths from manufacturer to customer. Someone needs to create a physical object, and sell it to the customer, usually through an intermediate.

Meet the Players

For now, we will assume that you have not yet fully planned your supply chain. While it will be most initially intuitive to think through your supply chain from raw material to finished good, doing so can lead you to skip important work, and miss opportunities that will later seem intuitive in retrospect. It's the advice I wish I had been given. Don't make the mistake of starting with your product—start with your customer and design your process around them. Put your customer first, and they will thank you with their wallets later.

Let's take a moment to get our terminology straight—we don't want to use the terms *customer* and *supplier* indiscriminately. Each of them comes in different flavors:

- A *consumer* is a customer who walks up to a shelf (real or digital) with some issue they need to solve. He may be hungry or thirsty, he may need entertainment, he may need to feel better about themselves, and it is for any of those reasons that he chose *this particular retailer* to walk into. He then walked up to a product that caught his eye, or sported a name he recognizes and respects. He inspects any messaging on the product, and makes an internal purchase decision before ultimately paying for and using the product.

- A *retailer* is a customer who makes a buying decision for what product goes on the shelf. Each and every product in the store is an investment of both real dollars as well as the opportunity afforded by a shelf. For a chain retailer, a single buyer may have regional, national, or even global decision-making ability on what products go where. Retailers base these decisions not only on whether they like the product, but also on the business model of the company behind it, the personalities at play, and their interpretation of consumer demand. The products they decide on could be brought to their attention by curious customers, the brand team themselves, or the brand's distributor.

  Depending on our product, there may or may not be established web retailers that will work for you. Your own web site could be a retail channel as well. This step is where the product hits shelves, and where we will spend much more time in Chapter 6.

- A *distributor* is a customer who is largely invisible to the consumer, but is the major player for the brand. The distributor physically runs the trucks between a warehouse full of product to their retail accounts. Retailers are the distributor's customers, and for the most part, a distributor will carry any product to a retail account that demands it. Distributors tend to be local or regional, though there are some national distributors worth mentioning. A start-up product company, however, is unlikely to gain national distribution off the bat. Distributors can be Direct or System and usually have their eyes open for new products that fit their portfolio. The distributor is the direct customer to the brand (read: writes your checks) and often has a sales force of its own to help move your product. Another critical step for which we will spend more time in Chapter 6.

- A *wholesale broker* can an effectively expand your sales force. Experienced brokers have longstanding relationships with retailers and distributors. Brokers can be difficult to get— they make the bulk of their money on a performance basis, and as such need to be personally sold into a product before agreeing to take it on. Once sold in, a good broker can help you grow without the overhead of sales reps. On the other hand, brokers are not *your* people, and will likely not represent the brand as well as you would. If they underperform, they may complicate your own expansion into their territory.

- The *manufacturer* is behind the curtain for your brand. To the customer, your company is synonymous to the manufacturer, though these are often different companies. Whether or not you choose to operate your own manufacturing, it will make sense to weigh the benefits of using a contract manufacturer (co-manufacturer or co-packer). A good co-packer will help you streamline your formulation, negotiate better with raw material and packaging suppliers, and even help find brokers and distributors for your product. Selecting a co-packer (or choosing not to) is one of the most critical decisions a young company will make, as it is a difficult one to change later. It is certainly an option to be your own manufacturer and to pack your own product. That would give you more control, but is also much more work. Although using a co-packer comes with a cost and a slight loss of control, it will free you up to focus on the business of building your company.

- In some cases, a *raw material broker* is needed to get your manufacturer key inputs for your product. While not always required, products with many ingredients or difficult ingredients can sometimes be helped by firms that specialize in finding raw materials. These companies may find rare or multiple ingredients for food, electronic components, or any variety of parts and pieces needed to create your product. However, they

Table 4.1: Key Production Process Considerations

	Low Economies of Scale	Large Economies of Scale
Simple Process	Self-produce prototypes. Digital supply chain first. Explore offshore production if labor intensive.	Act fast. The big players in this field will be able to move on this more easily than you.
Complex Process	Self-produce prototypes if possible; detailed concepts if not.	Find production first.

don't work for free, and the additional cost can be avoided with careful planning and clever sourcing. These brokers often also have relationships with your or other co-packers, as they will usually have the opportunity to share customers.

- A *raw material supplier* typically produces or consolidates the barest building blocks of your product. The quality, reliability, and price of their products echo through the entire process.
- The *raw material source* for most products may not be a company. For some snack and beverage companies, the source is the farm; for furniture companies, it may be the forests where they get their wood. You may never see or interact with the source of your raw materials, but knowing what they are can help you keep an eye on your risk of a price change, depletion, or even the effect of local politics.

This chapter is going to get into some of the legwork that you should do before setting out on actually creating your product. Table 4.1 has some high-level thoughts, too. If it seems a bit tedious, it's because there are a lot of moving parts in this business, and even people who are very well prepared often have a very difficult time in establishing a new product and a new brand. If you are anything like I was when I got started, you're thinking about it backward.

The Demand-Driven Supply Chain

When developing my product, I started the way many of you might have started: with a product concept. I thought that if I could just make the best product, that it would sell itself, and we'd all live happily ever after. That is unfortunately almost never the case.

A good product will not succeed unless it fills a need for its customer, and even then will suffer if they do not know about it, or are unable to get it easily. Building a brand for a young product is a labor of love, and stands a much better chance of being successful if it is better planned. The few quick conversations I suggest in this chapter (and even offer conversation guides for) could be the difference between you and the 95 percent of new product introductions that fail.

Getting back to the supply chain from before: the reason we want to start with the customer rather than the product is because they are your final decision maker. No matter how much your distributors and retailers may love you, no matter how beautiful your graphics and web site are, money changes hands only when your customer decides to buy. That said, getting to know what makes your partners tick will go a long way toward not only making your dream a reality, but in stretching your dollar while you're at it.

When I tell people that I was able to put a product on shelves in less than a year with less than $5,000, they don't believe me. By minimizing early mistakes, understanding your customers and your capabilities, and aligning your goals with those of your suppliers and partners, it will be easier for you to get your suppliers to buy in to your dream, to get customers to understand you, and to keep partners by your side. For simplicity, we'll consolidate the players behind and in front of you in the value chain, as shown in Figure 4.1.

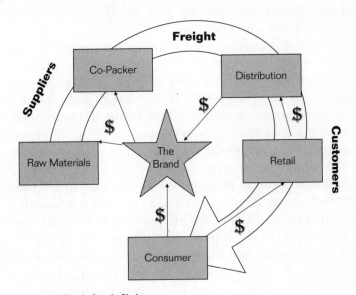

Figure 4.1 Simple Supply Chain

On the top of one's mind for both customers and suppliers is whether they are building a business for the long term—one with staying power. Suppliers that see your potential are more likely to relax their minimum order volumes, help you with your formulations, and connect you to people of interest. Partners that see the potential for growth into a great brand are more likely to give you better placement, more exposure, and less of a hard time. Perhaps more importantly, a brand with staying power will be much more profitable and fulfilling for you in the long term.

The flip side is that companies stick around when they create something valuable for their customers. While you could take an educated guess as to what that is, I personally believe that if you plan on investing your time and money into a project, it is worth testing demand and getting the product right.

Talk to the Right Customers; Ask the Right Questions

Consumers come in as many shapes and sizes as people on this planet. Indeed, each of us is a consumer in some way or another, and doubtless has been on the receiving end of many clever marketing campaigns. Think about the products you like and why you like them. While it is never easy to think of ourselves as easily suggested into liking one product or another, we as human beings are rational and emotional creatures who can be compelled by argument or excitement into a purchase.

Have you ever caught yourself wanting that really cool outfit that your favorite celeb was wearing? That perfect phone that looked so shiny and useful on TV? That fizzy beverage in a photograph surrounded by smiling people? We're just pretty little pawns to the machine. Now's your time to step off the board and become a player.

One of the first things you will need to do is come up with a quick summary of your product. When you're holding an early stage product, a prototype, or even your concept, people are going to want to ask you about it. Having a quick summary in your head will not only make your life easier (I must have given a hundred long-winded explanations before figuring this out) but will also make you more credible to key contacts who may be able to help you. You would be surprised at how many people around you have skills and contacts that could prove invaluable to your foundling project.

Fabian Pfortmüller, one of the founders of Holstee, has his own time-tested advice for first-time entrepreneurs who are trying to build a network, create a personal brand, and get the word out about their product.

There are four key steps.

1. *Pick a market:* Whether you're selling T-shirts in California or electronics in Sweden, know what market you're in and where your market is.
2. *Build a network:* Go to every event in the community and meet people. Give your 10-second pitch to everyone, and make some real friends. Be interested in what your network is doing, and be out there with your ideas. While this can be a bit uncomfortable, especially for shy individuals, Fabian says, "If it is painful, you're pushing yourself."
3. *Bring something to the table:* You're going to be asking your network for something: it might be sales, PR, advice, or contacts. So be sure you have something to offer as well. Be willing to share a story or insight, give some product, or run a promotion.
4. *When in doubt, be outrageous:* Memorable people are more likely to get a shot at a customer, a mention in an article, or an introduction to a key contact when the opportunity arises.

Exercise: Write Your 10-Second Summary

You may have heard about the 60-second elevator pitch that you should have ready, on the off chance you run into an investor in an elevator.

But what do you do when everyone you meet is a potential customer, partner, or investor? You don't have enough minutes in the day for that! You need a quick and to-the-point summary that will get your point across to anyone. This doesn't substitute for a real conversation, but will get a lot of the basic questions answered immediately.

You don't need to stick to this exact format—but it took me a lot of experimentation and ruthless word-cutting to get to.

Hey—I'm_____(name)_____and I'm working on a concept called _____(product)_____. It is a _____(product category)_____ that really solves the _____(problem)_____ in a new and better way. I'm looking for _____(what you need next)_____ and am really excited about _____(your next move)_____.

(continued)

> **Exercise: Write Your 10-Second Summary** *(continued)*
>
> This usually gets people thinking about what you're doing, and lets them know what you're looking for. I'll give you one I was using for a while, as an example.
>
> > Hey—I'm Vik, and I'm working on a company called Star Power. It is a starfruit juice—the first of its kind—and really gives people a great source of Vitamin C, antioxidants, and potassium in an exotic and all-natural way. I'm looking for distributors with a good grasp on their accounts and am excited to roll our new web site out this week.
>
> What's your 10-second summary?

Tie Your Customer to Your Product

I hope you've got that summary nailed down—because you're going to use it soon. While we've spent this whole time creating a cool idea and making sure it makes sense, we haven't quite put it out there in front of people. As you read through the next section—try to think about what kinds of questions you think are important, and what you think some of the answers are going to be—having a hypothesis can go a long way in helping ask customers the right questions. Ideally, after you ask a few of them, you'll have an idea about who your customer segments are, and what they think of your concept.

- *Determine customer segments:* There are billions of customers in the world and each of them is different. In an ideal world, you might want to tailor your product to every single one. One limitation of putting a product on the shelf is that (for the most part) it cannot be tailored directly for every single customer any more. Segmentation is a technique by which you can classify customers into groups with distinct traits that you can then tailor your product to.

  For example, if you were selling coffee, it would help to know whether your segment was coffee shop hipsters, globe-trotting executives, or active young moms. Each of them may drink coffee, but they do so for different reasons, at different times, and in different places. Grouping them into segments ultimately lets you serve them better.

Your goal in segmentation is to learn enough about your customers to keep your segments concise enough to be memorable, distinct enough to be meaningful, and important enough to be worthwhile. For example, another segment in the coffee example might be "occasional-coffee-drinking-airport-traveler-with-a-dog-in-an-apartment," but this segment is probably too small to be worthwhile, and impossible to pursue meaningfully.

When you're talking to people in the field, there are a few key areas to keep in mind:

- The *demographic attributes of a population* that are most objective, and are often used in government research for the same reason. These are easy, quick questions that you can ask your customers up front to later help you make better sense of the results. After all, when a customer tells you he loves your concept, it may also be helpful to know that he is an 18-to-35 young professional, college graduate, urban-dwelling male as well.
- The *psychographic descriptors* of your group that are more likely to be subjective, containing the thoughts and opinions of your consumer. These could include their values, lifestyles, interests, and activities. Along with their demographics, these can help you pick the right positioning with which to speak to them. Now you know that your 18-to-35 male also likes football and action movies, snowboards in the winter, and likes to eat dinner at casual restaurants. You might even know that he collects vinyl action figures and plays chess.

Now that you know who your customer is and what he's like, figure out where he spends his money. Be sure to include questions on his most and least favorite retailers, both brick and web. These tie back the 18-to-35 sportsman or geek to Best Buy and Toys"R"Us, and let you fully understand his segment.

Remember that the goal of this section of your survey or interview is to figure out all the ways to describe your customer. Given that you may have hundreds of these questionnaires filled out, good classification variables will go a long way toward making your results readable now and in the future.

- *Test the concept:* After you get the baseline categorization questions out of the way, you will want to ask questions that test your product and the legitimacy of the problem you're trying to solve with it. Sometimes, only an honest stranger can really tell us when we're eating a pie in the sky.

Before you launch your supplement to fight droopy ears or pocket tool for pulling thumbtacks, wouldn't it be helpful to know whether our customers are plagued by the problem? These questions are best posed as personal to the reader, making them answer whether the problem affects them, rather than whether they think the problem exists for others.

If your problem isn't garnering much enthusiasm, it might be a good idea to really think hard about your product. If you can't sell the idea, how will you sell the real thing?

Plenty of products exist for fun, and many of them do very well. However, assuming that you're an entrepreneur or a small team on a shoestring budget, your initial marketing will be considerably more cost-effective with a real approach to a tangible problem. Remarkable solutions to painful problems naturally lend themselves to viral customer sharing.

In addition to knowing what your future customers' problems are, it will be revealing to know their take on your solution. Before you spend time and money developing your product, it will be productive to know what kind of customers agree with you. You want to know what they think of your positioning as well, preferably again through questions that probe for their answers, rather than what they might say in a group discussion. Suppose it turns out that art industry young executives like your thumbtack tool, they may want to purchase it in a different way than the older auto mechanics who also like your product.

Your solutions should be articulated in such a way as to capture the imagination of your customers, and inspire passion on their response to you. Personally, I prefer a strong negative response to a lukewarm response. At least that way you know what they're thinking. A modest response will likely lead to a less-than-modest performance in the market.

Finally, you want to know if they would they buy or recommend the product. A simple question "Would you buy this product?" or "Select the price you would pay for this product" can go a long way toward giving you a sense of the viability of your project. Later, when you match these results back to the customer demographics initially collected, we will be able to build customer segments that are most likely to be receptive to your product.

A somewhat more complex question is whether or not they would refer this to a friend. It's a subjective question, and one that might get a different response in person than it would through the Web. There are a lot of good arguments for including it, however, that we won't go into for now. Just include it.

The Retailer: Where the Proverbial Rubber Meets the Road

While doing these surveys, you will get a sense of what kind of customers like your concept. These customers shop at retailers—the next stop on our homework train.

Retailers come in all shapes and sizes, and vary a bit from one category to another. Even within a category, similar retailers can operate in different styles with different sources—channels in industry parlance. For example, for foods, the supermarket channel operates very differently from the convenience store channel, which in turn is different from the natural foods channel. Good product design will be inclusive of your intended channels and retailers, and will make their lives easier.

Exercise: Grab Your Clipboard; It's Time to Talk to People

There are three primary goals to this exercise: To determine your customer segments, test product spec, and inform start-up strategy.

The questions you ask are going to be very closely tied to your concept, so I won't try to tell you what to ask. Instead, I can share with you a survey (see Figure 4.2) that I've used, and hope that it helps you with yours.

Using these and your own needs, write a brief survey that you feel captures every main thing you need to know, and ask it to at least 10 people.

What do they think of your product?

(continued)

Exercise: Grab Your Clipboard; It's Time to Talk to People (continued)

☆Star Power Superstar Survey

1. I am a
   a. Yoga Fan   b. Running Machine   c. Gym Go-er   d. Video Gamer
   e. Tech Geek   f. Adrenaline Junkie   g. Beach Bum   h. Globetrotter
2. My age is:
   a. 18-25   b. 26-35   c. 36-45   d. 46-65   e. 66+
3. I buy from this store
   a. Daily   b. Weekly   c. Every other week   d. Monthly or less
4. I drink fruit juice or fruit nectars
   a. Multiple times per day   b. Multiple times per week
   c. Once a week   d. Less than once a week
5. Overall, I think Star Power Starfruit juice is
   a. Life changing   b. Excellent   c. Pretty good   d. Terrible
6. I like Star Power because of the
   a. Antioxidant health   b. Vitamins and electrolytes
   c. Exotic story   d. Unique taste   e. Starfruit
7. The most important statistic about a product to me is
   a. Antioxidants   b. Calorie count   c. Sugars   d. Vitamins   e. Taste
8. I would love to see a Star Power starfruit blend with
   a. Carrot-Pineapple   b. Mango-Tangerine   c. Açaí-Pomegranate
9. Before now, I had heard of Star Power
   a. On the website   b. Posters in the streets   c. Blog/Facebook/Twitter
   d. Through a friend   e. Never
10. I want to get exclusive discounts and participate in fun contests.
    Please email me at _____ .

Thank you for taking our survey! Use this stub as a coupon to take $1 off of your purchase of two or more Star Power units. Live healthy.

Retailer: Collect these coupons and send them along with an invoice for a billback to Star Power, 389 Washington St, Suite 12K, Jersey City, NJ, 07302.
Customer: If the retailer won't honor the coupon, mail us two UPCs along with this coupon and a self-addressed, stamped envelope, and we will send you a rebate.

Figure 4.2 Starfruit Juice Survey

In all different categories, you can typically find two major types of retail: local, independent shops, which cater to a specific niche, and larger chain stores that can carry a wider variety of products. For now, we will focus on the independent retailer—they will be the first stop for our concept.

The differentiating benefit about independent retail is that the key decision maker is usually in the store and typically available. Most local retail is run by the owner or their family, and they have direct control over what goes on their shelves. Larger stores and chains, on the other hand, can have much more complicated processes to getting the product to the shelf. (We tackle them in Chapter 6 as well, but not in the initial phase of your product.)

The first step in selecting a retailer is to make a list of the top 5 or 10 retailers in your area that you think might be a good fit for your product. With the contact information of a few good distributors

Exercise: Meet the Retailer

In even the busiest stores, it is usually possible to meet the key decision maker by asking any employee to speak to the owner or the manager. This person, however, is not as likely to give you as much time in the meeting as the consumer was. This makes a targeted discussion much more important.

After your 10-second summary, you really want to ask two questions:

1. *What are their favorite products and why?*   Retailers typically care about how well a product turns over, and secondarily, how well it fits in to their portfolio. An upscale shop will be hesitant to carry a budget brand, and a grocery store is unlikely to carry electronics. Knowing the retailers' favorite products is like a crash course in what the winners in a particular channel look like. Note these—they will be important when we start to prototype our new product.

2. *Who are their favorite distributors?*   Although some retailers will initially allow you to independently place a product on their shelves, getting to shelves in a scalable way will involve a distributor. Also, many retailers don't do a thorough job themselves of scouting new products, but will take whatever their distributor presents them. Knowing who your retailers consider to be good (read: good selection, reliable delivery) will ease your work in searching for them. Ask for contact information—if you've done a decent job selling your concept, they won't have any issue sharing that with you.

Ideally, after your conversations, you should know what kinds of products do well at your favorite retailers and what they cost. You should also have a sense of what kind of distributor they like, the level of service they get, and how often they will take a new product from them.

in hand, get out there and meet them. Key contacts at distributors can be difficult to nail down; with a bit of persistence, though, you should be able to get in front of at least a few of them.

In your meeting, the real goal is to open the door to future discussions. The distributor is not only to be your initial customer, but is also a treasure trove of excellent contacts, industry knowledge, and your ultimate partner in the field.

Take this meeting just to introduce yourself, outline the concept, and confirm conceptions you've built so far about your customer and your retailer. The distributor has different concerns from the retailer because they have different customers and different constraints. In fact, the retailer is his customer! The distributor is much more concerned (especially for a new, untested product like yours) with what makes this product a good long-term investment, and what the person behind the product is willing to do to make it move.

These guys want *velocity*. They want the product to fly out of their trucks. Since you're not going to be able to promise them that (and if you do, they might not believe you), though, they will instead want a thicker margin and a marketing plan. There was a lot of work and planning that went into my first distributor deal, and a lot more misses than hits on attempted sales.

The only thing I knew when I started my search for a distributor is that I did not know nearly as much as I needed to, and that I certainly would not have time to do all the research myself. You got yourself an assistant, right? I used an intern that I hired (for free) from Columbia University for this job.

I laid out a project and called it "distributor reachout." I know, very clever. It basically involved applying the Inspired Method to selecting a distributor. We were talking to every single possible distributor in my target areas: New York City, New Jersey, and selected cities up and down the East Coast. Since we wanted get on the radar, I wrote up a press release and put it out to every industry publication I could. It was very brief, and got right to the point—a super-innovative new product with a great plan was seeking distribution.

I then had my intern drill every retailer we could, not only on who their favorite distributors were but who their contacts were there as well. We slowly but surely unearthed more than 50 distributors.

Exercise: Get Yourself an Intern

Unless you are yourself a student, they have two real advantages over you: They are at a stage in their life when learning is paramount, and are also have a different and younger vantage point.

Since they have typically fewer responsibilities and worries, you're much more likely to get a talented individual for fewer dollars, as long as the experience is worthwhile. Fabian from Holstee has taken on many interns for what he calls "survival pay." He gets them in exchange for the network he brings them through his company, the shared belief in the company's mission, and for the experience he creates for them.

I've shared the write-up I've used to get many of my own interns. You will note that although it isn't paid, it offers tangible benefits and takeaways written in a student's language.*

---

*Go to www.wiley.com/go/venkatraman for more information.

Manufacturer or Co-Packer Selection

Up until this point, all of the people and companies you've been speaking to and interviewing have been on the customer side of your product. You want distributors to buy your product from you, retailers to buy from them, and consumers to take it off the shelf. They hold a lot of the power in that relationship, because they can choose whether or not to buy your stuff.

On the other side of your supply chain, you're the customer, and the dynamic is very different. To the companies that will produce and pack your product, the ones that sell the raw materials that go into your product and your packaging, the ones that sell the services you'll need along the way—you're a potential source of fresh, growing income. The more potential you show, the better they will treat you, too.

For a start-up product to go as smoothly as possible, it is incredibly helpful for your suppliers to be bought in. When your suppliers believe that your idea is a good one, and that you are a capable force behind it, they are more likely to help you make it happen. They will be more flexible on initial pricing, more willing to create small batches for you (all of which cost them time and potentially money from other customers) while you get up to speed. Having a bought-in supplier won't just make your life easier—it can save you tens of thousands of dollars. Your supplier is your first investor.

Selecting a co-packer is therefore a more complicated business than just one who agrees to work with you. You want a true partner to your business, one who is going to bring some insight and expertise to your product, and is capable of flexibility when you need it.

The first step in selecting a co-packer is to collect as broad a list as you can of co-packers. Depending on what you're working on, this might be tougher than a simple web search, but you should start there. Look for "contract packaging," "contract manufacturing," and "co-packer," along with the type of product you're creating. For now, just capture everything you find. If you've run across any brokers or consultants in your industry, this is a good time to tap them for intelligence. I've found that even the guys who want to charge you for their help are happy to offer you some free advice for specific questions like "Which co-packers would you recommend for my concept?"

When you've got a fair list, write a quick e-mail that explains your product and asks the co-packer if they can produce it. Inevitably, some will say they're unable, and some may not even respond. However, the rest will likely get back to you with some detailed questions that will force you to think through details of your product that you might not have. Custom-molded parts? Corn plastic resin? Tin, steel, or titanium? Tunnel pasteurizer? Preservatives? What are the trade-offs? Here's when you ask those questions and really refine your product's concept.

Apply the Inspired Method to Selecting a Co-Packer

1. List: Collect a list as exhaustive as possible within a reasonable time frame.
2. Test: Test the options against your skills and vision, and your customers' and partners' feedback.
3. Cull: Eliminate options that aren't going to work. Be aggressive.
4. Pick and Negotiate: Select the one to three companies that make the most sense, while taking steps to reduce costs and improve benefits if possible.
5. Adapt: As circumstances change, repeat steps 1 to 4.

As you refine your concept in your discussion with one supplier or another, float your revised concept to all of them. Some won't be able to keep up—drop them. Hopefully, you'll get down to your top two or three.

Ideally, these top two or three firms are each able to produce your product and understand your needs. A decision now should be down to two factors: price and minimum volume. Nearly all manufacturers will have a minimum amount of *stuff* that they need to make for you, if any at all. This could be driven by the machines they use, the labor rates they have, or the way they buy their supplies. However, if they have bought in to your project and see your potential to become a big business for them, they will dig deep into their companies to help you make it happen.

The more difficult piece to capture is the sweet spot that overlaps quality, execution, and detail. A great price is not as helpful if product delivery takes forever, and a tiny order size does not help much if many of the details of your product are off. Personal relationships go a long way, too. Go and meet your suppliers, or at least get on the phone. These guys get so many requests from faceless, voiceless people that a call or a smile could easily be the difference in who does or does not get on the docket. Later, in Chapter 5, we get into ways we test your suppliers to keep them honest to the level of quality and service they promise.

The Bottom of the Chain: Find Your Raw Materials Supplier

Initially, your co-packer may or may not have the means and the network to source all your raw materials. If he can, he will usually have an honest assessment of the price and quality of their inputs, since they are for the most part passing those costs right through to you.

If your design calls for something your manufacturer cannot get, you're going to need to source it yourself. I've seen excellent product designers struggle sometimes to really wrap their head around the really tiny details that go into sourcing raw materials well. For example, if you're creating a new kind of women's bag, you might know all about its features, its shape, and even how to cut the fabric. You might not have thought about all the different types of buttons and buckles that are out there, or what brand, weave, and thickness you want in the fabric. In general, the manufacturer will want to know all the details of the product itself—the raw material suppliers will want to know all the details of the individual parts that make up your product.

What we need to do now is nail down these details while finding some dependable suppliers. First, you ask your co-packer. After all, they've walked down this road with tons of products, and often have an idea on where to get raw materials.

Whether or not your manufacturer is able to get you your inputs, you should have an idea of what exactly they are, and how differences therein could affect your product in quality or price. While your initial thought might be that it isn't worth your time to figure out all the granular details of all of your inputs—I hope to persuade you to do so. Your inputs really define the quality of your product, and once decided, come with a high switching cost. It's difficult to change suppliers once you've started working with one as your manufacturer and customers get used to the nuance the raw material gives them.

I had to learn this lesson the hard way. When sourcing my raw materials, I made the difficult decision to find my own supplier, even though my manufacturer claimed to be able to source it. I wanted to control every detail and own every relationship between the farm and my consumer, and was willing to put the time in to do so. After a lot of chasing wild geese, I found a great little company based in Washington who could get me all sorts of fun, exotic stuff. After all, though I had only one product now, I knew I wanted to create a platform for many products, which meant each of my suppliers needed to bring a level of scale with them. My manufacturer started using this to make my product, and learned only then that my customers didn't really like the taste. I was getting really tough feedback from some high-value groups. I wished right then that I had tested different suppliers and made the product myself before running it through the production machine and placing it in front of customers. I would never get those sales back.

Choosing a supplier is a permanent decision. You're married to them the moment you create a batch of product and show it to someone. There are four top areas to look at when qualifying a supply source:

1. *Quality:* The quality of your inputs multiplies into the quality of your product. If it is poor tasting, poorly collected, easily

broken, or has any other obvious defect, your product will share those as well. While it may not be worth your dollar to buy the absolutely highest quality possible, you should be sure you are buying components you can put your name on.

2. *Input life:* How long does your input last on its own? If it is a plastic resin or other inert material, then it might last nearly forever. However, if it might melt, decay, or spoil, its life is a critical concern in its purchase. In general, longer life is preferred, since your product will then enjoy a longer shelf life, and you are less likely to face spoils in your warehouse or on the shelf.

3. *Input use:* How is the input used in your product? How much of it is used at once? In the production of certain items of clothing or other softgoods, yards and yards of fabric are used at once. In general, the less of the supply that you need to commit to at once, the more flexible you will be able to be.

4. *Input pack:* How is your input material sold, and specifically, how is this different from the way it is used? For a while, I would purchase raw fruit puree from the farm 200 gallons at a time. However, the filling machine needed 500 gallons to run as well as possible. This meant I would waste half an order of raw materials for each order of product. Without good relationships with my suppliers, this would have come right out of my margin—but I was able to work with my supplier to buy half-containers of the puree to get only 500 gallons. This one little thing easily saved me several thousand dollars up front, and about 25 percent of my margin on the finished product.

Debate: Local Production versus Abroad

A big question that comes up at this stage is whether you should find production locally, or else try to find production in a place where they are proximal to suppliers or in a country better suited to production than your own.

Local production means your manufacturer is always on hand—a phone call away in your own time zone. The manufacturer can respond to questions and concerns, respond to changes if you have any, and in general can be within arm's length.

(continued)

Debate: Local Production versus Abroad (continued)

On the other hand, moving production farther away comes with its own benefits. Having the co-packer close to the supplier (rather than close to you) will save you money in transit. Having the co-packer in a different country, where the means of production and labor are less expensive will bring down your costs as well.

Having done both, I'll offer my perspective. When my packer was located in New Jersey, less than 30 minutes away from me in New York, he and I were always on the phone, and it was very helpful as we nailed down the concept. Eventually, however, I realized that my supply was in Florida for most of the year, and so we started using the Florida facility of the same company. We were so close to the supply that the farmer was able to drive my order over in his own truck, and my trucking costs fell to nearly zero. On the whole, I saved about 15 percent by moving from local production to supply-near production.

Then I started getting e-mails and phone calls from vendors across the world. Production facilities in China, Taiwan, Indonesia, and more were trying to win my support! After a lot of questions, I wanted to give a Taiwanese company a shot. He turned out to be a very compelling choice. Even though international production would mean that I need to ship my finished goods all across the world, I was able to save nearly 75 percent of my costs while keeping my product. It was like magic money that really enabled us to take the company to the next level.

I won't tell you if it's for you or not, as a global supply chain comes with unique challenges. It does take a bit more effort and time to speak to international partners. I lost a lot of sleep as I was routinely on the phone or video conference late at night because of the time difference, and disagreeing with e-mails and letters because of the language barrier. However, the bottom line benefited, and since I was running this business on nearly no money, the benefits outweighed the challenges.

The looming question here is: where can you find a supplier? What if you're unable to stumble onto one, and if your manufacturer is unable to find you the perfect partner? Then you need to follow the methodology laid out in this book to find one from scratch.

Let's go back to our trusty base options: the business directory, like a physical or digital white pages, and online aggregators like

Apply the Inspired Method to Choose a Supplier

1. List: Collect a list as exhaustive as possible within a reasonable time frame.
2. Test: Test the options against your skills and vision, and your customers' and partners' feedback.
3. Cull: Eliminate options that aren't going to work. Be aggressive.
4. Pick and negotiate: Select the one to three companies that make the most sense, while taking steps to reduce costs and improve benefits if possible.
5. Adapt: As circumstances change, repeat steps 1 to 4.

Tradekey and Alibaba. After a few quick searches on what you're looking for, capture all the available options.

Draft a form letter to a supplier that specifies what you need, what it's for, and how you would like it packed. Blast it out to them indiscriminately. Sometimes I find that I can contact tens or even a hundred suppliers in this way, depending on what the commodity is that I'm looking for.

As the questions start to flow back in, don't try to answer them one by one. If you've truly sent out a broad message, it will be impossible. Instead, give it a week or two and answer all the questions at once in a single broadcast. The questions you get will vary based on what item you are trying to get and how clear your original communication was. If you've contacted vendors across the world, it's possible that there may be a touch of language barrier too, but don't let that scare you.

At this point, your question answers would have scared off some suppliers and your read on their offering should help you whittle down the list. Work your way down to the top 10 if you can, and start quizzing them on some personal details.

How long have they been in business? Have they worked with a product like yours before? How flexible is price? Just like with your manufacturer, you want to make sure your raw materials suppliers are long-term, value-added partners that you won't need to swap out later. You're building a platform, not just a product, and they need to be able to keep up as you come up with new items. After you've had these discussions, ask them all to send you a sample of their goods so that you can really compare them. In many cases, you might think you've described what you want perfectly, but having to choose between multiple options will really bring a bit of laser focus to your decision making.

After you see which ones you like best, try to knock the price down one last time before selecting a vendor.

Summary

This chapter has been a whirlwind! If you've been keeping up (instead of just reading, you armchair product designers!) you should have a much stronger understanding than you did before of what your customers are looking for, who some key distributors are for your favorite retailers, and what both are looking for in a product. You should have spoken to a manufacturer who helped you really flesh out your concept and maybe even some raw material vendors who could make it all happen.

At this point you might be wondering, with all these players at the table—what does your company actually do? You're not going to create raw materials or mass produce your product. You're not a chain of stores, or a distributor, and you certainly can't keep it all.

Your job is the most complex, most rewarding, and most interesting job of all: to build this machine and keep it running. It's your job to prime the pump of demand and get consumers excited, to sell to retailers and keep them active, to work with distributors and keep them incented. As long as you do that, you will also pull through your manufacturer and raw materials and in the process, keeping a piece for yourself. It's a part-marketing, part-management, part-creative job that demands knowledge of your customer and your industry. Don't let that scare you, though—with the right systems in place, it will practically run itself.

For now, plan on some tough work to pull it all together, but in time, imagine a nearly fully automated machine through which demand pulls through stores, while sales forces push it through, all the while depositing money in your account.

When your supply chain is your airplane, and when it's pointed in the right direction, we're ready for liftoff.

> ## ⚠ Challenge: Focus
>
> While constructing your supply chain, you will be talking to a lot of different people, who do a lot of different functions in the interests of putting together something compelling for your vision. All of them may throw questions, concerns, and comments at you that could take your eye off the ball and drain your time unnecessarily.
>
> Your ability to stick to the vision for your product will be tested at every turn, and can save you a lot of time, confusion, and money. This exercise will try to help you build that focus.
>
> Find yourself a crowd of pedestrians. This could be at rush hour in the subway or at a sale at the mall. In the hustle and bustle of people walking in all directions, focus on a stranger 10 or 20 feet in front of you, and keep your eye on them as they walk in different directions, and as your line of sight is cut by others walking around as well. (Don't be creepy; this is just an exercise.)
>
> How long can you keep it up? How tough is it to stay focused as people bump into you, obstacles get in your way, and sights and sounds hit you from every direction?

PHASE II

LAUNCH

CHAPTER 5

Packaging a Product

All that is gold does not glitter.

—J.R.R. Tolkien

I was devastated when I first realized that my precious packaging was all wrong. After months of preparation, research, and math, I realized that it just wasn't going to cut it. "Gorgeous but unreal" summarizes the feedback I was getting from partners; "small and expensive" was the feedback I was getting from customers; "cool but difficult" was the feedback I was getting from consumers. In a world where 20-ounce plastic throwaway bottles were the norm, I was selling an 8-ounce glass art piece. The shape made it visually appealing but tough to drink from, the material made it heavy (and expensive to ship) and the production made it very expensive. I thought I was trying something bold and new, but it came across as super-premium and inaccessible.

By no means was I the first to come up with bold packaging. Back in 1987, an Austrian and a Thai launched a product that would change the world. As legend has it, they spent a year perfecting their product, but two full years creating their package.

For a start-up product in traditional channels, your packaging is arguably more influential than your product in early success.

Consumers, fickle creatures that we are, tend to make instantaneous gut-level decisions on whether or not we like something we see within moments of coming across something new in a store. When someone sees your product, will they love it, or will they wonder how some amateur got into their store?

You only get one first impression on a customer—make it work for you.

Dietrich, the Austrian, was an entrepreneur and brand master who understood the art and science of packaging. Chaleo, the Thai, understood the secret and chemistry of the product. Together, they went back and forth over what material to use, what size it should be, what colors speak best, what messaging and themes would most engender a strong following among their potential customers. While both were successful businessmen, neither had launched a product before, and wanted to take the time, effort, and resources to get it right.[1]

While one might argue that a great product should sell itself, a great package will grab attention, paving the way for your terrific product to do the convincing. Your package can also be a significant cost to your product, and getting it right can hit both your top and bottom lines. Packaging can be challenging to create, and heart-wrenching when your friends, customers, or partners think your baby is ugly or unconvincing. Then again, do it right and you could end up like Chaleo—the richest man in Thailand and one of my personal heroes.[2]

When I offer this advice, I often hear that package design is reserved for professionals—that a normal person like you or me is incapable of producing appealing design. In my experience, an amateur designer who is willing to learn the skill and has the patience to create several iterations will come up with a design that is as good as, or often better than a professional might have made.

We spend some time in this chapter outlining the basics of appealing package design and arm you with the tools to create something yourself. However, should you choose to go with a designer or a design firm, we also put some techniques in your pocket for managing and negotiating with them.

Planning Your Package

As we start to think about what kind of packaging you will need, and how you're going to get it, we should be cognizant of the challenges presented by more complex packages. This is often dictated by your category: your innovative breakfast cereal probably goes into a simply printed box, whereas your electronic gadget is going to need a molded or machined casing, packing material, a paper product box as well as a clamshell.

Table 5.1 gets into some of the initial considerations to take before jumping wholeheartedly into a particular package shape or appearance. Each time you take on a new vendor, you need to manage minimum order requirements, input and output constraints, and a host of other details (not to mention the relationship with the vendor's personnel).

Despite your category's apparent rules, the choice really depends on what your customer uses to judge the quality of the goods. In the beverage space, packaging is so critical to market approval that it can often be as big a cost driver as the product itself. In software or electronics, packaging is less critical because customers have placed more emphasis on the product within.

As you get into your discussions with suppliers for full packaging or for components, there are a few key terms you may want to keep in mind. Besides price, which you should benchmark off of multiple suppliers, you will want to know what minimum volumes

Table 5.1: Packaging Complexity

	Single Vendor, Simple Finish	Multi-Vendor, Complex Finishing
Stock Packaging	Having a single vendor create your package from stock components will keep things simple for you, and probably keep your costs down, at the expense of an elaborate package. For example: a printed cardboard box of a standard size, printed by your co-packer.	While keeping tabs on multiple vendors can be time-consuming, it is often the only way to get more complex details on your package. For example: a stock glass bottle that needs to go to a ceramic decorator for a fancy label.
Custom Packaging	If you need something specialized in paper, plastic, glass, or metal and can have it created and finished from a single company, you might be able to get the best of both worlds. For example: a custom clamshell for a kid's toy or the perfect-sized printed fold-up.	The sky is the limit in both creative ability and cost when stringing together custom work from multiple vendors. For example: custom-molded plastic casing that needs to go to paint-finishing and decorating at different shops.

they correspond with. You will want to know whether packing is done automatically or by hand, and how the packed item integrates with distributor systems and preferences.

Not limited to just packaging, an important question to ask any vendor when considering his services is that of *minimum volumes*—a reference to the number of orders the vendor must fulfill at a bare minimum to do any work at all. This is usually driven by the opportunity cost of labor or of running a machine, and can be difficult to talk your way around. For example, if a beverage filler needs to set up a filling and labeling machine to pour a certain volume, a certain size bottle and a certain formula, the bottler will often want to run at least a full day's shift for a single order. A company creating molded plastic parts may want to be sure it is running through a certain volume of plastic resin per order, and a company producing electronic hardware may need to balance the complexity and potential for your order with the other work that it may do with its limited capacity.

While you can sometimes mitigate the effect of minimum volumes, you still likely need to manage to them as well. This applies to any work or component that you need from a vendor. For example, when developing the supply chain for Star Power, we were purchasing several stages of work and component: A bottle, a printed label, a cap, a filling service, and a capping and labeling service whose minimum volumes did not always overlap.

Our initial setup required three vendors, each of whom had different rules: the glass packaging vendor needed us to purchase five thousand bottles, which we luckily were able to negotiate down to five hundred. The decorator, who would frost and label the bottles needed us to purchase the service for ten thousand bottles, which we struggled to negotiate down to one thousand for the first order. The filler needed us to purchase ten thousand gallons (which for our 8-ounce bottle amounted to 625 bottles) but had to also fit into 12-unit cardboard cases. Not including the thousands of perforated shrink seals and caps for the bottles, there was not always a perfect match between the volumes of the different packaging components we needed to get. In fact, I still have a few cartons of unused bottle caps.

Depending on your product, you may get to choose between *manual and automated methods of packing* your product and your case.

In other cases, the machine will not exist, and your case will need to be packed by hand.

If the machine does exist, you could decide this based purely on costs. Exceptions could be if your product is:

- Too fragile to be machine packed (for example, glass sculpture).
- Too cumbersome or oddly shaped to be machine handled (for example, sports trophies).
- Finally assembled by hand (for example, shoes and shoelaces).
- A collection of unassembled parts (for example, cufflinks).
- Expensive enough that the cost of the standard error rate, often 1 to 5 percent, is greater than the cost savings of machine-packed versus hand-packed (for example, high-end laptops).
- Required in a different case configuration than the machine can do, because of design constraint or customer demand (that is, a machine can pack 24 beverage bottles in a case, but the customer requires a 12-pack). This was the case for Star Power, my personal project.

If any of the preceding is true, then you should choose hand-packed or pick and pack over a more economical machine packing. The same applies for putting individual units into a case, and individual cases into a master case. When considering your case-pack you will need to strike a balance between keeping the price low for your customer, and keeping your costs low from your vendors.

After my staff and I spent awhile trying to manage the list of vendors we had going for my product's packing, we were able to find a single vendor who could create the bottle, print the label, fill the product, pack the cases, and even wrap the pallets. Because we moved from a glass bottle to a plastic one, we were able to machine-pack the cases rather than hand-pack them.

Case configuration, and the way your package *integrates with your distributor* is an important though less than critical consideration. Even though you may be far from a product, and even further from selling it right now, it will eventually become important to consider industry or category norms so that your distributors don't feel like you're twisting them in circles just to work with you. While many understand the challenge facing the entrepreneur, few will agree to be twisted. In addition, a knowledgeable co-packer will understand industry norms as well, and can answer this question partially until you have a stable base of distributors to call your own.

Also, there are more nuanced considerations in packing config-uration that do not present themselves at the beginning. A retailer who is used to purchasing cases of 24 may not agree to do the con-version math to your cases of 12, for example. This would result in half as many up-front sales as they compare the number of cases of your stuff versus that of your competitors. Or, a distributor who pays his reps $5 per case in commissions actually pays twice as much for the same volume with cases of 12 than with cases of 24. He then has less incentive to move a ton of your stuff versus the other items in his truck. Similar examples apply to pallet-packs. Initially, however, you should quickly compromise with your suppliers on this item to get a better price.

Stock versus Custom

The most critical packaging decision you would have to make early on is whether you will use *stock or custom packaging*. Stock packaging refers to what's already being made (typically for industrial appli-cations) and will be readily available to you nearly immediately, sometimes in volumes as low as a single unit. The advantage with stock packaging is financial—you save on the time and expense of designing a package, of fitting a mold, and of meeting a much higher minimum order size. On the other hand, you risk an undif-ferentiated appearance on the shelf.

Custom packaging is designed by you strictly for your use. With a custom package, you are much more likely to have a unique appearance on the shelf. You can have much more control than with a stock package. However, you will likely need to meet a mini-mum order volume over nearly every aspect of your package, which can vastly increase the start-up cost of your business.

This decision is based on three main factors: stock packaging availability for your category, the minimum volume of the custom package you want, and your capitalization. You could have a stock option that entirely fits your needs, or be able to negotiate custom packaging at manageable volumes. Or, you could be rich enough that it doesn't matter.

While hunting for the perfect packaging for Star Power, I employed a systematic approach that I recommend to you. I wanted to find a packaging option that stood out, and that I could test with manageable minimum volumes.

I started, as per the Inspired Method, by taking a total inventory of the packaging options available to me. There were glass and plastic packaging options from beverage and industrial applications. There were aluminum bottles and aluminum cans, and there were paper tetrapaks. I knew I wanted to strike a premium image, and was pretty set on glass or aluminum. There were few suppliers who could create custom options, and they came with 25,000- to 50,000-unit minimums. There were also some stock packages that would work—I could buy these 12 at a time. Given that the budget was nearly non-existent, I chose to go for the stock packaging. It was a compact bottle with a premium feel and weight, which I could get in low volumes. I purchased a case, not really knowing what I would do with it.

I then needed to decorate this bottle with some artwork, write some copy, and certain information required by regulation. This is when the next difficult decision comes into play. Labels tend to scale in price based on three factors—number of colors used, special treatments, and intricacies of the package shape. If your package was in a stock rectangular paper or plastic box, with a single color print, no special treatments, you might create extremely economical packaging. On the other hand, you may squander the one opportunity you have to convince your customer that your product is what you say it is.

Depending on the expected price of your product, and the margin left over for more intricate packaging you could decide to create a nicer label. If your supplier is using a digital press, there may not be an extra charge for a full color label. Also, flourishes like foil stamping (for some shiny flair) and acid etching can go a long way toward a truly differentiated label.

For my glass bottle, I decided to create frosted glass (using acid etching) and then baking on a ceramic label in a single color. It was gorgeous. Yours can be, too.

This brings up the point that there are actually two design tasks in creating an appealing package. The first is the structural design and selection of the packaging unit itself. The second is the graphic design of the label.

While each category is different, there are a few key elements that every good label has.

- Product name: It should be memorable, descriptive, and concise.
- Key benefits: It should quickly get to the heart of why someone should buy this.
- Regulated messaging: The place of origin, ingredient lists on foods, age band and choking hazards on toys, and so on.

Also, many good labels let you see the product, or even interact with it (try me!). Most of us are not graphic designers. You may even find the very task of label design seems very arbitrary. I will spend the rest of this chapter walking through essential design tasks that you should be able to build, and then allow you to make your own decision between whether you choose to do your own graphic design, or to hire someone to lay out the label for you.

If you feel you are creatively capable and emotionally resilient enough to design your own label, and bear to hear feedback on it, I recommend trying first to *be your own designer*. It is far less expensive than hiring a firm and you will probably grow professionally in the process. You will need to finalize the name (or get down to your top three choices so we can test them) as well as write some pithy copy for your key messages. You have to fill your packaging real estate with meaningful messaging, or choose open white space. You have to research the legal disclosures required by your industry and make sure to put them on there.

When working on Star Power, this was the route I chose. I felt reasonably capable as a visual designer and got to work selecting fonts and graphical elements (ultimately choosing a free, curvaceous font and a star as my design element). I researched FDA reporting requirements and created a nutrition panel and ingredient list that met requirements. I then spent a few iterations making sure my advisors liked the design before I settled on it.

Doing this work myself was difficult not only because of the technical skills that I had only an intermediate level of, but also because of the way creative work opens an idea to criticism. Any time you share your design with an observer (and you should do this as often as someone will look), he will tell you what he likes and doesn't like about it. It takes some practice to dissociate criticism of a design from criticism of the designer, but the final product is then that much more satisfying. Self-made, self-paid.

As an alternative to doing your own design work, you can *hire a design firm* or freelancer to do the same. There are some excellent,

Exercise: Mock-Up Your Package

Given what you know about your product and your industry, what does your ideal package look like? Would you want to copy the style of market leaders in your space, or do you have something new in mind?

Sit down with a piece of paper and diagram out what your package looks like in your head. The drawing does not need to be art, but should lay out roughly what information goes where. As an example, see Figure 5.1. I used a photograph from after the prototype since I didn't have everything mapped out beforehand.

If you have a pretty tight vision, lay it out. If you have multiple ways that all seem to make sense, lay them out, too. The more options you're able to put in front of a designer or your packager, the more likely you are to come up with a product that you're proud of.

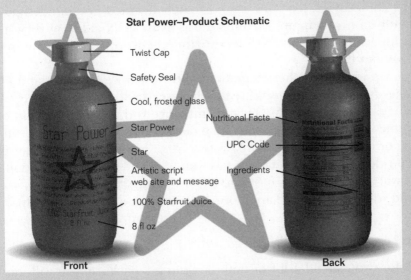

Figure 5.1 Star Power Glass Schematic

experienced, creative firms, many of which have done package design for both start-up and mature companies. While they can be expensive, typically in the tens of thousands of dollars, they will professionally assemble several packaging options, and have the right imaging in place for you to easily create materials, too. With some searching, and bit of negotiating, you can often get a firm to reduce their rates in exchange for an equity stake in your product. When operating on a shoestring budget, that can be an appealing choice.

Freelance designers are also a great resource for discrete projects like coming up with a packaging concept. I interviewed a lot of freelancers, and each time, would ask them to review my product and premise and come up with some ideas. Unlike many other types of service providers, it can be difficult to ask creative professionals (especially small shops or freelancers) to do something too *different* from their natural style. It will be worth the time and effort to team up with a creative who is in the same vein and style as your brand.

If you want professional help, but still want to dip your fingers in the design pool, you could consider my *hybrid approach:* Design your own materials, but have a professional execute your designs. While your results will vary, this option has recently become much more appealing to me. I am able to satisfy my creative impulses by mocking up or describing several versions of what I think my package should look like, and my extremely talented graphic designer deftly mocks them up. I'll often see as many as six different versions (with graphical nuances differentiating them) of each concept that I put out there.

We will review them together to see which we like best, and I'll take a shortlist of my top three to the streets and get customer opinions on the options. My biggest influence is the fond adulation or immediate dismissal of a potential design by a selection of consumers or by an influential store owner. Try to involve your customer in your design process—it will it save you time and money in iterations. It will also make your customers feel a closer partnership with you and your product, and are more likely to push it wholeheartedly.

Test the Package Compatibility

Before you spend a lot of time designing a package, you will want to make sure that you think through its implication on your get-to-market strategy.

A package decides many things. Besides the obvious first impression on your consumer, your package will play a deciding factor in how your product sits on its inevitable shelf, and could even limit the selection of accounts in your initial launch.

For example: in the beverage business, the selection of the bottle determines how well the product glides on the shelf, and the height of the bottle determines whether the product can go on a middle shelf or the bottom shelf. The choice of packaging material will affect logistics (as glass is heavier than paper, plastic, and aluminum). The decision to pack 6, 12, or 24 units in the case will determine whether chain or independent accounts offer more resistance to your sales, and will have an interplay with your eventual distributor's incentive program ($1 per case commission is twice as expensive in a 12-pack than a 24-pack).

In the hardgoods business, the type of clamshell package will dictate whether big-box retailers can put you up at the register, and in toys, the length of your package can have an impact on what percentage of the shelf is dedicated to your company.

A whole array of possibilities, opportunities, and limitations will be decided by the specifications of your package. Many of them will be largely invisible to you without some due diligence along the way.

In addition to getting your customer's support on a package, you will need the support of your manufacturing facility. Although they may not be as interested in the design (except as consumers themselves), they will be able to tell you if the dimensions of your package fit their equipment, and whether or not you will be exposed to additional charges or delayed timings because of a particular packing choice.

After figuring out which of your package designs are producible, walk in to the local branches of the retailers that lead your category. Study their best-selling items and see what similarities and differences they share with your package. Speak to store managers. If you are able, reach out to the central buyers and get their opinion. While not everyone will react warmly to this test, those who do could provide invaluable feedback, and save you much time and money.

When I was working on Star Power, I followed a similar strategy that I was later able to compare to my new peers who had products of their own. I created a close partnership with some great packaging partners, and created a few tangible prototypes of my favorite design.

In retrospect, I could have created three, four, or five options. I then took this prototype to the community thought leaders—the guys who wrote the trade publications, the regional buyer for a major natural foods chain in my area, as well as the owners of the leading distributors in New York City.

I learned three main things from them: The appeal of my package versus their best sellers, the credibility of my selling points versus what they knew about their customers, and key challenges I would face because of critical product choices. I had a glass bottle, which felt premium but would be more expensive to ship. I had an 8-ounce serving, compared to the 12- or 16-ounce servings of the leading companies, and I had a 100 percent juice where consumers tended to prefer watered-down, sugar-coated candy beverages. In total, this test cost me $500 to learn what many of my peers learned from their first production batch or their first focus group, a $10,000-to-$20,000 experience.

After the test, reflect on what you've learned and finalize your design using the feedback you have received. If you have followed this chapter properly, you will now have a detailed product mock-up or tangible prototype in hand, and you will be most of the way through building an extended team of unofficial advisors. You will have a relationship with a graphic designer or design firm that will serve you very well for the lifetime of your project. You will have a packaging supplier who now trusts your choices, as they have been vetted by your customer, making it easier to take future risks on you or offer your work higher priority without financial incentive. You will also have first contact with many future customers, which will prove invaluable when setting the foundation for your sales process.

Types of Packaging

When designing your package, the materials you select will have a measurable impact on the cost of your product as well as its appearance to your customer.

- *Corrugated cardboard:* A heavy-duty material made by pasting layers of paper together. The layers give this material strength, but also a thickness and distinctive ribbed look that are not always aesthetically preferred. Because it is paper, it is easily printed on as well. It is ubiquitous, and nearly any vendor can work with it, and it isn't very expensive to work with. It is also easily recycled and biodegradable.

It's typically used in all sorts of product packaging from the boxes for electronics to the cases for beverages. It has an industrial look that is usually reserved for packaging parts that consumers don't see.

- *Cardstock:* A sturdy material that is basically a thick piece of paper, cardstock is a useful paper packaging material in many cases for which corrugated won't work. Cardstock is much thinner than corrugated, and while less heavy-duty, is much more versatile. It is inexpensive, easily printed on, recyclable and biodegradable.

  It is typically used in all sorts of applications that don't need to bear much weight. It has a clean appearance that is used in many children's toys packaging, canned or bottled beverage six-packs, and cereal boxes.

- *Paper:* Although paper is the main ingredient in the card-board materials discussed here, it is also used in some of its own applications. It isn't very durable, but is easily available, versatile, and inexpensive.

  It is used in the stickers on vodka or other glass bottles, the tags on clothing (which count as packaging), as well as in the tissue paper that is often a subcomponent of another packing style. It is also used in cartons like juice boxes, orange juice, tetrapaks, and more.

- *Plastic bottle:* Plastic bottles come in all shapes and sizes, and in a host of materials. They can be as small as an energy shot or a vial of liquid pheromone or as large as a milk jug (or larger). They can be round or boxy, and can be molded to nearly any shape. They can be made in nearly any color, and from a few different types of plastic depending on what you need (high density, low density, polyvinyl, polyethylene, and so forth).

  These are used in beverage bottles, supplement bottles, some snacks, peanut butter, and more. Because of the degree of control the brand can have over the appearance of the product, and the relatively inexpensive cost of plastic bottles, they are a great choice if you can use them at all.

- *Plastic box or casing:* Similar to plastic bottles, plastic boxes can be used to hold nearly anything. Plastic casings can be used on anything with components that need to be held together as well.

  These are used for many electronics as well as DVD boxes. They can look like anything you want since plastic can be molded to nearly any shape.

- *Glass bottle:* Unlike plastic bottles, glass is expensive, heavy, and fragile. It does not melt easily but is fairly moldable. It is easily recycled, and can be decorated in a variety of ways.

  These are used for beverages, supplements, perfumes, and aromatherapy. They can withstand high heat, and so can be used for products that need to be pasteurized and filled while still hot (which would melt a plastic bottle).

- *Aluminum:* Metal packaging offers a distinctive look in some categories and critical functionality in others.

  It is used to hold beer and soda, often helping with certain types of treatments (like tunnel pasteurization). It is also used as packaging in decorative applications such as the outer package for perfume and watches.

- *Clamshell:* Plastic packaging that can be molded to any shape, and sealed in a way that is extremely tough and very annoying to open. It is also a great way to showcase small items along with some imaging.

  It is used to hold all sorts of small products, electronics, action figures, and more.

When selecting a package for my product, a beverage, I started with the glass bottle. The weight made it feel substantial, and the glass was cool to the touch. Ultimately, however, it would prove too expensive for a small business to create at a fair price and I started looking at other options.

Like the old cashier's dilemma, I really had just two options: paper or plastic. Paper packaging, like the tetrapaks used in many juice boxes or the cartons used for orange juice were dependable, recyclable, and inexpensive. I could print any graphic on them, but had little choice in their shape. Plastic (or high-density polyethylene to be specific) turned out to be even less expensive, and had similar benefits. While it was not biodegradable, it was easily recycled and the cost made it a no-brainer. I got my plastic bottles, label and all, for less than 10 cents each.

Also, I had to put these bottles in a case before I could sell them. Keeping it simple, we went with a simple white corrugated cardboard case with our logo printed on all sides.

Basics of Design

Most of us are not trained professional designers. However, any of us can understand the components that make a product package work and do our best to either fully design our package or at least create something compelling that we can hand off to a designer. We look here at some of those elements and see what you might be able to do to take your package to the next level. There are three key tasks as you create your product's label: Color selection, font selection, and the creation or placement of the various elements on the label.

Color selection is a highly contentious art—there is a lot of product psychology floating around about what the best colors are for your products package.

In my opinion, there are two schools of thought: to color the package like the product, or to color the package with evocative or brand colors. Customers who like a product usually want to see it. Do you prefer to drink a beverage out of a can or a bottle?

On the other hand, a new product needs to stand out on the shelf, and a differentiated color can often be the least expensive way to stand out.

When selecting colors for the packaging of my product, I wanted to stay with the all-natural theme I was going for, especially since most of the other products on the shelf did the same. My product

A Colorful Philosophy

If you believe the popular psychology, here's what I think many agree about colors:

Red: strength, passion, blood. Attention grabbing.
Orange: warmth, fire, food. Stimulating.
Yellow: Sunshine, energy, cowardice. Brightening.
Green: Health, money, safety. Relaxing.
Blue: Intelligence, trust, ocean. Calming.
Purple: Prestige, magic, luxury. Rich.
Black: Elegant, evil, death. Ubiquitous.
White: Pure, clean, peaceful. Goodness.

had a yellow color to it and so I made much of the package yellow (since I could not make it clear). By choosing a rather bold yellow, I also ensured that I would stand out on the shelf, as customers walking by would always see the bold, nearly glowing yellow right next to some darker shade of beverage. I chose to make the text on the package, and the color of the logo a dark blue (nearly purple) both because it offered a legible contrast from the yellow, and to imply some of the richness and intelligence associated with the colors.

The typeface you use for the name of your product and the various messages on your package can have as profound an impact on your customer as the message itself.

Classic tyepfaces like Times New Roman, Helvetica, and Verdana are universally applicable—aesthetic, legible, and simple. They are good to use for the text of a message, where the key is to really keep the typeface out of the way so that the message comes through loud and clear.

There are some cases, such as the nutrition labels on a food item, the country of origin declaration or legal disclosures to the FDA or FCC (should you need them) that are mandated to be of a particular typeface and size. In many cases, the preferred typeface is Helvetica, because of its clean design, fascinating history, and successful use in so many applications.

There are also fonts out there that are not intended for body text but instead for titles, headers, and logos only. These fonts have wild embellishments, bold strokes, and graphical elements that could be very useful to you as well.

A History of Helvetica

Helvetica was developed in 1957 by Max Miedinger with Eduard Hoffmann at the Haas'sche Schriftgiesserei (a type foundry, where they create typefaces for printing presses). It was intended to be completely neutral.

When it started getting popular, they changed the name to Helvetica (from New Haas Grotesk), from the Latin name for Switzerland. It is now the most widely used typeface in the world (even though now most of us use it on a computer instead of on a printing press). It is widely used in company names and logos, the U.S. federal government, the New York City and Madrid railways, and many more.[3]

Gothic, Old English, and Stencil fonts are popular, and there are many more than can be named or categorized. If you have an application that needs any of these, it will be worth your while to do the following exercise.

When I was first trying to design my package, I wanted to take a stab at it myself first before simply finding a professional to take care of it for me. It is my firm belief that we are all capable of good design, especially if we take a moment to study the world and ourselves for what is truly aesthetically pleasing.

Exercise: Typeface Selection

We're going to try to expose you to the world of available typefaces and get you to select a few and play with them. Your goal in this exercise is to find one body typeface for your messaging, and one novelty typeface for your titles or logo.

Go to 1001freefonts.com for what I find to be a very compelling selection of free and usable typefaces. Browse the typefaces by category, search for words that interest you, and even otherwise just poke around until you find some that you like.

Then, install them to your computer and type away.

Once you have your colors, messages, and typefaces sorted out, you will need to arrange them on the package. What should you put on the front? The back?

The front of the package is also the *facing*—the part of the product that faces off of the shelf and is seen first by the customer. The front of the package should have all the things you want to see in a first impression: the name of the product, a brief description of what the product is, and key information (size, weight, volume as needed). It is also where you have the opportunity to place any images that help your cause—pictures of your product, colors consistent with your brand, and company logo could all go right on the front.

The sides and back (if rectangular) or the rest of the surface (if cylindrical) is packaging real estate that you should use to sell your product and satisfy regulatory requirements. Describe the product if you would like, and describe the benefits your customer gets by buying or using your stuff. Tell your personal story on how you were inspired to create this product and why you want to share it.

Also, you should include any disclaimers that should warn customers of when *not* to buy, such as age warnings for small objects, allergy warnings for food and beverages, and whether any claims or images on your package are not exactly as they appear.

You might have seen something like the following on supplements: "This product has not been evaluated by the FDA. It is not intended to diagnose, cure, or treat any condition."

You may have seen something like the following on toys: "This product contains small parts and may be a choking hazard for small children. Ages 6 and up."

And something like the following on snack boxes: "Suggested serving. Enlarged to show detail. This product made in a facility that processes peanuts and tree nuts."

Each of them are meant to show a certain warning to protect your customer from any unintended consequences of using your product and protect you with a level of legal coverage in case your product is abused.

Exercise: Packaging Feedback

After putting the time and work in to pick out typefaces and colors and lay them out on a package, we need to see how you did.

Assuming you used software on your computer (I've seen this done in Word, Photoshop, PowerPoint, and Paint) print out the design and wrap it around your package. Is that the way you want it to look? If not, take it back and try again, or consider sourcing design help in the same way we sourced an assistant on eLance.

If you do like it, create a few packaging prototypes and show them to friends, colleagues, and any potential customers with the caveat that it is very much a rough draft. What do people say?

Pay special attention to questions they ask that are not answered in your messaging, or recurring questions that strike you as common sense (but may not be).

This probably would have taken you a fair amount of work and personal emotional investment, so try your best not to take any negative feedback too personally. The more you're able to address, the more likely you are to eventually come up with a successful product.

Remember: It took Red Bull two years of trying, testing, and iteration—and was worth every moment.

Summary

A critical component of your product is in its packaging and design. Packaging your package can be as simple or as complex as you make it; though using stock components in an interesting way can give you a premium, custom appearance without breaking the bank. Designing a package is a bit of an art, but one any of us can attempt it with a bit of patience and direction. Even decisions like color and font selection can be done carefully and effectively, laid out on a package and tested before deciding to take on professional help. So take a stab at making it yourself, and then see if a pro can make it better.

 Challenge: Create New Connections

We humans are creatures of habit. We'll do something a certain way once and stick to it for the rest of our lives. The biggest example of this is left- or right-handedness. We write with one hand, eat with one hand, and favor everything else toward one side of our body, which in turn favors one side of the brain. This exercise will try to make new connections between the left brain and right brain and open new channels for ideas to flow through.

The idea is simple—take an activity that you take for granted, like brushing your teeth, and switch hands. It will feel very strange at first. Your new hand doesn't know the intricate motions that have been learned only by the other hand. The first day this might seem impossible, and even after the first week might still be rather difficult. Stick with it for a while, though, and see if the new connections you build in your brain don't flow forth new ideas from the half of your brain that you've been ignoring.

CHAPTER 6

Produce your Product and Platform

When it comes to the future, there are three kinds of people: those who let it happen, those who make it happen, and those who wonder what happened.

—John M. Richardson Jr.

I had run on little to no sleep for several weeks, and was hitting the proverbial wall. In that time, I had learned a bit of Chinese, and spoken to several Chinese suppliers: companies that did everything from sourcing fruit from all over the world, to creating bottles, to full-on factories. I applied the Inspired Method to great success. Initially, I pit one against the other to negotiate them all to the same terms, and then haggled hard on price. I made few friends and made some people very upset. However, when I looked at the small pile of papers on my desk, I couldn't help but wish that the volume of work that I had done would look like a little more.

At that moment, 2:30 in the morning, Skyping around the world, we had assembled all the deals necessary to run an industrially produced test batch of my product. Our raw materials supplier begrudgingly agreed to sell a tiny volume of raw juice, our packager very hesitantly agreed to keep their prices fixed for less than a quarter of their usual minimum volume. My customs agent agreed to do my first import for free, and my international shipper agreed to use their trucks to do my delivery rather than sit my stuff at port. My distributor cleared some space in the warehouse to accept the delivery, and a few retail customers were already expecting a few cases. The ink was dry on all the agreements, prices and expectations were set. All I had to do was press the button.

By the end of this chapter we're going to try to get you to the same spot.

Taking It to the Next Level

Your product is your baby, and it is easy to go overboard trying to make it perfect off the bat. The first production runs are important for three reasons:

1. They will help you better understand your own vision.
2. They will help culture sales.
3. They will likely be the first time you are able to test all of your vendors and the links between them.

Done well, your production can be inexpensive, but will take some passionate sell-in. Most of the vendors in your production steps are probably designed for rather large economies of scale. When you ask for prototyping, they will complain that your project is costly and inefficient. Their first reaction will either be to deny you the possibility, or else to charge you a hefty premium for an order that does not meet their usual minimum volumes. Only by convincing them that you're on the same team and working toward long-term goals of mutual success will they be most likely to make exceptions for you.

We're going to take your prototypes to the next level, and run a small production batch that will help you develop the initial sales needed to properly mitigate the risk of creating stagnant inventory. This counts double if your product can spoil. The last thing you want for your product is to create a warehouse full of it and then start thinking about the sell.

There are a few things that need to be in place before you can run a small, cost-effective production:

- A Producible Vision
- Stock Components
- Good Supplier Relationships

A Quick Note on Terminology

I use the terms *prototype* and *initial production* interchangeably sometimes but there are two distinct concepts that need to be kept separate. Initially, your product is still being fleshed out, and you might create some by your hands in a facility not necessarily designed for it (for example, your basement). These are prototypes. What we want to do is move out of your basement and into the facilities of professional production plants. When culturing a new relationship with a supplier, the first sample products they give you are still prototypes for your brand, just not ones you've made yourself—since these are likely still evolving and hence part of the concept. Moving production out of your basement and into a facility will help you standardize your product, understand your costs, and focus on building a brand rather than fabricating one item at a time.

A Producible Vision

As unique as your product may be, its first iteration needs to be created by equipment and processes that already exist. Have you ever wondered why concept cars often look different from the ones that make it to showroom floors? There is a balance you will need to strike between the costs of production, the resources available to you, and your concept. This need not be forever, but will be true of the maiden production run, especially if you are trying to do this on a minimal budget.

By now, you should have an idea about the kind of things manufacturers in your industry are able to do. You should also have an idea about regulations you will need to meet, and standards to consider keeping since all the major players do. When I was developing my first initial production run for my product, I had to track what seemed like mundane details, but hold thousands of dollars in savings. Beverage filling machines can fill any bottle, but if the diameter of the nozzle is the same size as the previous product on the line, the filler does not need to retool the machine. Helping your supplier by maintaining some of their standards shows them that you understand their business. Changing some of these details can be a time intensive process that will cost you several thousand dollars without much functional gain (for me at least). FDA and CFSAN regulations led me to pasteurize my product, but that meant my packer needed to be able to pasteurize (basically bringing my product to near boiling temperatures) and my packaging needed to receive a hot fluid without melting.

My first package concept was wildly shaped and stoppered with a cork. Yours may have custom-machined components, molded plastic, or hand-sewn details. All of these have an exponential effect on production cost, especially when working on a minimal budget. Using stock, or off-the-shelf available components will go a long way. Often, you will be able to create something with minimal compromise to your product, and in effect, you are asking your suppliers for a few samples of something already in their office, rather than asking them to commit man-hours and factory time to making you a freebie. It's a far more friendly ask.

This won't be possible in all situations, and if your design mandates a few components that don't exist because they are core to your innovation, don't lose hope. Use the innovation of your product to get your supplier excited. Remember, your supplier is your first investor—your win is his win too.

Stock Components

Stock components are available for all sorts of applications. Plastic and metal hardware, boxes, bottles, labels, casings, and most other components are available off the shelf. For any component of your product that performs a well-defined function, you should be able to find a stock component.

Stock components often come in less exciting shapes, rectangular boxes, cylindrical bottles, and other bits and pieces that may not have the design appeal of the specific curves that you want. However, you, as the creator, need to get to the core of your product's true selling point. For example, if you were creating an electronic product, whose selling points included the ability to play music, take pictures, and jump on a wireless network, you could likely build this product's prototype out of stock components in a plain box while developing the necessary capital to create the more aesthetically pleasing production model. This is because the selling points are in the function.

However, if your product was a beautifully designed paperweight whose primary function was to look good on your desk, the design likely needs to be more fleshed out in the maiden production run.

Unfortunately, however, a product is rarely this black and white. When I was developing my beverage, I knew that both were equally important. The functional benefits were determined through consumer research, (which you should already have under way for your product) and the appearance determined through a study of existing best practices and the eye of a good designer. For example, I knew consumers were into antioxidants, which have some proven (and some not-so-proven) benefits, and that they tended to purchase glass bottles with a premium feel. Using available components and processes, I was able to create a very appealing, frosted glass bottle with a ceramic label, using the vendors I had been in discussions with for a month. The first two came to me for free. Now I just needed to fill them with product.

Good Supplier Relationships

As you think about what is most important to you, consider Table 6.1. A solid supplier relationship is critical in the early stages of producing your product. After all, your suppliers are doing business

Table 6.1: Form versus Function

Product Cost\Selling Point	Form	Function
Inexpensive	Inexpensive packaging is usually stock material and shape. They tend to have simple geometric forms and may be undifferentiated from other products using the same stock components. You could later choose to get more expensive packaging and a nicer form.	You may need to focus on the core function of the packaging to keep the costs down. That might mean not having the collectible bottle cap, the special stackable casing, or the biodegradable plastic early on.
Expensive	If the form of your package is more important to you, some customization is possible with a bigger budget. Injection-molded plastic parts, blow-molded glass parts, and custom-machined wood or metal parts all come with steeper manufacturing and setup fees than the stock packaging, but are more likely to give you a differentiated image at the shelf.	More customized packaging comes with opportunities to add functionality to your package as well. Anything from collectible or stackable components, built-in coupons, or built-in bottle openers could be possible depending on your product and your need.

with multiple brands. Some are making them most of their money—successful products from big brands, perhaps. Those are likely to be low growth—most suppliers also keep a few products that promise to be their next big bets. Today, you become the next big bet. How can you make your suppliers buy in to your product, your company, and you to create your first batch as cost effectively as possible? Your suppliers need to understand your vision and its implications for them, and they need to like you personally.

Now you may wonder why this is important. I certainly did. As you work on making your product, you will have enough creative and organizational work to keep you and your assistant busy. Why spend more time and effort selling in your suppliers? You're the customer—you should always be right. The challenge comes in when asking a supplier to bend the rules for you. They need an incentive for them to do so. Specifically, your contact at the supplier will need to pitch your idea to his boss, and they to theirs until the right person hears your story. This story is going to compete not only with all the other new projects out there, each of which has been packaged to sound like a dream come true, but also with projects from existing customers or internal parties at your supplier. You will only be successful by having an idea that is unique in at least some capacity, whose concept speaks to trends in your industry, and through a competent spokesperson—your contact. If they don't have the passion for you and your idea, it won't happen. Your suppliers are your first investors, and we are going to have to sell them well.

My philosophy is that every dollar and every minute is valuable. So is it worth it to spend more time negotiating down your maiden production run to save the cash? Absolutely. The time spent learning your suppliers and negotiating will be valuable not only for your knowledge of what may be at least a partially new industry, but it will also strengthen a relationship that will later pay dividends for the both of you. Triple benefit: Save money, learn more, build a relationship. As a bonus, the money you save on your prototyping can go toward testing the process, your package, and your product.

Let's Get Practical and Get Some Help!

Now, back to your product. Is it easily and inexpensively made? Are you a skilled enough craftsman to make your initial prototypes yourself? If so, you might think you should skip this for now, and you may be right. However, it's my position that the entrepreneur should be building a business, and it is tough to build a business if you are also the manufacturer. So even if you are able to make your own product, read on with an open mind. It may save you a ton of time and heartache.

Let's get tactical. To properly and accurately have someone else build your product, you will need to articulate in no uncertain terms exactly what it is you need them to do. Fortunately, most product categories come with well-defined ways to do this, often called specifications or a *spec sheet*. Most manufacturers won't have an issue sharing the format or sample content of a spec sheet with you.

In addition to specs, you will likely need some images to help communicate the holistic vision of your product. Photographs of your prototype work well, including internal pictures if there are any mechanics or electronics beneath the surface. If your product is a food or beverage, as mine was, the specs are often a formulation, a sort of industrial recipe—a way to produce your good on the machines available. It's a best practice to enter a nondisclosure agreement with anyone you share your specs or formulation with. If you don't have one, feel free to start with mine. (Go to www.wiley.com/go/venkatraman for an NDA document for suppliers.)

Creating a good set of specs can be an exercise in ruthless self-evaluation. We need to lay out exactly what the input materials are, in exactly what quantities, and all the steps to combine them into your product.

When I was developing my product for its first industrial production, I had some sense of what I was getting into. I had a phone-call first-name relationship with my packaging supplier, my co-packer, and my raw materials broker. I had learned some of the jargon for my category—beverages could be *flash pasteurized* (heat treated to sterilize) and *hot filled*; Packages could be PET (plastic) or *flint* (glass); *decorations* (the label on the bottle) could be *shrunk* (plastic heat-shrink printed labels) or *ceramic* (a special kind of ink baked on to the glass). Each have interesting elements, pros and cons, and more importantly, gave me the credibility I needed to secure my prototypes for free. While not critical, being able to speak the language of your industry, and having some knowledge of the materials used in production will show your partners that you're the real deal, and save you from having the wool pulled over your eyes by a fast-talking fox.

Before all of that, however, we need to establish the baseline. Without a common ground across which to evaluate ourselves and multiple suppliers, we may not know whether or not we're truly getting a good deal.

Nailing Down the Details

First, let's get back to that listing of suppliers we collected in Chapter 3. If you have not already done so, a good web search or two should yield at least a starting selection of suppliers. I like to have at least 10 at this stage, but this may not always be possible. Keep in mind that depending on your product, your suppliers need not be in the same country as you. I've created great relationships with beverage companies in Mexico and Taiwan, clothing factories in Thailand and India, and artisans of all kinds in the United States through this process. Using multiple sources but identical criteria is the most holistic and standardized way to gather actionable information on a new category or service.

Keep track of contact info for the companies on your list in a way that makes them easy to use. I prefer a spreadsheet on which I can keep name, address, and e-mail address (see Table 6.2) separate for quickly merging customized communication. For U.S. companies, a bit of searching the Web and business listings should get you a good list. Indeed, you'll find some good international companies this way too. However, don't overlook companies like TradeKey, Alibaba, Elance, and others who allow businesses and freelancers from around the world to post themselves in well-organized categories.

If your product requires multiple suppliers (or *could* require multiple suppliers), include the specialists and the generalists. For now, don't worry too much about specificity—the goal of this stage is only to create a robust list of companies.

With a good list of companies in hand, we're going to sort through them and request a ton of information (RFI) to figure out

Table 6.2: Sample Supplier Contact List

Company Name	Contact	Country	Avg Lead Time	Min Order	Willing to Send Free Samples?
Vik's supplies	Vik	US	2 weeks	1,000 pcs	Yes
. . .	. . .	. . .	. . .	. . .	. . .

Apply the Inspired Method to Selecting Suppliers

1. List: In Chapter 3.
2. Test: In Chapter 3.
3. Cull: In Chapter 3.
4. Pick and negotiate: Understand key levers, while taking steps to reduce costs and improve benefits if possible.
5. Adapt: As circumstances change, repeat steps 1 to 4.

which ones will fit your needs. It is important to go into this stage with an open mind. It's entirely likely that the company with the best fit may not be the one you think of at first.

Step 1: The Sell-In

This is the most important part of your initialization—the sell-in. Most people don't view their vendors as stakeholders—after all, you're the customer here. However, assuming the vendor sees your vision without having to explain it to them first is like asking them to read your mind. Some of them may give you the benefit of the doubt, but your retention rate throughout your negotiations is guaranteed to be higher if you're able to convince your suppliers that you're onto something. A successful product means a new channel for growth, good press, and a sense of satisfaction for them that is likely more exciting than the work they do for larger clients. Sell your heart out before trying to negotiate anything.

In your initial discussions with a new supplier, act as if they were your customer. Ooze passion about how your product will change the market, about how much thought you've put into this, and how hard you're going to work to make them successful. Let them know that you understand the risk they take by working with you, and how much you would appreciate the opportunity. After all, if you cannot inspire suppliers to work with you, it will be difficult to make them compete for your business.

Step 2: Tap Competition

There are two goals to this stage. The first is to educate ourselves about the industry, this category, and the dynamic that suppliers have among themselves and with creators like you. The second is to provide an objective means to compare suppliers and come to an informed decision on which ones to use. With all else equal, I think the best supplier is the one who gets the job done on time, at the best price, with minimal direction. They also need to have a high level of integrity, be responsive, and be willing to send samples. Remember that we need samples! If there are other things that are more important to you, keep them in mind and feel free to edit the following. After we collect all of their info, we will make them compete for your business. After all, you can only work with one of them.

1. *Supplier basic information:* What countries does your supplier do business in, and how much are their annual sales? How old are they? Can they reference specific key client references? Do they have any project management functions? Use this space to learn a bit qualitatively about the suppliers as well, and let them speak to their strengths. We will need this information later for supplier segmentation.

   Using the contact list generated from Table 6.2, add as many relevant details as you can glean from these conversations.

2. *Product and service listing:* Look back at your own list of materials and services that you think you need to build your product and list them out. Here we'll give the supplier a chance to quote preliminary prices on each of the components you need. We need this not only to see the price points, but also to see what each supplier is capable of doing. This is also a good place to check out their quoted minimums for each component—they may not all be the same. For example, my initial request looked something like Table 6.3. The italics represent an illustrative response from a vendor.

   While not all suppliers will fill this out properly, it will go a long way toward setting your expectations about where you might go with negotiations on price. Minimums and lead times will inform an objective comparison across suppliers.

3. *Value engineering:* Unless you're a true expert in all aspects of your supplier's business (which I certainly am not) it's likely that your initial proposal may not make optimal use of their resources. I'll often devote some space to asking the supplier

Table 6.3: Request for Information

	Minimum Volume (Units)	Price per Unit (at Minimum)	Next Level Volume (Units)	Price per Unit (at Next Level Volume)	Lead Time (from Order Date)
Plastic Bottle 8-ounce	1,000	$0.15	5,000	$0.10	2 weeks
Plastic Bottle 16-ounce	1,000	$0.25	5,000	$0.20	2 weeks
Glass Bottle 8-ounce	5,000	$0.50	20,000	$0.10	1.5 weeks
Glass Bottle 16-ounce	5,000	$0.85	20,000	$0.50	1.5 weeks
Bottle label plastic	50,000	$0.01	100,000	$0.005	3 weeks
Bottle label glass	100	$0.10	1,000	$0.05	3 weeks
Product mix and fill	500	$0.30	1,000	$0.10	1 week
Cardboard case	100	$0.20	1,000	$0.15	2 days
Case printing	100	$0.05	1,000	$0.01	1 week
Case packing	1,200	$0.05	10,000	$0.01	1 week

if they would change my spec in any way to increase efficiencies. Supplier efficiencies could be one of three possibilities: material use, supplier's relationships, and leveraging industry norms.

One of the easiest savings areas to pick up earlier on is material use and selection. These savings usually come from an industry or company standard on the way input materials are purchased or packaged. They could also come from a manufacturer's superior knowledge of substitute materials. For example, suppose your product used a printed paper component that you initially designed as a 4 × 5 card. If all the cardstock initially starts as 8.5 × 11 stock, a good supplier might suggest changing your design to be 4.25 × 5.5, which would save 67 percent of the cutting work, and leave you with a larger card (that you might have wanted anyway). You would never have known unless you asked. Alternatively, the manufacturer might suggest an identical yet different stock that is entirely acceptable to you. Again—you only need to ask.

There are also savings that come from the relationships your supplier has built as a result of their time in business. For example, when selecting a bottle for my product, I was faced with dozens of choices from just as many companies, many of which created identical stock product. By working with my supplier to use the ones that he found reputable, and was already buying a large volume, I was able to save 30 percent on my quote and cut my minimum requirements almost completely.

Finally, there are savings that come from standard practices within the company, and are often a bit more nuanced for each product. These may not have anything to do with the external constraints of material use, but internal standards due to existing customers. For example, when creating supplier relationships for my beverage, we found that the filler had all of their filling machines outfitted for a 22mm bottleneck. Using a bottle with the same opening would mean the filling machine would not need to be retooled. This kind of step is a fixed cost—so when larger companies are considering larger orders, they may not mind as much. But for us, testing a new product, the cost of retooling on an order that would be close to the minimum volume, these small fees can double your cost.

4. *Terms and price breaks:* Initially, we asked pricing only for minimum volumes. For almost all supplies and services, the minimum volume has the highest price per unit, and as you are able to take larger volumes, you will be able to negotiate for lower prices per unit. Assuming success for your product, you want aggressive price breaks for larger orders so that you can achieve superior economies of scale as you grow.

In addition, your initial order probably will require payment mostly up front, or at industry benchmarks (perhaps full payment in 30 days). As you build trust with your suppliers, you will want to get payment terms that are better than industry benchmarks so that potential hiccups with your customers don't put pressure on your production. While we get into more details in our discussion on supply risk, it will be important to establish flexible and open payment terms with your suppliers from the very first conversation. Many suppliers, especially overseas facilities, are likely going to want payment up front. See if your suppliers are willing to offer 15, 30, or 60 days (prenegotiation). I was able to get full open terms from my manufacturer on the second order itself.

5. *Sample spec:* It is entirely likely that your initial description of your product or prototype will be in a format different from that used by your suppliers. Unless you are extremely diligent, you may overlook one small detail or another that would result in some extra back and forth of e-mail or phone calls that you can avoid with a better spec. Also, a good, complete spec makes your product portable from one facility to another, and will go a long way toward a credible negotiation. I like to ask up front for an example format of the way they like to take instructions, just so that I know exactly what all the parts are that they consider. Not all vendors will give this to you, but those that do are more likely to understand your position and take a realistic view of the market they are in and the service they provide. This always wins bonus points from me.

Supplier Negotiation

If you've done the preceding right, you should start getting back completed versions of the proposal document that you sent around to all the suppliers on your list. Some of them will fill out about half of it, some will write random (and sometimes hilarious) comments on it, and some will fill it out perfectly. They all should have been generous with reasons on why they are great partners.

If you don't get back as many responses as you hoped (at least 60 percent), send an e-mail communication to truant suppliers with a firmly worded prod. You can use the one I provide here.

Truant Supplier—Final Reminder
The purpose of his letter is threefold: to remind the supplier that you exist, to reinforce the sell, and to impose a firm deadline that implies other suppliers have responded.

Dear Supplier,

I hope this message finds you well. It has now been three weeks past the deadline set to respond to our company's RFI.

Initially, we approached your group because we heard excellent things from our colleagues and your other clients, but as yet, are disappointed not to have heard from you. We realize that this is a busy time of year for all of us, and assure you that the few minutes it would take to fill out our document will be time well spent.

Our company has created a product that will revolutionize <u>our</u> industry, and we are confident that you might be a trusted partner and reliable vendor who can share in our mutual good fortune.

If we do not hear back from you in one week, we will assume that you are not interested in our business, and will award this work to another supplier.

Thank you for your consideration.

Best regards,
<u>*Vik*</u>

There are many ways a negotiation can go. Our goal, however, is to conduct a negotiation that not only gives us a good deal—whether that is purely price, flexible terms, or free samples—but also sets up a relationship that we can live with in the long term. Remember that it unlikely that you will want to change suppliers later, once you have product and details nailed down. Getting to yes is important, but getting *past* yes is what keeps you in the game.

Many people's first instinct is to drill their vendors on price. I prefer to drill them on broader value. Remember that right now, we're looking for free prototypes. Price matters, but I would gladly give a 5 percent premium to a vendor willing to work with me at my level. Second, lower prices often mask cut corners in workmanship or quality assurance (though not always) and may be offset by stiff terms. I would again gladly give up 5 to 10 percent to a vendor with a great quality guarantee (read: takes returns or chargebacks) and flexible terms. Remember that a good deal is not just the one with the best sticker, but the one that is equitable enough to be sustainable for all parties involved.

First and foremost, however, is your value proposition to your vendors. Keep in mind that you will initially be the smallest possible customer for any of the suppliers on your list. Unless you are bringing particularly deep pockets to the table, you will likely stay small until your demand engine is up and running. What you are really asking is for the vendor to invest his time, money, and personnel resources into you and your product for a delayed payday.

I cannot repeat enough times—your suppliers are your first investors. Start by repeating the sell that you've given all your suppliers at the beginning of your progress, but improve it with all that you've learned in the process. Make yourself both easy to work with and an exciting engine of growth. Talk numbers—your suppliers want to hear about how you are going to move large volumes of your product. Your vendor is a stakeholder, your investor, and great source of advice. Share your vision, even the gory details. Share your inspiration—after all, you're a human being, with dreams and passion. Get them excited! Bring them into your inner circle and share a small secret or two. Building some rapport will lend you a much better negotiation. Personally, I start my best negotiations by taking my supplier out for cocktails.

I'll keep my advice simple: Have you ever been to the local flea market, where (if you're like me) you haggle voraciously over tchotchkes just for the fun of it? Challenge the price just to see how flexible it is, often antagonistically? Don't run supplier negotiations for your product that way.

While the techniques may prove effective nonetheless, the more important point for a good supplier negotiation is to lay the groundwork for a potentially long and mutually beneficial relationship—not to chip away so hard at the price that you become an unprofitable headache of a customer. I am not suggesting to overpay—a good price, slightly below market, is a great goal. However, a price too good to be true, way below market, is often unsustainable. You don't want to get your company up and running only to find that your producer won't take your phone calls anymore. I typically apply one or more key negotiating levers, none of which involve haggling unreasonably or a blind pursuit of the lowest possible price at all costs.

- *Benchmarks:* One of the primary reasons we sent out pricing requests to multiple suppliers is to get a sense of what the market rates are for a product or components such as what you need. This way, when approaching a discussion on any point—whether that is price, payment terms, or value added features, you can start your asking point with a fact. "The market is telling me X," rather than "C'mon! Lower your price, won't you?!" I'm not kidding. Be an informed negotiator and your vendors will respect you more (and likely give in to the things you ask for, if reasonable).

  There has been more than one occasion when I or one of my colleagues has entered a negotiation with a simple statement: "We're very experienced in this industry, and we know the benchmarks." An overcharging supplier will be quickly brought down to earth if that idea is conveyed in a credible way.

- *Principle:* Another lever to pull, when benchmarks are tough to come by is that of a particular mutually agreed-upon principle. For example, if you can both agree that the market demands a certain price for your product; you can reverse engineer the costs and try to hold your supplier to them. A reasonable negotiator will realize that for their deal to carry any long-term value with you, it needs to be long-term sustainable for you as well. Other principles could include reasonable shipping times, availability of resources, and more.
- *Value or barter:* Negotiating is tough if one side feels like they are getting a worse deal than the other. Since you're not going to want to pay more to your supplier for a particular product or service (at least I don't) I like to keep in mind what I'm bringing to the table in nonmonetary resources that I'm willing to share. For example, I can offer an interview on my blog, an introduction to a key player I know, a shot at future cooperative marketing, or anything else I may have that I sense my vendor wants.

The Art of the Barter

As a new entrepreneur on a budget, you will want to save every penny possible. In fact, if we could get stuff for free, we would take that, too. However, since there is often no free lunch, the next best thing is to barter some of the value we bring to our product for the things we need along the way.

The key to the barter is knowing when either your product has a lot of real value to the other party, or when the service you need is of relatively lower value, has a low variable cost to the other party, or is at risk of going unused.

A great example is office space. A landlord with extra desks and no one to fill them often faces two options: let them go empty or take whatever he can.

Experienced entrepreneurs Fabian Pfortmüller and Sol Khan used this circumstance to their advantage in two very different ways.

(continued)

The Art of the Barter (continued)

Fabian, one of the founders of Holstee, realized that his team needed to stop working in the founders' apartments and needed a respectable place to meet with vendors, clients, and business partners. One such business partner had them in one day when they were also having a brainstorming session. Always interested in solving a problem, the Holstee team stuck around and threw in their two cents. They were so impressed that they offered them an office, if only in exchange for their time and ideas on occasion.

Sol, a stand-up guy and founder of comedy magazine *The Comical*, needed an office in which to keep his occasional staff and in which to meet advertisers and clients. One such advertiser was having trouble filling their office, and *The Comical*'s team was able to trade a few ads for much needed office space.

Other entrepreneurs have used product barters as incentives for their distributors, as prizes for customer contests, and even as collateral for loans. What can you barter for?

In the Negotiation: Asks

It's tough to negotiate with someone when you don't know what you want. *Asks* are the things you want in the negotiation, and should come with an understanding of what drives their business and what is a bit more flexible.

- *Order minimums and flexibility:* My first question is nearly always on minimum order quantities—*MOQ* in the lingo of many manufacturers. Why not price? A great price means nothing if I need to buy 5,000 widgets to start with. Initially, when you may not have all parts of your design finalized, it would be nice to place orders for one or two units or cases at a time. I'll linger here until I am either able to negotiate away the minimum, or get my supplier to acquiesce to free samples.

   This is your chance to get free samples. I twist all my levers hardest here. Free samples can help you build free prototypes that you can show potential customers. Good prototypes will help you understand demand much better than drawings.

- *Price, price breaks, and payment terms:* Pricing is a tough science to follow sometimes, especially since your suppliers are going to understand their pricing better than you are. However, what you can do is a careful comparison of these three key elements of pricing and put a bit of pressure on to see how flexible their prices are. Will your suppliers be more flexible on price per unit if you are more flexible on price breaks? Given your situation, it may make sense to give in a little on price for more aggressive breaks and terms.

  The actual dollar price per unit is the most obvious starting point. With all else equal, you want your item to cost less. Would you rather pay $1 or $1.10 per unit? Less, obviously. Depending on what the item is, sometimes there are complex economics behind price per unit, and your supplier may have strict floors to stick to, and price parity to keep across their customers. It never hurts to ask, and often (especially for overseas suppliers) you can shave 10 to 15 percent right off the initial price.

  Price breaks define how your prices change, as you are able to purchase larger batches of product from your suppliers. While you may not think about this up front, if your product takes off, you will need to be set to scale up and meet that demand. Would you rather pay $1 per unit initially and have the price break down to $0.75 per unit for 10,000 units or $1.10 per unit initially and have the price break to $0.75 at 5,000 units? The latter would save me $1,250 when I get to 5,000 units versus the former. I would pay the extra the 10 cents if I had the confidence in myself and my product to make it happen.

  Payment terms determine when you need to pay your supplier for whatever you're buying. Up-front terms require you to pay before the order even goes though, and COD (cash on delivery) terms require the full payment upon receipt of the product. Ideally, however, you would want to pay later. Net terms (Net 15, Net 30, or even Net 60) allow you to wait awhile before payment. Also, you can sometimes ask for a discount for paying before the cash is due. Two percent 10 Net 30 terms would mean that the buyer can take a 2 percent discount if he pays the bill within 10 days, and otherwise, the full amount is due within 30 days.

In a perfect world, you would ask your suppliers for longer terms than you give your customers so that you're never stretched for a payment. For example, if you're able to get Net 30 terms from your suppliers, offer your customers Net 15 terms and use their money to pay your suppliers within a comfortable 15-day window.

- *Lead times and timing:* A topic I will bring up only if the quotes are very different from what's expected is that of lead times. In most industries, lead times are set by production cycles and logistics (that is, shipping times) and tend to be very difficult for vendors to change. This is when the benchmarks collected from your RFI will be important. If a vendor that you really like seems to take twice as long to send an order, by all means ask.

- *Idea generation:* The last lever I push on is less on the exact constraints of production and delivery, and is often not really an ask at all. Some supplier representatives, however, are going to be more interesting, knowledgeable, experienced, and pleasant than others. Some will have a great list of clients that puts them in contact with industry VIPs and keeps them on the pulse. In a pinch, I have found that a good supplier rep can go a long way toward keeping your ideas in check, consistently thinking of new solutions and ways to engineer value, and just make your entire experience much more pleasant and effective. For a first-time product designer, this kind of supplier can be the difference between a good product and a remarkable product. While not worth overpaying for (in my opinion) it's the kind of soft value that I keep a lookout for when selecting a supplier. I recommend the same to you, especially if you would personally need and appreciate their expertise.

If you are able to build a friendly rapport with your vendors through this process, you can probably also ask them for information on their other clients, their rates of growth, and the kinds of terms they get. This way, you can not only compare benchmarks across suppliers, you will be able to compare your quote to other quotes at each supplier and build a truly comprehensive understanding of the business. Highly recommended.

The First Full Production Run

At this point, if you've worked through the process diligently, you should have one to three suppliers from whom you have good prices, a decent rapport, and a verbal agreement to make you free samples or at least an approachable minimum order for testing. Having more than one supplier at this stage will give you the last bit of crucial negotiating power—after all, if only one supplier provides you a good prototype, you're married to him after that. If you're still able to make a choice, however, you've got the upper hand. An upper hand I guard as tenaciously as possible, especially when I don't want to spend the dollar muscle to buy it back.

Exercise: Supplier Selection

It is time to make a deal. If you've been following along, talking to customers, learning about the industry, and cleaning up your concept, you owe it to yourself to take the next step.

Find a supplier for each part that you need, and for each service that takes you from one step to another. Get a price that's fair. Be up front about your situation, and don't commit to make any purchases until you're ready. Ask for free samples! Offer to pay the shipping to make it painless on your suppliers.

Make it happen—we're almost there, you negotiating shark, you.

Summary

In this chapter we try to move from the handmade prototypes we have so far to factory-produced product. We considered stock and custom packaging options and created a detailed product space. We sourced vendors using the Inspired Method for all our parts, and negotiated pricing and terms. With the suppliers we needed and created the deals that we're going to need to get from raw materials to finished good.

! Challenge: Perseverance

When working on your product, you are probably going to come up against an obstacle. It's probably going to happen more than once.

You might get really deep into a negotiation and have a supplier disappear on you. You might get an inch away from a sale and have a customer back out. You might pay to create prototypes and find something wrong with them that you didn't foresee. If you stop there, it's failure. If you keep going, you can look back on it later and laugh about how you got past a little speed bump.

Get down on the floor, you're about to do some pushups. First, think about the most pushups you've ever done. If you haven't done any pushups, then imagine how many you think are possible.

Start knocking them out. Do 10, then another 10, then do 10 more. If you start getting tired, keep going. Are you close to the number you wrote down? Keep going. Are you at the number you thought possible? Keep going.

Collapse on the floor when your arms feel like they can't hold you up. Lie there. If you stop now, it's over. Do five more. Do one more. Collapse again but don't give up.

Do one more at a time until you absolutely cannot move. Remember this feeling—unless you feel this way again, you are not allowed to give up on your product.

PHASE III

ROLLOUT

CHAPTER

7

Get Distribution, and Get on the Shelf

The salesman knows nothing of what he is selling save that he is charging a great deal too much for it.

—Oscar Wilde

In 1876, an 18-year-old boy named Milton realized that he loved candy. In fact, he loved it so much that he got apprenticed to a candymaker in Philadelphia, and wanted to devote his life to it. As it turns out, Milton had a gift for candy. He learned the art of caramel quickly, and started a little caramel company, content to produce sweets for his customers in Lancaster, Pennsylvania. After selling that company, Milton was now a wealthy, successful entrepreneur, and set his sights on what was then a brand-new idea—creating chocolate with milk.

Like most new category beginnings, people were at first resistant to the idea, and his first few customers were hard won. He stuck to his art. With time and determination, people came to love his milk chocolate, and his manufacturing process brought prices lower than fancy handmade chocolates of the day. Milton's company turned out to be so successful and his company so beloved, that they eventually named the town after his $30 million business—in Hershey, Pennsylvania, and the country embraced "The Great American Chocolate Bar."

By now you are halfway to your goal. We've gone from concept to product. If you've been playing along, you might have a prototype or a produced product already. How does it feel to hold your product in your hand?

Very few people see their dreams distilled into a tangible product. Celebrate! Now comes the tough part—taking your wonderful product to the people who can make your life much easier or much harder.

There are two key players who stand between you and widespread consumer exposure: the retailer and the distributor. In many industries and categories, retailer and distributor penetration are imagined to be prohibitively difficult. I have heard many different reasons from otherwise experienced and successful businesspeople on why selling to consumers is impossible. I'll tackle some myths up front, but remember that every product you see on the shelf started as a concept—a concept that someone like yourself lovingly nourished and grew into the product you perceive it to be.

- Myth: The chicken or the egg? It's very difficult to get into a retailer without a good distributor, and it's very difficult to get a good distributor without a bunch of retailers. How can one person expect to do both at once? It must be impossible for me.

  False. By far the biggest rationale I have heard on this topic is this circular argument. Distributors are in constant competition with their rivals and are very sensitive to how their portfolio compares to others, as well as what sorts of products their accounts like. You represent a potential competitive advantage against the other distributors around them if you play your cards right. On the other hand, retailers tend to understand their consumers, and many take pride in the variety of goods available in their store. If you sell them properly, your product is a feather in their cap, as well as a new way to attract a particular customer.

- Myth: The market is so big and unpredictable, and I'm no expert—only big companies can successfully introduce a product.

  False. While the stories will vary from one industry to another, the big guys often are *least* successful at creative new product introductions. The truth is that launching new products is usually a less predictable, less profitable endeavor than bolstering their core business. It makes more sense to let the assortment of entrepreneurial brands fighting it out in the market prove themselves a bit and then acquire them for what it might have cost to develop them anyway.

- Myth: This is blind luck. Who knows what customers want and whether or not I can even make a product? The people who do these things are crazy, lucky, or both.

  False. Stories are often told retrospectively by entrepreneurs and inventors about how they happened to be in the right place at the right time, or how their creation happened to stick. In reality, successful brands and products are driven by both tireless promotion and calculated action, under carefully observed conditions. Your product stands every chance of making it to the shelf if you are willing to follow the methods and exercises laid out in this book.

- Myth: I'm not comfortable with sales—I'm not a salesperson. I don't have the contacts or skill or training, and so on.

  False. There's no magic in sales. If you are able to explain the benefits of your project, write them down, or explain it well enough for someone else to write it down, you can sell. The best sales guys I know are not the best talkers, but the best listeners. Figure out what your prospect wants, and then offer back to him the facets of your product that fit.

Get On a Shelf!

That isn't to say that selling your brand new product with just a prototype in hand is going to be easy. Unless you have a breakthrough solution to a plaguing issue, or a marvelous technological innovation on your hands, you're going to have to pound the pavement a bit to learn how sales work in your industry. If you're like me, your product is probably pretty cool, but not exactly groundbreaking. I'm assuming for now that your product has a few real benefits, a genuine innovation or two, and is aesthetically pleasing—in other words, meets the bar set by probably every other product in your category.

It's very likely that any retailer you speak to is going to ask you about distribution, and that any distributor you speak to will ask about retail penetration. I think it makes more sense to shoot for retailers first, for two related reasons: your cost of failure is lower with retailers, and they are just easier to get access to.

You are inevitably going to screw up some of your initial sales. Since there are fewer distributors than retailers (often by two or three orders of magnitude), you don't want to use these rare and valuable customers to practice your pitch on. They are busy and proud, and not likely to take a second meeting (it can be tough enough to get the first) with you unless you are coming back to the table with considerable results or something different. In this case, losing a single sale could keep you out of hundreds of accounts. Don't be discouraged. Even if you have experience with new products in your industry, it's likely that you'll make some mistakes on your first test of your initial product.

Retailers are also just more available. Depending on your category, there are likely to be several potential accounts in your area, some will be chain accounts, but others will be independent stores, whose owners you can probably ask for in the store. By talking to a wide variety and number of accounts, you will get a feel for their reception, and better understand how they fit into the landscape.

The primary goal for your initial product should be to guide your decision of what aspects of your product will need to be changed before production. While you could try to also develop sales, give them away, or brag to your friends—doing so without reaching your customer would be a waste. Even a well-conceived prototype will miss a detail here or there, and some initial product will be completely off the mark. It doesn't matter much. As long as we use the initial product for meaningful customer interactions, we will be armed with the changes people want to see in your product.

The way we approach this has a lot to do with the volume of product available, and on how it is used. A single durable product item can be shared with hundreds of customers, whereas a single consumable product item can be had by a single consumer (or maybe shared among the members of a small group). Also, if you have a lot of initial product, you might be able to get a broader response by sending samples out to industry thought leaders or authority figures, but if you have only a few, you will be likely limited to sharing it with people you can get in direct contact with.

Exercise: Your First Retailer

It is time to take your product and put it on a shelf.

- *Pick the right retailer:* Some products that do a brisk business at the corner bodega will struggle at a big box, and vice versa. Every product has a channel that works best: food in a grocery store, apparel in a clothing store. Pick the right channel and a store size that makes sense—based on similar or competing products that are already out there.
- *Set up the meeting:* Go to the store and ask to speak to the manager. If it's a small store, it might already be the person you're speaking to. If not, get a phone number, e-mail, time he'll be in—anything.
- *Prepare your pitch:* Introduce yourself and your product. Describe its benefits and tell your story. Tell them all the ways your product is better than what's out there, and about the message you personally want to share. Tell them how fair your price is, and how much money they could make with you.
- *Make it happen:* Sometimes retailers will tell you about how they don't have room for new products, or how they don't understand your benefits. Maybe they don't believe your price or your proposition. They may not even want it for free if you don't have a distributor or proof of insurance.

Don't take no for an answer. Even if it runs counter to your normally easy-going personality, push through. A sale is *always* made: either you're going to sell them some product, or they'll sell you a reason they can't take it. Which will it be?

The very first time I put my product in front of a true consumer—not a friend or family member—was a nerve-wracking experience. The culmination of so much emotional investment was sitting right on the table, poured into sample-size cups for people to try. A computer printout of some product benefits was lying on the table as well, getting a little wet because of the melting ice nearby. We wore t-shirts with my company name on it that I had spray-painted in my garage, and stood next to my brother, whom I had brought along for moral support. I felt like it was amateur hour at the supermarket.

It was our first demonstration, and hadn't picked the best spot in the store. It was early in the morning on a rainy Saturday, and nobody was coming to our table. Fifteen minutes crept by, each one slower than the one before it, and each one building the anticipation of what would happen when a customer tried my product. What if no customers came to our little table? What if they hated it? What if they had a question I could not answer?

Sure enough, we started getting a trickle of people at around 11 A.M. As soon as we started talking, my anxiety melted away. They weren't grilling me the way the retailer did—they were more interested in my story, what the product was, and why it was interesting. Then they tried it, and for the most part, had pleasant reactions. Some people didn't like it for one reason or another, and I wrote down their feedback. Some people thought it was great and picked up a few bottles for purchase.

I had brought copies of the survey I created for my concept test many months before. Every customer interaction is a learning experience, and I wanted to be able to report customer sentiment back to the retailer when I pushed for a bigger sale. While you might initially think your retail customers will automatically reorder your product, building that relationship will initially take a bit of well-reasoned follow-up.

When testing my Star Power concept, I had a few prototypes made up for free, and after discussing with a few local retailers and some friends who ran beverage companies, decided to take the

---

Reminder: Main Parts of a Customer Interaction and Some Bonuses

1. Segment information: Age, gender, profession, hobbies, preferences, habits.
2. Opinion: What do they think about your product's name, appearance, function, price?
3. Suggested next steps: What would they want to see done differently, and why?
4. Optional: Incentive—Why should a customer take your survey? Better results with a good incentive.
5. Optional: Contact—How will you continue your discussion with this consumer?

This way, when speaking to a distributor, as you will do next, you can credibly say something like: "Young professional males from 25 to 30 really liked the appearance and name of my product, and strongly approved my price point. They suggested that I change a few of these attributes, which I'll do before the next batch. How many can I sign you up for?"

plunge and really test my idea. I had 500 bottles created, and set up sampling sessions at different types of retailers. I analyzed that there are three primary places customers purchase a beverage, and tested all three. They could get some while grocery shopping at a grocery store, typically to stock up for later. They could grab some in a convenience store, typically for immediate consumption, or they could pick one up with a meal, usually lunch, perhaps a sandwich or something quick like that.

I sampled my product in grocery stores, bodegas, and delis, and accompanied the samples with the survey in Chapter 3. Note that I first collect self-identified segment information, followed with opinion questions, followed by suggestions. I incentivize the survey with a $1-off coupon (I allowed the retailers to sell my samples) and collected contact information. The incentive was something I tested to increase the number of respondents to my survey (20 percent more!), and the contact information seeded a few test newsletters as well as a social network strategy.

I found that customers in upscale grocery stores were much more likely to like my product than the other two channels, and that they tended to be split between two segments. The first was young professional female fitness enthusiasts who liked my product for its benefits. I called this segment "Yoga chicks." I also had a segment of typically older (35 to 50) gentlemen who were likely to be white collar, well-traveled, and liked the product for its nuanced flavor and story. I called this segment "Globetrotting Execs." I could then use the personality of these two customers not only in discussions with other customers, but also as people to keep in mind when shaping messages. I recommend you try the same.

If you do this correctly, you would have done a test of channels and customers, across what we hope is a large enough sample to be representative of your customer base. In the process, you might have gotten some great suggestions on improving your product, strengthened some business relationships you can use later, and learned a bit about your market. Not bad for a few days' work.

In my discussions with retailers after a sampling or testing event, I'll ask similar questions to what I ask my consumers. Most often, however, the first two are self-evident: The retailer's category is often dictated by the type of store they run, and they are going to like a product if their customer likes it and if it fits with their portfolio. However, they will often have great advice on the appearance and

A Note on Online Sales

Depending on what your product is, online could represent a large opportunity.

Unlike the brick-and-mortar world, online retailers can be physically anywhere, and can transcend channels—Amazon sells not just books, but *everything*. Or you can eschew the channels and set up your own web site.

A web site is a must, but web sales are not guaranteed. While there have been a few products that built a following online before hitting stores, many consumer products demand trial and demonstration before purchase, and for that reason, it is my personal opinion that the web site supports brick-and-mortar sales, not the other way around.

If you have only a few items in stock, and are content to sell them slowly, then spend more time on the web site. Perhaps your product is one that can go viral based on nothing more than a photograph and a promise.

The market tells us that most successful products, billion-dollar brands, need people to buy them and channels to carry them, which is why it is the focus of this book.

Apply the Inspired Method to Selecting Distributors

1. List: Populate a list of distributors you can find.
2. Test: Check with retailers to see who the best are.
3. Cull: You don't want to work with *all* of them.
4. Pick and negotiate: Meet, sell, negotiate. Lather, rinse, repeat.
5. Adapt: As circumstances change, repeat steps 1 to 4.

positioning of your product, having seen many products fail and succeed on their shelves. A question like "What would you change about this product to make it super successful in your store?" can lead to as long a discussion as they have time for.

On your way out, however, ask them for their favorite distributor—who are they ordering products like yours from? Most retailers will be more than happy to share their distributor as well as their contacts there. Indeed, a good distributor makes their lives as easy as possible. Yours, too.

Distributor Reachout

This is when you show me the money! By now, you should have some good sell materials, experience with retailers and feedback from consumers. Time to bring that to the table and actually sell to a distributor in your target market. Here are three steps.

1. *Populate list:* Your list should have a few names already on it from your discussions with retailers. Depending on your category, you may or may not be able to find more distributors through web searches. For example, some of the top beverage distributors have web sites, but many snack distributors do not. In addition, many great local distributors of all sorts are regional, family-owned businesses that may or may not have the inclination to put up a web site. If they don't already take orders that way (many are phone or in-person only) they don't have many incentives to put up a site.

   However, your category may have some great people you can find with a web search on "candy distributor," "toy distributor," and so on.

   The goal of this phase, however, is to get their feedback on your product, and book some preorders. You don't need a comprehensive list just yet. Get as many as you can and take action.

2. *Summarize retail test:* Now that you have a list of people you can talk to, let them know that you've done your homework. Write up your results from the retail test you just finished. It should include the names and types of retailers you tested, the characteristics of consumers who liked your product, and the ways in which your finished product may be different from the initial product you're going to present.

3. *Follow method:*
   a. *Write query letter*—Using the preceding write-up, customize a letter to each distributor, requesting an informational meeting. Remember that if this sounds like a request for a sales meeting, they may not be as open to speaking with you. However, if it is the voice of an entrepreneur who is trying to learn and build something valuable for them, they are more likely to be willing to spare an hour of time for you.

b. *List companies*—Keep track of the companies who agree to meet you, and connect with your contact by phone beforehand if you can. Are you speaking to a company owner or an operator? Is your contact the same as the one who makes buying decisions? Both of those answers will be useful before entering the room.

c. *Informational discussion*—When in discussions with a distributor, imagine working with them. The distributor is the guy who pays your salary if he becomes your customer. He's your advocate, eyes and ears in the street, and sometimes your sales force as well. He comes loaded with industry expertise and experience, and if you're lucky, some techniques that have worked on products similar to yours. Besides the questions you would ask a consumer to feel out your distributor on your product, you're going to want to find out a bit about where they fit on your map. As you meet more of these guys, you will need objective ways to compare them, such as the number of accounts they service, the size of their fleet and sales staff. This is important because a distributor relationship is long-term and often restrictive, and you should be comfortable with the capacity of a partner. Also, you will want to know what other products you will be sharing a truck with. Distributors often are good at selling certain things because of the nature of the accounts and staff that they have; some, however, don't sell at all.

- Distributor operation: How much distributing can your distributor actually do? How does he move a new product? How many accounts and how many trucks? What kinds of accounts (chain versus independent)? How big is his warehouse and is it shared? Does he subcontract routes or own them all? How does he get new accounts? Does he like to push or take orders? What does he require of his suppliers? (Some need a staff commitment, mutual sales targets, marketing spend, and so on—good to ask.)

- Finances: How much margin does he take on his products? How much do his retailers take? (This is often done by keystoning, in which each player takes a fixed 30 to 40 percent margin.) What does he think a fair price is on your product? What is the average price of his products? How are they packed? (How many units in a case? How many cases on a pallet?)

- Product portfolio—What else is on the truck? Any products that could be competing? How many new products have been in and out of his system? How confident does he feel about new products? Does he think you and your product would be a good fit?
- Competitive plan—How did he get to where he is (company history and personal history)? Where does he see your industry going? What is his next milestone? Where does he see his business in five years?

d. *Discuss next steps*—There are two ways that the end of your discussion can go. If you sensed excitement and interest in your product, you can try to close a sale. If not, you can still go for the sale, but may be better off keeping the door open for an improved sample product.

- It's important to be transparent with your distributor on this point. They will be used to placing orders that they can receive the next day, on terms they will try to dictate. However, if you have done a good job of devising an exciting product, you can try to swing some weight of your own.

e. *Bargaining chips for an early close*—There are usually three main reasons a distributor would be interested in buying your initial product:

- Territory exclusivity: Offering a distributor an early exclusive can go a long way toward both a good relationship and an easier sale. If you like the way they operate, float the idea of giving them an exclusive in the areas they operate in. In some categories, exclusivity is table stakes, but in others, it's a dealmaker.

  In industries in which exclusivity is the norm, the various distributors are each going to have definitive portfolios since they can't share brands. In this case, it's critical to the distributor that you're speaking to keep his portfolio more interesting, robust, and profitable than his peers. Mention sometime during the discussion that you're meeting with one or two other local players and see his reaction. Sometimes the best defense is a good offense, which means good things for you.

- Low-risk terms: If in the course of your discussion you find that the depth of your diligence is insufficient to pique the interest of the distributor, then you will need to consider playing cards that reduce his risk. Consider what happens if you don't keep up your end of the bargain—he might pay you for a shipment of product, and if he is unable to sell it, will face a loss of the entire value for your product. However, if you are able to offer payment terms, such as Net 30 or Net 60 day terms, or guarantee the sale of the product (that is, buy it back if they can't sell it) then doing business with you will be a much less painful ordeal.
- Personal preference: The most tenuous way to get distribution is when all of the preceding are not overly impressive, but the decision maker at the distributor personally likes the product. It may be because of the appearance, the benefits, the story, or for any reason, really. Maybe the contact likes you as a creator. However, the personal component of a buying decision is not to be underestimated. It is the toughest to predict, but a wild card that can often fall in your favor.

In all your discussions, keep one eye on the sale and another at the sky. The big picture matters in this business. If you learned through your discussions that your initial product was not quite right, go back to your suppliers to revise it. Keep in mind all the feedback, and balance the costs of implementing them to the costs of not fully addressing the segments from which they came. Some feedback will be more invasive than others, and you will need to play a creative role in prioritizing which ones matter more to you than others. However, nothing would be worse than pushing through the first sale and losing the distributor because of retailer dissatisfaction, only to realize that a few simple changes could have kept your business running much longer.

In my experience, feedback comes in a three flavors.

1. *Name and graphic design feedback:* The most superficial of feedback, and the kind that you should have the most flexibility in dealing with. If your name is not as appealing as it could be, or your font and color choice is not as differentiated as it

could be, take this back to the drawing board for the cost of a few hours of design time and a new domain name. Highly recommended.

2. *Product feature or benefit feedback:* Some of the feedback you get will be on the function of your product. For example, a snack bar may be too rich in calories, an electronic may have the wrong type or number of connections, a toy might be the wrong material. These tend to have more involved and more expensive fixes. A supplier that gave a free product on the first round may not be as friendly on round two. Changing shapes and materials of custom components may have mold and machining costs as well. If you are able to address any of these feedback points without sacrificing too much of your vision, I recommend it.

3. *Core concept feedback:* You will occasionally get feedback about your idea itself. This can be some of the best or least useful feedback, depending on your goals. Then again, not only will you be least likely to want to change it, but it may also not be the right thing to do. No matter what your product is, there will be some consumers who don't like it—no one product will be all things to all people. You may sometimes need to make the difficult determination that a bit of feedback needs to be thrown out entirely, and that a certain customer may never come to like your product.

When weighing out the options, consider your goals. Is your goal to build a successful, scalable products business at any cost? Is it to test a rate of return on as few dollars as possible? Or is it to put a product in front of people and just see what happens?

You will likely need to refine your initial product at least once, and repeat the steps of testing with the various stakeholders. While it may seem daunting at first, the difficult work can be done by the different people on the extended team and the end product will be something that is both immensely satisfying to you personally, as well as something that meets an expressed consumer need.

Most important is defining your channels for sale. Depending on your industry, a good distributor will recognize the merits of a good product, and will appreciate the persistence and tenacity of a good product creator. I strongly encourage speaking with distributors in your industry, both big and small, and making allies out of them.

Sometimes the best negotiation is done over a nice dinner or a few cocktails—don't be scared to take them out, and when you're at the table, don't be afraid to state your needs.

Holding a product, product price, and a distributor deal, the world is your oyster.

Tactical: The Distributor Deal

Your distributor agreement may be the single most important piece of paper you will hold. Although you will need to rely on the strength of your relationship with your distributors for the little things like influencing them into opening their big accounts, and in getting their advice on any aspect of your product. You will need to rely on your agreement for much stickier situations, like when your distributor "forgets" the price you agreed upon, or when his payment is due.

A good distributor agreement should have a few key questions covered—the kind that you don't want to bring up when either you or he has more to lose: First and foremost are all the prices and terms, then any references to a support program, territory, exclusivity, and termination, which are all necessary clauses to have early on, and will help stem any arguments that may otherwise come up down the line. In this section, we will discuss the key elements that should be in your distributor deal.

The key component in the agreement is that the distributor is agreeing to buy your product. While the amount of that purchase can be settled in invoices that you write as you go along, the *price of the purchase* should go in this agreement. If not, you risk having to negotiate and haggle at the time of each order.

Also, having a fair price break structure will help avoid the haggle as well. For example, you may have an introductory price for a small order, like a single pallet, and have the price break when they purchase a half container (or truckload), which could be 10 or 15 pallets, depending on your product, and again when they purchase a full container (or truckload).

If your product relies heavily on certain inputs, like plastic resin, or a certain agricultural product, or even the foreign currency where you produce, you can place a clause in this section that pegs price changes to an underlying index for your key inputs. For example, if you used a facility in Taiwan and paid them in yuan, you might want to say that a greater-than-10 percent change in the dollar-yuan exchange rate would let you increase your price by 5 percent.

While you're unlikely to actually use it, you can place an auto renewal clause here too, stating that each year, the agreement lives on, and your prices increase 3 percent or match national inflation.

This is also a place you can include your suggested retail price (SRP) for the distributor to use in his sales. Given that the distributor likely uses a keystone pricing process that guarantees his margin, your SRP needs to make sense with your price. For example, if you want to set an SRP of $5 at the shelf, the retailer (who typically has a similar keystone policy with your distributor, let's say a 40 percent margin) will purchase this item at $3. The other $2 is his margin—$2 is 40 percent of $5. The distributor then will want to buy this from you at $1.80 per unit—$1.20 is 40 percent of $3. As long as your price is there or lower, your SRP makes sense. If not, we're going to need to raise the SRP or reconsider some of our costs.

Just as important as the price you're paid, are the *payment terms* that state when and how you take the cash. While 30 days is a standard in most industries, most product start-ups I've met ask new distributors to pay for the entire first order in full up front. Whether or not your distributor will agree to that is between you and him.

When agreeing to any payment terms, keep in mind both the terms you have with your suppliers—you probably want to have the same or better terms with your distributor. If your suppliers give you Net 30 terms, you are going to want Net 30 or Net 15 terms from your distributor. This way you can try to avoid being stuck in a receivables gap.

You will also want to take into account the typical turnover rate of products in your category. If you're selling milk, for example, your distributor might move full containers each day. If you're selling juice, your distributors might sell a full container only each month. The milk guys get paid much more promptly than the juice guys.

Until this part of the agreement, we've been taking from the distributor (price, terms, and so on). Now we give a little too, because our product won't move itself. Even if your product is the best thing since sliced bread, your distributor is taking some risk in bringing in your new product. It is our job as the brand to help them move it.

Incentive Clause

The distributor's primary incentive has to be the profit he makes on your product. If your item is unprofitable, this whole discussion is a nonstarter. That said, it is possible to sweeten the deal for your distributor through thoughtfully placed incentives that can help him help you get to the next level.

Incentives are for both the distributor and their customers, and don't always need to go into the main agreement. They are used to get the distributor to sell harder, the retailer to merchandise better, and the consumer to try. Before walking down this road, keep in mind that the brand has to pay for any promotional programs at the price that customers bought in parallel.

I used to roll out incentives each month to my distributors and they were just fine with that. However, in a case in which the sale is more difficult and the distributor is looking to you to make his life easier, a few quick incentives in your agreement can go a long way.

There isn't necessarily a comprehensive list of incentives, since they really can be as creative as you like. I do strongly believe, however, that the brand is responsible for incenting every action it wants its partners to take. So if you expect your distributor to promote new accounts as well as reorders, they need incentives. If you want their reps to put up your point of sale (POS), that needs incentives.

For example, though you may start your relationship with an order for a single pallet, your own projections may show that the market will support a full container (let us assume 40 pallets in this example) of your product each month.

To help the distributor get there, you might want to take it in baby steps. Perhaps first is a buy-nine-get-one-free deal to help your distributor pick up 10 pallets. Then, if he picks up a half container (or half truckload, depending on where you're coming from) you might keep the buy nine–get one (so buy 18, get 2) and in addition take 5 percent off the price. When he's able to move from a half load to a full container, you might take another 5 percent off. In this case, don't worry about overdiscounting—you will more than make it up in the freight cost savings.

The easiest kind of incentive to communicate, but trickier to actually do, is to simply pay the distributor's reps directly for their efforts. Most distributors will be okay with this, as long as the conditions of your incentive don't hurt sales of their other products.

As a rule, assume that an incentive of 10 percent of the reps' weekly pay should be perceived as meaningful. So if you're selling a product for which the sales reps make between $1,000 and $2,000 per week, you could have a $100 to $200 target in mind.

You also need to know how much your product can move based just on the market, which might be 100 cases a month. In this case, a $1 per case commission will net the rep $100, and if this incents him to sell twice as much, then he could make as much as $200. Too low a commission will prove ineffective, as the reps already are making commissions in the due course of their jobs, and too much incentive will destroy your margins.

By setting up a competition, you can make your incentives work even harder for you. Sales guys love a good competition. In many ways, sales is itself a competition that plays out every day. By creating a contest for your distributor's sales reps, you can channel their competitive spirit into sales for you.

The key to a good competition is a goal that is just out of reach, a prize that is just a little too nice, and a number of winners that is just small enough for the reps to have to play musical chairs. For example, if after a month or two of sales, the average rep sells 10 cases of product and the best rep sells 20 cases of product, a good contest goal might be 25 cases in a month. If your usual incentive is $1 per case, a good prize might be worth $50, but could be a $200 item cleverly bought on sale. If your distributor has 10 sales reps, perhaps there can only be two or three winners (only one, and the reps would lose motivation after the first guy hits the goal; too many and the challenge doesn't seem exclusive enough).

With a good contest, communicated the right way to your distributor, you'll have some winners, and all the reps would have hustled hard for you during the promotion.

Exercise: Distributor's Incentive and Support Program

Test the theory that a lower price and some interest is enough for our product to compete. Even if that's true, it won't happen without some incentives to the distributor to try extra hard to get accounts for us.

(continued)

Exercise: Distributor's Incentive and Support Program *(continued)*

Do a little bit of math to see how much you can afford to give up per case. If you've kept the recommended 50 percent gross margin, you should be able to afford 10 points or so in incentive payments.

Example: One of my old programs

Accounts: Buy 5 cases, get 1 free
             Buy 10 cases, and get 3 free

Dist Reps: $1 per case sold to new accounts with POS
             $1.50 per case on reorders
             Open 30 new accounts (5 case min) to receive an MP3 player
             Top sales rep (50 cases sold min) receives a flat screen TV

Support: 50 brand T-shirts
             1,000 Window decal POS
             In-store sampling as needed

Promotion Clause

The first and easiest kind of promotion you can do is to give some product away. While this may initially sound like a terrible idea (after all, you created this thing to sell it, make millions, and retire), it is critical early on to get people to try your product and love it before it will fly off shelves. Besides, if your product is good, and valuable to your customer, the initial giveaway should repay itself ten fold (or more) over the course of your relationship with your retailer.

Depending on your costs, it may make sense to go with an offer as rich as buy one–get one free or something more humble like buy 10–get 1. In either case, the distributor can be instructed to use this rule in his sales, and then bill you back at cost.

Similar to freebies, a sale or percentage off on your product can be used in cases in which your product is too costly to give away. Retailers for these products, like high-end electronics or designer clothing, are less likely to expect freebies as well, and so an initial sale can help build accounts that are otherwise unsure about carrying your stuff.

While some distributors may not be set up for handling sale prices, most will accommodate you on this as long as they agree that it is a good approach to selling your product.

Also, depending on your product, a good distributor will ask for point-of-sale materials as well. These could be anything from pens with the company name, to T-shirts, to window decals, to anything at all. While this does not necessarily need to go in the contract, (indeed you don't want it to) a distributor may ask for support that will include these kinds of giveaways as well as marketing and promotional support from you in exchange for taking on your new product.

Territory Clause

For some distributors, territory is critical. They want to know exactly where you are letting them operate, especially if there is exclusivity involved.

For local players, you could define territory using streets in their neighborhoods, and for regional players, you can use zip codes or counties. National distributors often have descriptions of territories that are full states or parts of states.

However you decide to articulate this, it is important because when the time comes for you to add more support, or when you want the distributor to service particular accounts it will be helpful to point back at this document so both parties know what was agreed to.

Return Clause

Although you will likely make your agreement with an optimistic spirit, it is a good idea to spend part of the agreement setting a foundation for what may need to happen in a case when the distributor needs to return product.

As difficult as it may be able to hear, it is possible that a distributor is unable to sell the product. Perhaps it is because his customer base does not like your product, or perhaps it is because he is selling it wrong. What happens in this case? Can he give the product back to you for a refund?

In an ideal world, your distributors would agree not to send you any returns, but that is unlikely for your new product. It would be ideal instead to sell them only as much as they can sell, and in case they do need to make a return, to offer 50 percent back.

Also, if your product can expire, a proposition should be here as a spoils policy as well. I've often seen brands agree flat-out to take back any expired product.

Exclusivity Clause

Exclusivity with your distributor is a double-edged sword. Do you want to use multiple distributors in the same territory? Your distributors will probably not like that at all. Would you want your distributor to carry another product like yours?

In most categories (candy is one exception), distributors will not operate at all without exclusivity. For good reason, too—two distributors in the same territory are likely to resort to competing on price, and destroying one another's margins. This effectively makes your product much less profitable for them. While you may seek not to have any exclusivity, it is likely that your distributor will require this as a condition of working with you.

Termination Clause

Finally, every good agreement needs to come to an end. In the best case scenario, you may one day need to give this territory to a larger, stronger, less expensive distributor as you outgrow them. In a worst case scenario, the distributor may not wish to do business with you anymore and want to cut you off.

Without a *termination clause*, you risk a thornier argument than the discussion that would bring you to this step. What happens if one party owes money to the other? What happens to your mutual customers?

In many cases (and this was very surprising to me at first) your distributor may demand a termination fee or a buyout. This is meant to both discourage termination and help a distributor recover from the loss of revenue that your departure represents.

Ideally, you will want to suggest a termination clause that allows you to leave the distributor after a notification, which makes it more difficult for them to drop you, and has no buyout at all.

Hiring a Sales Team

It's not easy to recover from a bad beat. I learned from the "Florida Failure" (see next page) that putting too much in the distributor's hands and operating without an agreement left them too many outs and

The No-Pay Distributor and Having a Solid Agreement

It was the middle of the afternoon on an otherwise nondescript day in the fall when I got the e-mail. A distributor in south Florida (a market I had been trying to enter unsuccessfully for a while) was interested in taking on our product. It was almost too good to be true!

I did some research: Although there wasn't much written about them, some of the people I knew in the beverage business were working with them, and they had a fairly impressive plan.

When I connected with the owner of this small operation (a man whose name I'll omit here) he seemed like a genuine guy with a passion for beverages. We wanted to get a quick start, in time for snowbird season (when some Americans from the northeast start their seasonal migration to their second homes in Florida). After reviewing our terms and pricing, I settled for a signed invoice and sent a couple of pallets of product, some POS materials, promotional T-shirts, and everything.

We had big dreams. Publix, the major supermarket chain, was interested, as was a local marketing and PR shop. I had recruited some local talent to help with sales and personally got my hopes way up. I found hookups to local events like a celebrity golf tournament and a fashion show and poured my heart into making this happen. I saw this as my opportunity to build a market that could take over when New York City slowed down in the winter. So much so, in fact, that I allowed him to run a buy-one-get-one-free promotion for the first two months.

The owner of the distributor was excited, but already showed signs of what was to come. Instead of going after the grocery and lunch channels, he wanted to put the product in hotels. Instead of working with the PR firm I recommended, he wanted to keep his own PR guy. Instead of sharing the sales reps I found, he wanted to sell on his own. I wanted to go down there and visit, to help grow our mutual business—but he always seemed to be just a bit too busy.

Then one day the song changed. Abruptly—like a DJ who was still trying to learn. I was a villain now, who had forced him to take the product, and who shipped it to him without his approval. I didn't have a plan to support him, and didn't really want him to succeed. Now that he thought of it, he didn't think he would be able to pay me.

Then he just disappeared.

left me holding the bag. If I was going to sell product, I should have my own team.

Even if you have had direct reports at a day job, it is very different from having your own employees. While the need to train them and make them successful is the same, the downside is very different. An ineffective report can be annoying. A bad hire can bleed you dry.

I had nearly no experience with hiring when I decided that I needed a team. I did some quick math and decided that a sales rep could support himself with a modest number of sales per month, which, of course, *anyone* could do. However, if I could, I would take on some help for free, and the rest of it on a commission basis.

I made every mistake in the book when I started looking for an intern. I asked for too much and offered nothing in return to people who wouldn't make good interns anyway. To make matters worse, I did this in an untargeted way on a major job site that was full of so much noise and so little talent that I was not going to get anywhere.

I went back to my old campus at Columbia University and started reaching out to the student professional groups on campus. In particular, I approached the Columbia Organization of Rising Entrepreneurs in the hopes that some of those students would appreciate my struggle. I wrote a letter to the students asking for their help as an alum in exchange for a cool experience in which they would have the opportunity to influence major decisions in a start-up, meet customers, and otherwise get to play entrepreneur for a while.

I was inundated with applications—and didn't know what to do. I went to Josh Wand, founder of Bevforce and one of the coolest people I've ever met. He has had a ton of experience hiring people for his clients and is typically full of insight.

When it comes to hiring talent, he says, an intense interview process is a must. In fact, multiple interviews are ideal, especially compared to simply reading a resume. Even within a single interview, it is better to have a multifaceted approach. Besides asking questions of fit, which really don't tell you any more than whether you might personally get along with the candidate, give him a situational question that he needs to reason his way out of. Give him a personality test (like the Myers-Briggs test from earlier in this book) and ask questions that test his ethics.

In all his years of headhunting, Josh has learned that most people, even the most-driven high performers have a part of themselves who just want money and stability. To that end—commission-only jobs are a tough sell. While it might sound low-risk to you up front, people need to eat and if they feel the pressure of their commissions, will always have one foot out the door. The same goes for equity— you might think you're making a huge sacrifice by offering your new

Example: Interview Questions

There are as many interview questions you can ask as there are people to answer them. However, in my discussions with Josh and my experience interviewing many candidates for roles at several companies, the following categories roughly cover the questions I think best distinguish good fits from poor ones.

The only exception is the case question, which is a type of situational question. I reserve those for ex-consultants and more senior personnel. I could write a whole book about that and not say enough, so I leave it out here.

BASIC/FIT:

- Why did you apply for this position, and why should I hire you?
- What is an accomplishment you are proud of?
- Give an example of a time you failed, and how you handled it.

SITUATIONAL:

- If you had a great team member who brought consistent results, and you found out had an alcohol problem, what would you do?
- A customer comes to you upset about an order and wants to return an order, but the return would mean you lose all the commission for that sell—how do you respond?
- Nonwork: You're planning a party for a close friend and it goes much better than expected. The venue is packed and a VIP guest (or boyfriend or girlfriend) shows up late and is unable to get past the bouncer. What do you do?

BRAIN TEASER:

- How many Ping-Pong balls could you fit inside a 747?
- Four people need to cross a river late at night. It is too dark to see across, too deep to wade. There is one boat with a flashlight that you must use to cross. Each of the four rows at different speeds: one can cross in 1 minute, another in 2, and another in 5, and the last in 10. The boat moves only as fast as the slowest rower. How can you get everyone across in 17 minutes?

PERSONAL MOTIVATION:

- Would you rather have a high salary with a low bonus or vice versa?
- If you were making a sale, and the customer offered you a cut in exchange for a lower price, what would you do?

Not all of these questions have a correct answer, but many of them will give you a window into the applicant's experience, intelligence, ethics, motivations, and more.

hires a stake in your company, but unless they share your vision and passion (and even if they do) they can't take that share to the bank.

Even a very low base is better than no base. With a bit of digging, I found out that one of my distributors was offering his people $250 per week in base, plus 5 to 15 percent of sales. Some of his guys made over $1,000 per week. Distributors have the benefit of multiple products, however. For a company selling a single brand (like yours and mine), the base needs to be higher to keep people engaged.

After two different failed attempts at hiring a commission-only rep (one lasted two weeks; one lasted less than one), I decided I should take the plunge on a real employee. Josh's advice rung in my

Josh Wand—Insight from an Expert

Josh is a guy who has seen a lot of products come and go.
  What he's seen people do well:

- Build the product yourself before giving that task away. Outsourcing has become very trendy, but you will get better quality if you're able to do the tasks yourself before hiring it out.
- Don't be a "me-too." Create a product where there is real demand and it is underserved.
- Do a solid strengths, weaknesses, opportunities, and threats (SWOT) analysis. If you're inexperienced, that's okay. Do a lot of industry research and take on an experienced partner.
- Focus on customer service. And invest in having a tight brand identity, including consistent visual cues, and messaging themes. These two things can make even a tiny company seem competent and professional.

  While you're at it, try to avoid some of the things that he's seen bring companies down:

- Don't expand too quickly, or advertise to the wrong customer, or you'll spread your limited resources thin.
- Don't hire a PR company to do "personal interest" stories. You might like seeing your name in print, but your customers don't care. They feed the ego, not the wallet. Focus on the company.

  Josh told me once that too many people think entrepreneurship is this easy, glamorous thing. Building a business is not lavish, he says, nor easy. In fact, in his mind, it is the most difficult thing in the world.
  "Building a business takes thick skin, a strong stomach, and balls."
  Well put, Josh.

head each time I spoke to a candidate: "Don't think the job seeker is lucky to work for you; that's ego talking. Good talent has tons of options." I interviewed some experienced candidates and some newbies. Some transplants and some locals. Some old and some young. Everyone seemed promising.

I'm the kind of person who tends to see the opportunity and potential in others, which can be a dangerous thing in a hiring situation. I worked my way down to two equally promising candidates: one was a veteran from VitaminWater (a beverage company that had recently sold for a breathtaking $4 billion) and a referral from a trusted advisor. The other had applied to a job posting, was a veteran from Voss (a beverage company that was a pioneer in premium waters) and a recent transplant to New York City. They both had terrific experience, an enthusiastic disposition, and a plan of attack ready for my brand in New York City. One of them thought my offer was too low. I hired the other the next day.

Having a new employee is a little bit like having a new puppy. You have to teach him everything from scratch (even though she was an experienced salesperson) and everything he does is somehow adorable. I gave every tool my little start-up had, and even created new ones on the fly. Through a bit of luck and some strong networking, I came upon a list of accounts in New York City. Nearly 100,000 addresses, names, and phone numbers across all five boroughs were at her disposal. A small group of field-marketing flexible staff were available to do demos in store (including me) and sales support for key accounts (me) along with a host of POS materials and giveaways, and all the wisdom she could glean from our distributor.

She had a slow start. She was out in the streets, meeting accounts, sampling to customers, and learning the brand. No sales the first week. She's learning, she said—feeling better about this whole thing. No sales the second week. My distributor asks me—are you sure your rep is doing anything? "Sure," I reply," she booked an order!" Three sales the third week. For a few days I can't find her by phone or e-mail. No sales the fourth week.

At this point, nearly everyone is telling me to shut this experiment down. I'm paying out $500 per week for nearly no return, but I still see the potential. I stopped most of my other activities and put all of my time and effort into making my salesgirl successful. I sent her to successful accounts to see what worked, I walked accounts with her to help get sales, and sent her on ride-withs or trips with the distributor to see how they operated and sold.

Finally, I agreed with the advice Josh had given me so long before—"A bad hire is one of the most expensive mistakes a company can make," he said. Not only did I lose the salary and expenses I gave her, but lost a month of my time, and a prime month of sales in my biggest market.

Opening a distributor or two is only half the battle (or less). The only way your product really blows up is if the people like it, and they tend to shop at retailers.

In many ways, opening a retail account is a lot like opening a distributor. The retailer is your customer, but also your partner. In all likelihood, he is initially making more money per unit than you are. Although the retailer brings a certain cachet to your product (especially if he is a well-respected player, locally or nationally) he only has that cachet because of his products. He knows that you represent a potential long-term profit center for him—you just need to convince him that you've got something.

On the other hand, getting retailers is easier than getting a distributor since they can buy a case or two of your product at a time, versus the distributor who is looking at a much larger purchase. It is for this reason that you may have a set of retail accounts long before you have a distributor.

Retailers that are part of large national chains have a pretty standard process by which they review new products, usually on a category review schedule that you can ask them for, and a laundry list of things they look for in a product. For the most part, however, it is support.

The retailer is going to want to know your case allowance or how much money per case you plan on spending in promotion for him, whether or not you will demo the product in store, and whether you are willing to pay for premium placement or a display.

Have you ever walked into your favorite store and there are some young, attractive people telling you a bit about some new product? Have you walked down the aisle and seen the towering displays of printed material and product for specific companies? How do you think they got there?

Local retailers are easier to approach, most often since the decision maker might be the store owner or manager and is on the premises. Seek these out and make your case. Are you able to answer their questions? Can you build the confidence needed to take on your product?

In an ideal world, every single retailer that takes on your product should be better off because of it. If you're bringing value to the table, don't be afraid to tell them why and how much it's worth.

My first sale was to a small chain of stores in New York City and New Jersey called the Garden of Eden Gourmet Market. As the name suggests, these stores were perfectly curated collections of fancy foods from all over. They had small companies and large ones, hundreds of types of coffees, teas, olive oils—you name it. I e-mailed the owner more than 10 times before he let me meet with one of his store managers, and when I did meet, I made my case passionately, and crossed my fingers that my decision maker liked the product. "Let's get six cases and see how it goes," he told me. Boom.

I delivered those cases myself, late one night after I got out of work. I wasn't making nearly enough to quit my job, and so squeezed in sales and deliveries in my nights and weekends. I carried the cases into the store myself, brought the manager a T-shirt, and helped put up the decals to guide customers to the product.

"People aren't going to buy this stuff themselves, as much as I like it," he said. I was going to have to come back in to share it. I planned on coming on a pleasant Saturday morning, when I thought the morning grocery crowd might be out in full force. It turned out to be a rainstorm.

I hung out at the table in an eerily quiet store. There might have been no one in there except me and the store employees. Great, I think to myself, I'm not only wasting my time, but the retailer is going to think no one wants my product! My brother, who I brought along for moral support, had gotten bored and was wandering the store.

Then I realized that I had come a long way from being just a guy with a dream. In that moment, it didn't matter what my distributor, retailer, or even my consumer was thinking. I had taken my dream from concept to shelf.

Summary

We started this chapter by thinking about the approach to the market and met some interesting people. We learned what distributors and retailers were looking for in a product and took it to the streets.

We got feedback from customers, and deconstructed a distributor agreement. Not everything is guaranteed to go well at this stage, and even hardened entrepreneurs can struggle with early sales of a product. Ultimately, with passion, an open ear to customers, and a flexible approach, you can take your product to shelves and start selling to your many future fans.

❗ Challenge: Seeking Alternatives

The sales game can be challenging in more ways than one. Not only do you need to persuade the guy on the other side of the table to believe what you're saying, you need to do so on multiple fronts. A good price can be weakened by poor payment terms, and a great deal can be undone by a poor termination. An effective sales arrangement can be weakened by poor enforcement or nonexistent incentives.

Sometimes you need to compromise on one to get movement on another. You need to walk down one path just to see if another opens. In this challenge, we're going to seek alternatives in another situation.

Think about a place you'd like to go to nearby. If you normally drive, drive; if you prefer to walk, bike, or rollerblade, that's fine, too.

Most of us have "the way we know" to get somewhere. Don't take that way. Make a few wrong turns, get a little lost, and then try to follow your instincts, down side roads, through new neighborhoods, past unfamiliar stores, until you get back to where you wanted to go.

Wander down roads that turn out to be dead ends, and shortcuts that turn out to be scenic routes. No asking for directions or navigational instruments allowed.

CHAPTER

8

Demonstrate Local Success

Success is the ability to go from failure to failure without losing your enthusiasm.

—Sir Winston Churchill

I t was late at night when it first happened to me. I woke with a start, and sat in bed, looking out the window at the lights of New York City. Did I really think I could do this? Many of my close friends thought I had already accomplished a Herculean task in creating a product, managing an international supply chain, and ultimately getting it to market. I didn't see it that way. In my mind, I had tripped and stumbled into somehow making this thing work— what if my luck ran out? I had a couple hundred accounts in three states, each of which had their own challenges. Each new account sale was a battle, and as a result, every distributor had a different incentive program. Each one had difficulty paying their invoices on time. Winter was coming, and customers and team told me that it was going to be my biggest challenge yet. I was running on no sleep. I was making money, but pouring it all back into the business. I had interested investors, but none had fair terms for me. As far as I had come, I was still very far from the explosive return that I sought when I first got in to this venture. I wasn't alone either—I learned that many entrepreneurs have a moment when they realize that they've made some progress, but the path forward seems as daunting and confusing as what they've passed. When you have your gut-check moment, will you push on?

Sol Khan, founder of the comedy magazine *The Comical* was in a beat-up van driving on the highway late at night. He and his team had bought this van as part of a not-quite-fully-thought-through attempt to save money. They had just left the printing press that produced their magazine and were discussing the plan for distribution the next day. They were going to drop the stack of 10,000 magazines in front of the local college and use that as a base station for volunteer drivers who would take them to all the accounts they signed up. For all intents and purposes, it was a solid, if bootstrapped, plan. Mid-discussion, smoke starts coming out from under the hood— quickly clouding their vision with billowing black plumes.

"We thought the van was going to explode," he says. It was 3 A.M. on a random highway and they were sitting on one of the biggest investments of their lives. They pulled over and thought hard about what they were doing. Was it worth it?

Bad investments happen to all of us. We buy something that seems perfect at the time, and it then turns out not to be. This decision is tougher to make when the roadblock is something less replaceable. Uri Weg is the founder of Evolvist, a green-minded web product and service that helps customers find and track green businesses and locations. He felt like he had done the impossible—he had pulled together a group around his idea, raised some money, and built a web site. Then, when he was going to demo his site in front of thousands of spectators, an issue with his page threatened to shut down the show. Frantically, he called his web developer, who did not care enough about the project to stop what he was doing and help for five minutes. The demo struggled through when it should have wowed the audience. Uri realized then that his whole team (not just the web developer) was not filled with people who cared about the vision, and could not be relied on to get it done. He got rid of all of his underperforming team members. All his work seemed to be in vain. He had a decision to make: keep the project running, or shut it down?

As a product creator, it's up to you to stay strong, keep in front of your customer and your team, and not to fold when you hit speed bumps.

Ask Sol and Uri. They both decided to pick up the pieces, learn from their mistakes, and rise from their ashes like phoenixes.

The challenges you face on your journey only lead to failure when you give up.

■ ■ ■

With product in hand and a distributor by your side, you're feeling unstoppable—but this is when the harder work starts. Show your distributor that you're a partner by demonstrating sell-through. We got into this business to breathe life into an idea, but we will stay in this business only by creating a system that will reliably create the product and take it to market. Up until now, we've focused on sell-in. Sell-through describes the opposite phenomenon as sell-in: the ability of our distribution and retail partners to move the product to customers, and allow them to order again.

Viewed in an opposite light, what we've done so far is create a product and push it into the channels around us. The remaining job is to remind our consumers that our product solves a meaningful problem at a fair price, and that they should get out there and pick it up.

In this chapter, we're going to go back and look at all the activities that we glossed over while focusing on making our product and getting it to the shelf. Building a sustainable promotional strategy, especially using all the tools and options that are available to you was probably not on the radar when hustling your boxes to the sale. Longer-term strategies like an ongoing guerilla campaign, the collection of spokespersons, and an expansive web and PR strategy need to be in place to ensure that your product is well positioned to stay relevant and with mindshare.

In addition, revisiting our partners with whom we cobbled deals together and taking a moment to reassess and optimize can go a long way for both your bottom line and to improve the effectiveness of your supply chain. We'll fix your web site, tweak your pricing, and recheck all aspects of your business so that it is incented in the right direction, and running as smoothly as possible.

The Three Ps

Now that you've got some product, you have to help it move. Your first few account sales will help tell you a lot about what will and won't work for you. It is your chance to test different price points, promotions, support offers, and more to see what is really going to stick. It's also a chance to test a few different types of retailers to see which attracts your ideal customer. In all likelihood, it may be true that your first few accounts are not profitable at all. Depending on your product, retailers may expect their first order to be free—a free fill—or otherwise may want to try the first order on consignment. Trust your product—you've worked for it this long, now ask it to work for you.

Sales and promotion are two sides of the same coin. Salesmanship will take the product off your hands and to the customer. Promotion will help you persuade consumers to take it off the shelf, and enable them to like it and share it with their friends. Both take time and resources, so we will need to choose how to choose best.

My recommendation is to try a few different promotions and a few different support promises to see what is most effective in your category. Some options are presented in Table 8.1.

At first, you will lean on your retailer to bring your customer to you, but ultimately retailers depend on their brands and products to bring customers to them.

When merchandising your retailers, focus first on *pricing, placement, and point-of-sale* or *POS* (the three Ps) to build organic adoption. The price is one of the key differentiating factors in a purchase decision for the vast majority of products. The market is the best place to take initial inspiration for your price—people will only pay a little more or a little less for a product than they are used to for a similar item. However, there is a catch—you cannot dictate how much your product can sell

Table 8.1: Promotional Activity versus Sales Support

Promotion and Sales Support	Low	High in-store activity, marketing campaigns, above-the-line advertising.
Low	If your brand is catchy and your product is truly innovative and satisfies a pervasive pain point, you may be able to create sales without promotion or support, but this is unlikely for the early stages of any product.	A great appearance and a compelling value story will go a long way toward helping sales with low promotion. Also, a demonstrable product experience will help customers quickly understand your message, and make them more likely to share it.
High—Free products, aggressive pricing	Aggressive promotion without support can work for products at budget prices, especially those that fill an expressed need.	If your product needs a lot of promotion and broad promises of support in order to make sales, I would recommend making sure your margins allow for a sustainable practice.

for, only what it is advertised at. This is why your price is the *suggested* retail price. Upscale retailers may choose to charge more, and budget retailers may choose to charge less, but many consumers associate a certain value to the manufacturer's suggested price. Initially, I recommend keeping it close to the average for your category, unless you are specifically seeking a value or premium play.

There are compelling reasons to stray from the mean. A low price, accompanied by messaging that indicates that a new and exciting product has a low price for a limited time will encourage customers on the fence to jump in and try your product. A price much higher than average, if accompanied by a premium appearance, differentiated benefits, and in a market that will bear it, could do just as well.

Within a retail location, there are different kinds of real estate. Placing in prime locations like window displays, endcaps, checkout, cooler doors, custom racks, and other high-visibility spots are excellent. The bottom shelves and back corners are where new products go to die. Then again, prime real estate can come with both outright fees as well as the quiet expense of having to create the display or endcap.

Walk into the store and do a bit of your own research. What do you see as soon as you enter? What product is displayed in the best spot right now? If you go over to the section that would make the most sense for your product, what catches your eye? If your item is a smaller impulse buy, would it go by the register?

Sometimes, the best placement is your own: through custom racks or high viz options.

When Shelf Space Is Scarce, BYO

Custom racks are hard to miss. Walk down the candy or cereal aisle in your local supermarket and there's bound to be a giant, cardboard, folded-together shelf, touting some new product or flavor. Walk down an aisle in your local big box and you're sure to see a floating shelf with an item on sale or some neat little thing for you to look at. At the front of your favorite clothing store, I'm sure there is a bin or a rack with some new or sale product that you just *had* to look in to.

Not all custom shelves are created equal. High-visibility shelving, sometimes just called *hi-viz*, includes the often-overlooked empirically super-effective places to put a new product. In beverages, it's the suction-cup racks on the cooler doors. In electronics, it's the demo section where a few products are out on the floor for people to play with. There you can put your product front and center without haggling for shelf space.

While every layout is different, the best real estate is often going to be where the customer enters, where they pay or exit, or in a place where they can experience your product. If there is space to put a poster, a custom rack, or something similar that you're willing to make, that could work just as well too. Ultimately, you want your product to be front and center somewhere in the retailer—don't fool yourself into thinking that your early customers are going to search the store looking for you.

Once your product is in a store, it is your responsibility, not the retailer's, to move the customer to your product and sell it to them. Effective POS materials will capture and entertain your customer from the moment they enter the store, direct them to the stocking location, and compel them to make a purchase.

Every retailer has different POS that they will allow a brand to bring, and each category has different POS that makes sense. Most retail channels have a place for at least some of the below:

- *Decals or static clings*—Available in a few different sizes, clings are vinyl decals with a very light, easily removable adhesive. They could go on windows or glass doors, or any other smooth surface.
- *Danglers or shelf tags*—Signs that hang on or near the shelf your product is on to add a bit more information in an attention-grabbing way. They have an adhesive tab that is separated from the messaging by a strip of paper or plastic, and normally go on or under the shelf.
- *Price tags or channel strips*—These small signs go into the groove on the shelf that normally holds price and product information. Usually only an inch or so tall, shelf strips offer just enough space to put your company name on a burst of color to stand out from what might otherwise be the simple, store-printed price tags.
- *Banners*—On rare occasions, a retailer may like you enough to let you hang a banner from the ceiling or stand one on the floor. These can be pricey—my hanging banner cost close to

$100, and my floor-standing banner more than $200. If you do make some for your retailers—be sure not to let them throw them away.

- *Aisle interrupters*—These little tags pop out from the aisles and beg to be read. They sometimes carry coupons that beg for the product to be tried. They can be extremely effective in some stores.
- *Pole signs*—These signs are most often used near the cash registers, where the poles hold up the number signs for checkout.
- *Barrel or bin wraps*—If your product could go in a barrel or bin, it might be worth creating a good one.
- *8½" × 11" sell sheets*—The sell sheet is a critical tool, but it is unlikely that you will want to give them to consumers. This is material for you and your distributors to use while opening accounts.
- *Automatic sampling or coupons*—Although you will want to be in front of your consumer to talk them through the experience of your product, there are times when you can't be in enough places at once. Coupons for a new product can help people get over the initial hurdle of trial.

A POS strategy, however, is not for the faint of heart or easily defeated. While most independent retailers will encourage some signage (it helps sell product, after all), many larger retailers will not be in favor of scattered POS. They usually have dedicated channels like endcaps for that. All of them will have an opinion too. If getting feedback from your friends and consumers wasn't difficult enough, get ready for a retailer with a firm idea of his store deciding whether your signage fits with *his* brand or not.

While I won't endorse it here, more than one successful product entrepreneur has told me about how he would sneak POS into a store that may or may not want it. When he thought no one was looking, he would put decals on the doors, shelf strips on the shelves, signage in the aisles. It isn't illegal, after all. The retailer makes the decision on whether or not to tear down your materials—but you can certainly still put them up. Awareness is king for a young product.

Often, when a retailer objects to your POS, the more collaborative way to get around that complaint is to create materials in partnership with your retailers that do some work for both of you.

For example, you could create window displays that advertise your product while improving the stature of a small retailer. You could create a rack that holds your product but allows the retailer to display something else as well. You can create push/pull decals for the doors. All of these ideas should have appealing imaging and text, ideally in a way that is clever, humorous, or in-your-face as consistent with your brand.

Support Your Sales

In addition to merchandising, most retailers, especially shrewd ones, will want to know what kind of sales support you plan on offering to help them turn your product. There are a few ways to address this.

Above-the-Line Numbers

The first way, and the way that many established companies would put it, is in terms of a number—a promise to spend $10,000 or $200,000 marketing your product specifically for that retailer. This is often mostly above-the-line marketing that is run in specific media properties the old school way.

However, above-the-line marketing is tough to track, expensive to place, and not necessarily a high return on your investment (ROI). While there are some great ways to get a deal—would you believe I negotiated an ad in a major leading men's magazine for $10,000 (over 90 percent off the rack rate)—we're trying to build a brand on a budget. I would not recommend spending your initial marketing dollars on advertising even if you can afford it. Most aspects of good marketing have a cost associated—to keep the dollars low, you will usually have to throw in something else, such as your product, your time, or both. When executed well, quieter, experiential, relationship-driven marketing can go a long way.

In-Store Demos

One of my favorite ways to support a retailer, and a way that costs no cash at all, is to do demos in-store. Once a week (more or less), go back to the retailer and explain your product to your customers. Connect with your consumer—get feedback, answer questions, share your story personally. After a while, I was having so much fun that I would have *paid* to do this. In a business where your customer is often behind your distributor or behind a web site, this is one of the few ways to really meet them and make it real.

The downside to doing in-store demos is that you can only be in one place at a time. So when you're doing demos, you aren't being productive for your business. You also can do only one demo at a time, and may be neglecting other retailers. The solution: clone yourself into brand ambassadors.

The first time I met Keli, she was sampling another product at my local Whole Foods store. I watched curiously as she gave a quick story to groups of customers each time more genuine than the last. She seamlessly answered questions from young parents, playful children, and senior citizens, each with their own concerns. She was pretty, professional, and articulate. Ladies take note, that's how you move a product. Sorry, guys—some things are just easier for women. I recruited her immediately.

I recruited two more as well: one who was bilingual and had experience with beer promotion, and a guy who worked for another beverage brand by day, but was able to sell and demo product for me as well (don't worry, not a competitor).

Between the four of us, someone was always available when a store needed a demo, as determined by the sales reps who went to the accounts. Using Google Documents, I created a schedule that the sales reps could enter demo requests into, and the demo team could raise their hands for. The demo machine practically ran itself after that.

Guerilla Marketing

For a little more time than an in-store demo, or a lot less money than above-the-line, you can do some guerilla or other unusual marketing that is consistent with your brand and product. For example, a beverage company once put giant straws in trashcans around a city, the implication being that people were drinking garbage if they were not drinking their product. A sneaker company might stencil designs onto the sidewalk, reminding people that their shoes are important. An electronics company might put on an outdoor display with their products that gets people involved and interacting.

One day, perhaps out of hubris or perhaps out of boredom, I decided that street billboards were the right strategy for my company. I knew ROI could be low, but I figured that since most

How to Build a Self-Sustaining Demo Machine

Scheduling and running in-store demos can be some of the most rewarding but most time-consuming work. It's fun when you're doing it leisurely, but like most things, loses a lot of its fun value when it becomes a chore.

Here's how I took myself out of the loop and made my customers happier in the process. The sales rep gets a demo, and puts it into the sheet. The demo rep looks at the sheet and does the demo. All you have to do is look at the sheet every now and then to be sure the demos are getting done.

- Getting demos is not difficult. Since it helps the account sell product, and does not cost them anything, most will let you set up for a few hours and do your thing.
- Doing demos is not difficult. Show up with your product and explain it to people. You can usually even ask the account for a table and basic supplies.
- The sales reps who got the demo are already tracking it if they are any good—ask them to track it using your document. Although more sophisticated solutions could be built, Google spreadsheets works just fine—share it with them and ask them to fill in key details (address, demo date, and so on).
- Getting demo reps does not have to be expensive. At $10 to $15 per hour, you'll make back their pay if they can sell even one case (by my math, at least). Let them know their goals and keep them to it.
- Share the request sheet with your demo team. Ask them to select the ones they are going to do, and schedule it with the stores. Don't be too worried; see second bullet.
- Share your training. Use the same documents you've created for your sales reps, or for investors, or even for yourself to train sales reps. Once they know what to say, they can simply say it during the demos.

of my customers were just wandering into stores off the street, the street would be a good place to remind them of what I was up to.

I called the outdoor company that managed all of New York City's subway and street billboards, and tried to get him to part with some information. It worked too well—a subway billboard in New York City cost $300 per month, or roughly the cost of leasing a car. I didn't have that kind of money. That's when I remembered my friends at Attack! Marketing.

As it turns out, they have a service called *wild posters*, which are what they sound like: posters that go up in the urban wild. At a fraction the cost of billboards, I went for it. Five hundred posters of my product went up all over the city, but in focused clusters around my favorite accounts. However, it seemed like a waste to put them up with no way to see whether they were engaging people or not. So, in addition to looking just plain awesome, I put a call to action on the poster: people could send in stories of themselves and why they were stars and I would post them on the blog. It worked out—lots of people saw the posters, and people were sending in stories of why they were awesome (which made for fun blog posts). Accounts reported an increase in awareness and even my distributor was happy for the support.

Celebrity Endorsements

Does your category have local authority figures that you can reach? Meeting them and getting their support doesn't need to be expensive—just some time spent being your charming self should do. Having a celebrity (even a D-list local one) or an authority figure of any kind stand behind your product can go a long way, especially in the founding stages. Consumers respond to the advice of authorities. For example, if your product has any health or fitness application, a doctor could give a great endorsement. If it has a design or aesthetic edge to it, a local artist could lend his voice. With a bit of diligence, a good alliance does not have to cost very much at all.

Seth Tropper, the founder of Switch2Health knows a bit about this. Through a mix of persistence, luck, and passion, he teamed up with a pro basketball star who is both a great brand fit and a skilled product ambassador. Although Seth and his team, including Gautam Badri, their killer head of biz dev, are experienced entrepreneurs, they certainly aren't flush with celebrity contacts. They are normal guys like you or me who aren't scared to share their story and hope for the best.

Seth says that the better way to get celebs and authority figures on your side is to use the Icon Approach. Rather than finding an influential person and using them to be influential, find an icon in your field who is passionate about what they do, and also happens to be an influential figure.

"So much of it is luck," Seth says. "We just push it along." If your product promotes fitness, like theirs does, find a figure who is already into your topic, rather than giving some random celeb the hard sell. If your product promotes health, find a doctor with expertise and credibility in your specific area, rather than just any doctor who will let you pay them to stamp an MD on your product. The most important part might be just to keep your eyes open—the S2H guys met their NBA star's agent by chance, and made a deal. After that, the floodgates opened. How did they do it? Two basic steps:

1. Get the meeting.
2. Make it happen.

If your product is inexpensive, or has a specific function (for example, packaged foods, beverages, problem-solving inventions, and so on) you might get a lot of experiential marketing mileage by simply offering to share your products with events that serve a similar customer. Almost all customer groups have events that are important to them, and getting involved does not need to be expensive. While event sponsorship can sometimes cost thousands of dollars, I have secured full sponsorship packages for products of mine, including cooperative marketing, branded materials, and more for just-a-moment cases and some of my time.

My best advice for approaching event sponsorship is to make sure that the attendees are the right customer and that there is mutual value. Star Power sponsored a gala for a collection of dance troupes in New York City, and a coalition to support the arts. We created a signature cocktail—the Green Gatsby, and printed

---

Seth Tropper and Gautam Badri's Advice to the Aspiring Product Entrepreneur

Don't think that just because you fill a need that people will buy your product. You need to market the hell out of it. Don't develop your product in a vacuum—you will never know more about what your customers want than they do.

So what do they think you should do? Know your market before developing your product, and focus on doing one thing really well. Being the best at something is going to make a better selling point than being moderately good at a variety of things.

It's easy to have ideas—many of us have them. What's tough is taking action and committing fully. Know your strengths and don't give up. If at first you don't succeed— *"you only need one yes."*

the cocktail on the venue's stationery as well as donated a bunch of product to the planners. The attendees loved the cocktail, and sales proceeds of the drinks went fully to the charity.

What local groups or events can you approach to integrate your product into their offering? Would your product fit into the concerts of local bands? Perhaps the local book club? The local recreational soccer tournament? There are always relevant events, waiting to be uncovered and unlocked.

Public Relations

A critical component of awareness for your product will come from your public relations (PR). Besides the general thrill of seeing your company's name or your own emblazed in print, PR helps a business get in front of a bigger audience and appear much grander than they are.

PR runs on angles. Similar to the way we needed to work on search engine optimization (SEO) for the web site in terms of what people are searching for, we'll do that here for what the editors of magazines and newspapers are looking for. The best angles are both timely and respond to a compelling need. For example, a cookbook product could have one angle that includes a recipe that is healthy, quick to make for working families, and aesthetically pleasing. Reach out to the trade publications in your industry—the ones that have information for you by being an expert in your field. Trade pubs are sometimes the easiest to get published in as long as the angle is reasonably good. So come up with one to three angles on your product and circulate them. Put them up as press releases and see who comes back.

However, anyone can write a press release—that's the part that's public. To get even better PR, the other half helps too. Building relationships with bloggers, columnists, and reporters can go a long way when your angle is one they cover. I've seen much success for myself and others through finding a few kindred media spirits who cover the topics we're playing in. As long as what you're doing is interesting (and why else would we do it?) the right angle will make it print-worthy.

Along with the PR channels, every industry has trade shows at which you can go to meet and mingle with people in your field. When you are in contact with the trade pubs in your field, ask them to send you the calendar of key events, which I will simply take.

The combination of trade shows and well placed PR can build tremendous and long-lasting hype.

Web Marketing with the Three S's

Your web strategy is going to involve not only your web site, but also some free advertising with search engine optimization, search engine marketing (SEM), and social network marketing (SNM)—the three S's. I spoke to David Whittemore, online product expert, a good friend of mine, and a fellow entrepreneur. He has a lot of experience with web-based sales and web marketing.

First things first—your site. If you haven't made one yet, your product needs a web site. It doesn't need to do back flips, but it should clearly and attractively display your product. When you get started, you can quickly plug in to Google Checkout. When you can manage it, you should be able to take orders directly on your web site. Initially, you would have some good content describing your product, and when you can manage it, you'll want to have a where-to-buy map, as well as a private area for distributors, retailers, and other partners to order POS and download materials.

Your web site can be as simple or as dynamic as you like, but without making it search engine–friendly, customers who are looking for you (or perhaps don't know about you yet) will have difficulty finding you and are more likely to stumble on to a competing or substitutive product. Although search engine optimization has turned into a somewhat secretive and expert-driven topic, Dave says its core remains the same: findable web sites are up to date, on topic, and well-integrated into their communities.

Search engines like new, updated stuff. Actively update your content—blogs are great for this. There are many free, usable blogging platforms, like Blogger and Wordpress that you could get up and running today. Take the time to write insightful blog posts or thoughtful commentary on industry news and you are more likely to have readers and customers respect your brand and content.

Search engines also point customers at specific things that they search for. Your web site is obviously about your company, brand, and product. However, to connect your web site to a surfer who is looking for it, you need to discuss the topics they are looking for. This seems straightforward but is much tougher to execute. For example: suppose you are selling a widget that makes a great paperweight, and your brand is about fancy home décor. Your web site's content should discuss all the things your customer might search for: interior design, décor, housing, real estate, modern art, still life, paper, offices, coffee tables, and any other tangentially related topic that will allow your web site to be relevant to the people who are searching for what you have to offer. SEO experts will talk about meta tags, XML trees, keyword placement, and more. Unless you expect to generate a lot of your sales through the Web, however, a bit of simple SEO will be enough to help you test your site and make it findable. A bulk of your time at first will be spent opening and supporting accounts—your web site needs to exist only as a mark of legitimacy and perhaps to encourage the occasional web order.

Lastly, search engines like sites that are integrated into that community. A beauty of the Web is that interesting and complementary ideas can be easily linked together. The logic follows then that if your product and its effects are interesting, complementary sites will all be linking to you and you to them. The challenge with a new site is that no one is yet linking to yours. However, by starting to write blog articles about complementary topics, linking to other interesting content, discussing key people in your field, and occasionally soliciting authors of complementary content to link to you, you can integrate your web site into the fabric of your community over a few articles and nearly no time.

A Remarkable Product

David's advice comes from his perspective as an entrepreneur, professional product manager, and the president of the premier New York City entrepreneurship community. He says that successful companies don't just have a good idea, they have *remarkable* execution. *Remarkability*, in his opinion, is a combination of professional appearance, aesthetic appeal, and a certain level of surprise and delight that can't help but make a good impression on a customer. In all likelihood, every successful product you've seen has done something remarkable compared to all of their competitors who have failed.

Dave's advice:

- Have a laser-like focus on what is new and special about your product.
- Know what new behavior you are testing your customer for.
- Cut away the frills early on and focus on the core of your offering.
- Get the idea out there rather than be developing it forever.
- After confirming the problem, see if your solution works by tracking key metrics.
- Go the extra mile on delivery to make it extra-pretty and extra-professional.

Besides optimizing your web site to be found through searches (organic traffic) you can also do some search engine marketing and advertise on search engines to appear in the sponsored area and drive traffic to your site (through paid traffic). Google is an obvious choice, and Yahoo! and Miva are also effective and less expensive options. SEM works by bidding on keywords—if we take the earlier example of the widget, you could bid on the keyword *décor*, which, being popular, may be around $0.50 per click. This means that if you budgeted $50 toward this marketing, you would be nearly assured of 100 clicks. Assuming a 0.1 percent click-through rate (the ratio between the number of people who are served your ad to the number who click on it) you are getting 100,000 impressions for your $50. That's nothing to sneeze at.

Your customer belongs to a segment of customers just like them, with similar tastes, views, and preferences. Many of them are going to be using similar social tools, like Facebook or MySpace, to track their friends, Meetup to organize groups, or LinkedIn to discuss work. Reach them here through social network marketing. By tying your product or the problem you solve into one or all of these, you will allow happy customers to share your idea, discuss its merits, and broaden awareness at nearly no cost. While viral ideas are sometimes difficult to predict, a customer will usually appreciate a genuine outreach by a company that cares. Social networks can be unforgiving when a product does not represent sufficient value, or when a company does not seem genuine, so put some thought into creating a truly valuable experience for your customer for them to share through social networks. Good ideas can be as simple as sharing a discount with only your friends through Twitter, or a Facebook group, and as complex as creating an online game in which your customers are incented to interact with you and each other, strengthening your product's place in their circle. Simply having a Facebook page and a Twitter account does not make good social networking. The crucial step is to engage your customer in a genuine dialogue.

Mission: Possible

At this point, if you've done everything right, you have successfully taken your product from concept to shelf. You came up with a cool concept, had it made, sold some, and have started thinking more broadly about marketing, PR, and strategy. A tremendous accomplishment—very few people see their dream products fully fleshed out, let alone created or sold. Now is the time to make sure that this machine you've built is properly greased, and that all the wheels are turning. Here's where we go back to the rough edges and polish them, go back to our old contacts and freshen them up, and make sure that we're set for a long curve of profitable business.

If you don't revisit some of the details that you may have glossed over in the beginning, like pricing, incentives, and the deals you've made with your partners, you risk building your house on a shaky foundation—one that can come crashing down at the most inopportune moment.

One floor underground on a perfect night in New York, I was having dinner with Eric, my distributor. He was telling me about his life, and about how he was a trained jeweler, but put down the gemstones to pick up beverages. He said to me—"Vik, in this world, ninety-five percent of people just exist. They earn money and spend it. They live and they die. Five percent of people understand what we're doing here. Out of that, three percent own businesses and experience real freedom. One percent of people have the heart to see their own product happen."

The numbers didn't sound right, but the sentiment was spot-on. "It's not easy," I replied. "No, it's not." He agreed. "Cheers" and the clink of our saké glasses echoed the potential of all the people quietly creating products with one eye on their desks and another pointed up at the sky.

If you so choose, your journey really just begins here. After all, you've made considerable investment, certainly emotionally if not monetarily. Creating a product is almost like having a baby—everything it does is amplified: every sale is a celebration and an unhappy account is personal failure.

Until now, it is pretty likely that you have had your own fingers in some element of the manufacturing, distribution, sales, and marketing of your product. You need to slowly extricate yourself so that you regain the freedom that this business was supposed to bring you. One of the benefits of a product business is that once established, you are not necessarily personally needed anymore—the product is what people associate with. You just need to build a process that keeps customers engaged, and keeps product flowing.

Sometimes, when your product is made by your own hands, when your sales are always in person—because people like you

A Quick Reminder of the Inspired Method

1. List: Complete.
2. Test: Complete.
3. Cull: Complete.
4. Pick and negotiate: Complete.
5. Adapt: We spent a lot of time on steps 1 to 4 up front. Now that you can see the big picture, we go back to all our players and make sure they are up to snuff.

rather than your product, it can be difficult to step out of it. However, if you've been following the advice of this book so far, you should have most of the pieces in play to start trusting the experts that you have assembled around yourself and this product.

Optimizing the Role of the Co-Packer

At this point, I hope you've been taking notes. It's inevitable that most of your customer surveys, retailer tests, and distributor reach-outs came with some sort of feedback on your product. Your faithful co-packer has probably put up with conflicting instruction, changing designs, late-night disturbances, and more. Mine sure did.

Then again, perhaps you never got that far, and have only now been able to speak to a few co-packers and figure out whether or not one of them is right for you. Perhaps you shared some responsibility with them—for example, you may have had the package created and put your product into it yourself.

If you have a production product that you are happy with, and that you are able to sell to retailers and perhaps a distributor, you should extract yourself from the production process. Change your role from *active participant* to *decision* maker. Your involvement in production is likely to be tedious, time consuming, inconsistent, and a liability risk should anything go wrong with your product. Allowing a good contract manufacturer to put your product together will eliminate all of these issues.

If your co-packer is not effective, can't make your product or implement your changes, and for whatever reason does not see the value in your enterprise, you will need to sort this situation out. When I reached this stage, I ended up changing co-packers when we hit an impasse on price. It was not easy, and not something I would wish upon anyone else.

Then again, if it isn't going to work, you're better off cutting the cord quickly, cleanly, and early. Go back to your list of co-packers. With a product in play, retail and distribution partners lined up, you will find this round of discussions much easier than the last.

Defining the Responsibility of the Distributor

It is pretty typical for the people behind a young product to do a lot of the deliveries themselves. Even when I had three different distributors operating in my market, I still found myself occasionally going to stores to do case drops, shake some hands, and talk to customers. There's nothing wrong with that, especially if you've been maintaining relationships with retailers. In fact, this may at first seem like the simplest arrangement: after all, you can make sure you like the placement on the shelf, you can talk to your customers, and you are in close contact with your product.

These are all great things for you to do, especially as you learn more and more about how your industry works. However, if you are the only person who can carry product to some or all of your accounts, your time will be spent servicing existing accounts during the crucial hours of the day when your time is better spent meeting customers and building business. Also, you will find yourself losing opportunities to meet key players or attend events because you are your own infrastructure.

What is more important, though, is that you will find yourself stretched between the jobs of salesperson, delivery driver, payment collector, relationship manager, and other roles that can sometimes be mutually exclusive. How can you maintain a jovial relationship if you are also the one who has to turn the screws in a sales meeting, and play hardball to collect checks? You could, but probably not all as well as you could do any one of them. A good distribution partner will let you focus on the ones you want to do, while handling the day-to-day deliveries and payment collection. Many will also help you sell and build new relationships.

If you've been operating without an agreement, now is when you should lock your distributor down. As long as your own sales force is small, and your delivery fleet nonexistent, the distributor is probably your most important partner. Get an ironclad deal together that you both can live with, and sign it.

Then again, if your distributor is ineffective, late with payments, weak on the sell, and unreliable—don't sign anything. Find yourself a partner who values your vision and your product. Again, this time around, you have a product and an account list. Getting a new distributor will be simpler than getting the first one.

Incentivizing Sales Personnel

You will be your first, and often most effective sales representative. However, even if you're professionally trained and operating at full steam, you might be able to visit only 20 to 40 accounts in a single day—and that's if you're in a market where many accounts are clustered together.

If you enter a market with a bit more suburban spread, and if you want to focus on building the business rather than single account sales, you are going to need a few good salespeople. At first, you may be able to lean on your distributor's reps, though often, your distributor will ask or require that you support them with sales as well. It's inevitable that your first or second sales rep will struggle a bit, as you learn to distill your knowledge and passion onto them while struggling with a tiny budget. I've been there. Ultimately, however, great salespeople exist, and you will want them around you to take your message to your key accounts, and to bring a level of expertise that you may not have about your industry.

That doesn't mean you should ignore the distributor's people— your ability to use both well could define your success in a market. In the last chapter, we discussed incentives for the distributor and their reps that were designed to keep your product at the top of their minds and keep them excited since they might be dealing with dozens of products. How will you incentivize your own rep, who has only your products to offer?

The answer, unfortunately, is: it depends. It depends on your industry and the market rates for talent. It depends on the experience and expectations of the candidate in question. It depends on the product you're selling and the potential you believe it to have. Ultimately, it depends on how much you're willing to part with— because if you hire them at all, it will be for exactly that much.

What is most important, however, is that each industry has its own standards. If you don't know them, you can typically find them out by asking your distributor—after all, they stand to gain directly if you hire people to support them.

However, there are few options that are great fallbacks.

- *Per case incentives:* Per case or per item incentives are most straightforward. This is most transparent since the reps will be able to track how many they've sold (which keeps it simple and leads to potentially fewer arguments over pay). A whole dollar amount like $1 or $2 per case will keep them excited as long as it isn't viewed as trivial.
- *Percentage of sales commissions:* In situations where order size can vary a lot, a percentage works, like 5 percent of gross sales. The percentage also helps you keep margin calculations simple, in which the whole dollar amount might be a tricky percentage of margin. However, having to do any math at all risks disagreement with the reps—is it 5 percent of gross or of net? Who gets to calculate that? Without an automated system, I avoid this route.
- *Acceleration tiers:* When ticket prices are relatively low, accelerating threshold incentives can be included as well, for example, $1 per case up to 50 cases a month, then $3 per case thereafter. These kinds of incentives have a positive selection effect as well, since stronger reps are more incentivized than weaker reps. I've had guys make great sales for me, and I would throw in incentives that they didn't even know were coming—tickets to a game, a shiny watch, anything to keep those sales numbers up.
- *Competition:* If there are multiple sales reps in a pool, a competitive incentive can be layered on. Salespeople are naturally competitive, goal-driven individuals. You already know that's important to them, especially if you are already running a program for distributors' reps. Why not make the competition work for you? Have competitions with compelling prizes (but do the math first): for example, the rep who has the highest sales this month gets a free flat screen TV.

Improve Your Web Site

When first you launch, it is likely that your web site is a bit cobbled together. Even if you've decided early on that your web site was an important channel for you, there are going to be parts of it that beg for refinement.

Once your machine is up and running, pour a little more heart into the web site. Even if you don't sell a single widget there, it is your most easily accessible face to the world. The web site is what your customers will see when they look you up, what your distributors will see before you meet them, and what potential partners will see first when deciding to work with you.

A great web site might cost more than $5,000—though not too much more, if you're smart about it—and is well worth that price for a gorgeous and content-rich first impression.

The web site is also a great place for you to share your thoughts on the market, exciting updates for your product, discussions with customers, and more.

Exercise: Launch a Blog

Is it mandatory to have a blog on your web site? Certainly not. However, people expect fresh content, and have been shown to value companies that show that they're listening. What better way to do that than by having a blog on your site?

If you've held off so far because you are daunted by the task, don't be. Setting up a blog these days is very easy.

- First, you will need to create an account with a blog provider—the big ones are Wordpress and Blogger. Both are free. I happen to like Wordpress since it can run nearly invisibly, but I will focus here on Blogger just because it is much easier. Go to blogger.com and sign up.
- Come up with a name for your blog. It could be your company's name, or perhaps something clever that's close by.
- Decide on your blog's central thesis. It should not be just to write about your company—nobody wants to read about that yet. Make it instead about the problem your product solves, or one of the benefits your product provides.
- Write your first 10 posts. They don't need to be novels, but should be long enough to say something interesting.
- Publish! Set aside some time each week to write a few posts, and schedule them to publish every day or every couple of days.
- Publicize your blog by putting its link in your e-mail signature, on your Facebook page, and sprinkled into your discussions.

Changing the Price

More than one brilliant product designer has launched a great product at the wrong price. Of the three Ps (Pricing, Placement, POS) pricing is the most complex to revisit, and it is inevitable that you will consider changing the price one way or another.

On the one hand, you may find that your product sells too easily, and that perhaps you've undervalued yourself. Can you inch the price upward without scaring away your customers? On the other hand, you may find that your margin is not as wide as you wanted (it nearly never is) and inching the price up will help you fund better marketing and incentives.

In either case, this is testable and noncommittal. Since it is likely that you've signed a pricing agreement with your distributor already, you can't very well just demand more money. However, explain your situation to him and he may be happy to help—after all, he can't make their money off of you if you aren't happy. Ask him to test sales at a higher price and ask your reps to do the same. As long as you're within spitting distance of competing products, accounts should not complain that much. Having proven the feasibility of the price increase, take the price higher at the next chance you get.

The other scenario is also possible. Perhaps your sales are softer than expected despite your most brazen efforts at blowing them out. Perhaps you're unable to reach a particular target audience because you've currently priced them out. You want to lower the price to bring up your numbers. This is a slightly more dangerous situation. First, lower prices echo through your supply chain and will definitely hurt your bottom line. Four bottles of $1 water make as much money as one bottle of $4 water. Second, you aren't setting prices—your distributors and retailers are. I've seen stories in which a brand struggles to reduce its pricing and the distributor pockets the difference instead of passing the savings through.

You do have an option available to you: Test your price point first through consumer incentives—coupons. Print coupons or have them digital and get them out to whomever you can. I've been known to hand coupons out in accounts while asking customers to please try my product. If the incentive works, perhaps you offered 50 cents off or so, and then do some math to see what you would have to change to make that work. The retailer and distributor are not likely to squeeze themselves too much for you—you will have to change the price you sell at, and then check the retailers later to enforce the change.

Manage and Track Sell-Through

Are all your customers new customers? All your accounts new accounts? When you get started, they will be. As you get rolling, however, you should start to see accounts reorder, and of course, your distributors should reorder. The important metric is your reorder rate. If you have 100 new accounts this month, how many of them reorder? How many reorder the month after? How long does it seem to take them between reorders?

If you're growing primarily by aggressively getting new accounts, it won't be sustainable for long. Reordering accounts are giving you free money for effort you already spent on the sell. Lapsing accounts represent time and resources wasted on the sell or an opportunity squandered through poor execution.

Good reorder rates vary by category, though proper account selection, merchandising, and support should keep you as close to 100 percent as you can manage.

Summary

Your product represents a great challenge and tremendous potential. It could bring fame, fortune, and celebrity. It is certain to bring strong lessons to learn and interesting people to meet.

While we covered some of the tangible incentives you can set for your staff or for your distributor, the whole machine that you're building is greased by the smooth sweat of collective incentive. How thoughtful you make them, and how you harness them to work for you will define your experience and ultimately your success.

At the very bottom, your customer purchases your product because he is incented through your offer to make him better in some way. The retailer is incented to carry your product because he makes 30 to 40 percent on the sale to that customer, and he only knows about it because your sales rep was incented to walk through the door. The distributor is incented to help build your product, because the bigger it becomes, the easier it is to sell, and the better his 30 to 40 percent margin gets. If you need his help, a broker is incented to make 5 percent on his sales to multiple distributors.

The payments you take are funneled to your suppliers, who are incented to make a product you like, so long as you'll buy it. What's left in between is poured back into POS material, guerrilla marketing campaigns, and PR. It goes into the prizes for your sales reps and your travel expenses to meet your clients. It goes into giveaways and sales, coupons, and business cards. It goes to the graphic designer who makes your images, the web designer who makes your site, and the masseuse who calms you down when it gets overwhelming.

What's left after that could make you a legend and a billionaire. Enjoy the ride.

❗ Challenge: Take Calculated Risks

Learn to play Texas Hold 'Em. If you know how to play, play more often. Poker is repeatedly cited as the common thread among successful CEOs—second only to golf. I'm not encouraging you to gamble huge amounts of money—just to understand the feeling of sitting around a table of opponents who are trying to read each other's moves.

In many ways, poker approximates starting a business on every hand: you're dealt some cards—your product. No one but you knows how valuable they are, or how you are going to use them. As the flop, turn, and river come out on the table, people try to sell each other the notion that they have the best hand, predict the future, and make the best out of what they had. On each round, we go through a pricing exercise, placing the right bet that will let us make each hand as profitable as possible. Finally, at product launch time, we show our cards and see who had what, who merchandised his hand the best, and what it was worth.

9

Financing Primer

*He that is of the opinion money will do everything may well be
suspected of doing everything for money.*

—Benjamin Franklin

In 2007, an entrepreneur named Tej had an idea. Not just any idea, but an epic idea. To help companies reach international audiences through web video. He knew he could do part of this on his own, but it wouldn't be enough. He needed a team, and he needed to pay them—so he set out to raise some money. The first few times Tej pitched an investor, he didn't know what to expect. He spoke to the people he found by searching for investors. He got a crash course in tidying up his documents and his pitch, but also in humility. They didn't want to invest.

However, with a bit of time, the word got out that he was looking for capital, and he would end up having meetings with investors who heard of him through a friend or through family. He learned something surprising—the best angel investors don't call themselves angels at all. They were wealthy individuals who just liked investing in interesting people and their businesses.

At this point, Tej had raised some money, but not enough. The quest to raise financing was consuming him, and it took his eye off the ball. They were supposed to be building a product. Instead, he had a precise and sophisticated way to keep track of the conversations they were having with investors, and finally closed some more capital there, too.

Now, Tej has capital, a great team, and a lot to say about his business. In this chapter, we explore some of the different ways you can finance your product, some of the documents you will probably need to create to do so, and tackle some potentially contentious questions around company valuation and the terms of a deal. Although raising money isn't easy, even in good times, with a good idea, clear pitch documents, and an understanding of this game, anything is possible.

It Takes Money to Make Money

Anyone who tells you that you can make a solid, sustainable products business from nothing is either naïve or misleading. With the rare exception of artisans who can craft an expert product with their own hands, and build a business slowly and organically over years, we've got to be able to put down some capital for inventory, production, and marketing. It all starts with the first idea and the first dollar.

Money is an interesting thing—it means so many things to different people. Before I walked down the path of entrepreneurship, I thought money was this thing to be prized—value incarnate that I should earn slowly and hoard up. While I still think it is valuable, I now think of money more like fuel. Burning it well can take you places, bring life's experiences, and teach you endless amounts. In fact, it's like a magic fuel that refills itself as long as you're burning it right. There are a lot of places your financing can come from: yourself, your friends and family, angel investors, venture capitalists, or the banks. If you're lucky, you might qualify for a grant or be able to win a competition, too.

We can be extremely diligent about what we spend it on, buy it only when we badly need it, and stretch out when exactly we need to pay for it. We can bootstrap, work for capital, or try to pull sales figures and use them for financing—but your company will probably need someone else's capital at some point. That's not to say that building a business is expensive—every dollar wisely spent will come right back. In this section, we're going to explore the various ways you can get funding, and some of their pros and cons. Hopefully, by the end of it, you will have a sense of what you're willing to give up, and how much risk you're willing to take in the pursuit of capital.

Your Own Pockets

Initially, you are going to be your first and best source of capital. The money is going to come from your own pocket. The amount you can afford can vary wildly, based on whether you're employed, a student, or old-money wealthy. When all you're doing is meeting potential partners and sketching prototypes, this shouldn't be onerous at all. However, when you're purchasing raw materials and prototypes and shooting for the moon in sales and marketing expenses, it might be.

Friends and Family

After you need more money for growth than you can afford, you should reach out to those close to you—friends and family (F&F). They are the next set of people who are likely to invest because they believe in you and have known you all your life. Your parents, rich uncles, and close friends might be willing to lend or invest a bit of their hard-earned money as capital for your business. In fact, it is possible that friends and family might be willing to invest that capital at a much better valuation than an institutionalized investor, which means you give up less of your company now. For this reason, friends and family money often carries young products to

---

Tapping Your Network

You might be surprised at how much the people around you want you to succeed. Your friends and family are more likely to understand your motivations, hear out your plan, and believe in you earlier than a stranger might.

In fact, your friends and family also know a bunch of different people, some of whom may be looking for an investment. If you make it known to your circle that you're looking for capital and you have a plan to keep it safe, you might have an easier time finding it than you think.

Taking friends and family money might seem free, but it certainly isn't. Holding the hard-earned dollars of people closest to you can be a lot of pressure. You've promised them success, and they want you to succeed. Now make it happen!

the next level, where they are now small, sustainable businesses with proven propositions. While this depends on your means and your network—people usually go to F&F investors for $250,000 or less.

Angel Investors

After F&F, your next stop will be wealthy individuals who are not your family. Angel investors are experienced but not institutional investors who can offer a substantial capital injection and fuel explosive growth to a national or strong regional operation. They aren't your friends, and so you will want much more diligence, value proposition, and documentation in your pitch, and they are not going to give you as cushy a valuation as your family might. They will want their pound of flesh.

Beware of companies out there that call themselves *angel firms* or *angel groups*. There are many sketchy or actually fraudulent companies that call themselves angels but are really out to destroy companies. However, there are also angels who *are* rich and relaxed, and just want to do something cool. Unlike venture capitalists (VCs), angels are in this game because they have had their fun and want to hang out with entrepreneurs, or perhaps to tell a story about their fun little venture at a cocktail party. While they are usually serious, successful businesspeople, they bring with them a lightness not usually observed with VCs. Companies typically go to angels for less than $2 million in funding.

Venture Capitalists

Next, your product company will be ready for venture capitalists or a strategic partner to get you ready for a blowout to a rock-solid contender, or exit to initial public offering (IPO) or acquisition. Venture capitalists are in the business of finding successful concepts and building successful companies. Depending on the firm, they will want to take a business from small or even concept to sale. The sale could be an acquisition or perhaps an IPO (where your stock sold to the public markets) and the VC looks to make a sweet return.

These guys tend to have a focus—not all VCs will invest in a product company, but most of the success stories have one of these guys backing them up. VCs are a powerful force for a start-up—they have business expertise, potential partners, and client contacts. Once they come on board, they will hold 10 to 40 percent

Inspired Method—Selecting an Investor

Selecting an investor is in many ways similar to selecting a distributor. They hold a lot of the power since they are the ones offering the cash. However, just as the distributor seeks a superior product for their catalogue, an investor seeks a superior company for his portfolio. A variation of the Inspired Method can be applied here to help keep track of all the investors you're seeking.

1. List: Do a bit of homework and list out all the investors you can find out about through your network and your research. This includes not just the investors you can find through VCs, but your parents, doctor friends, rich uncles, and the neighborhood Lotto winner.
2. Test: Although they will be testing you in every meeting—you should test them, too. Find out about their experience in your space and their network for your support. What's most important to you? Do you want their experience and help or just silent investment?
3. Cull: Many investors may not have the experience you need, and some will likely turn you down. An investor relationship is a lot like marriage: a long-term partnership that is messy to get out of. If the deal doesn't seem right, it isn't unheard of for a start-up to refuse capital.
4. Pick: You need to make a decision based on all the important factors. How much capital, at what cost, and from whom.
5. Adapt: If over time you need to take on another investor, or further investment from a current investor, roll back through this process and make it happen.

(perhaps more) of your company and be extremely interested in your success.

While every firm is different, VCs tend to invest when companies need millions of dollars, and have the promise of returning a hundred times that amount or more.

Traditional Banks

The bank is the next stop when you can't or don't want to sell a stake in your company to equity investors. The bank exists for this purpose—to lend money to people who will make good use of it. When you need money, why not go to the people who deal in money? But cash isn't free, especially from the bank. Even if they like your business, they are going to want some security for their loan. They might want a piece of your house, if you own one, or else a piece of anything else you have.

If you're able to get a loan that is unsecured, it will likely be small and for an exorbitant interest rate. The same is true of borrowing indefinitely from your credit cards, which is a decidedly bad idea.

Then again, there are some exceptions. In many states and countries, local governments sponsor and promote loans to promising "Small and Midsize Businesses" often shortened to SMB loans or SMB programs. These programs are special as they include a subsidized interest rate and often a government guarantee—so Big Brother watches your back if you should need him. Also, interest groups often organize programs for specific groups—there are tons of programs and easier loans for small businesses owned and run by women and minorities.

When the banks won't give you something for nothing, you still might qualify for factoring. Factors are a form of receivables financing, where you show the bank proof of orders from customers that have not yet been paid—perhaps because they have long payment terms—and the bank offers to lend against them. However, as the name implies, there are more factors involved. The size of your business, the history of your customers, the product involved—all play a role, and each lender does it differently.

For example—your first 50 customers might have placed orders and signed contracts. You may not actually have any of that money for a while—depending on your terms and the way you've set up client relationships. Factoring would let you borrow half the amount of the receivables (or close to that) as long as the bank believes your customers will pay.

Grant Programs

In some places, for some projects, and for the right founder, you can get free money from Uncle Sam for your endeavor. While this can be difficult in the United States for profit-driven companies (there are more available for nonprofits) many countries offer grants for promising entrepreneurs with promising ideas, especially minorities.

Seth Tropper, the founder of Switch2Health and PlasmaSol, was able to get grant financing for his start-ups by persistently applying to local and national grant programs that can be found on grants.gov .Erik Nilsson, the founder of the innovative start-up, Cubis, was able to get grant money for his start-up at the municipal idea center in Sweden.

Each city and country have different options to give away money, and they merit at least a bit of due diligence before being written off. Although grants are often only for projects that directly benefit the city or country in question, it's always possible that your project fits the need of a particular group, and the grant might get you financing and a customer. It's sometimes a long shot, but easily worth half an hour of your time.

Entrepreneurship Competitions

Unlike soccer and rugby, entrepreneurship competitions have cash involved even at the minor leagues. Your local university, your small business club, even industry organizations have business-plan, elevator-pitch, and design competitions that you and your product can enter. Winners can get thousands of dollars, connections to key players, exposure to customers, and more.

Sol Khan, the founder of *The Comical*, needed to get to the Aspen Comedy Festival to get fresh content, advertisers, and publicity for his start-up magazine. He was, however, tight on finances, and a flight to Colorado seemed almost frivolous. Undeterred, he booked his ticket.

Feeling the pressure from this move, Sol entered an elevator pitch competition—one where entrepreneurs compete to summarize their company and ask for money in one minute (a bit longer than the 10-second pitch we worked on earlier). Although surrounded by more experienced entrepreneurs with high-tech projects, Sol won the competition through good prep and a funny pitch. Leap and the net will appear.

Your municipality, college, and local professional group probably have business plan and pitch competitions all the time—many of which are free to enter. Doing so will not only get you valuable practice at speaking in front of a crowd of decision makers, but also could get you to meet some cool fellow entrepreneurs.

Buyer Beware

Keep in mind, however, that getting financing for your venture is not all gumdrops and teddy bears. Investors and banks are not in the business of losing money, and will take every step possible to limit their losses in the event that you don't work out. In return, you should be educated on what terms are important in your deal, and structures like corporations and limited liability corporations

(LLCs) to limit your liabilities. If all else was equal, that might be enough for you to go toe to toe with an investor. However, you are probably on your first or second deal, while many of these guys review hundreds of deals.

Don't be a sucker. If you let an investor take you for a ride, they will. I had an advisor who thought all VCs were *Vulture* Capitalists—looking to pick apart a company and screw the founders. While I don't think that's the case, it would be a travesty to pour your heart into building a brand and a cool product only to lose it when you're ready for financing and growth.

Make no mistake—investors in your company are not out to do their civic duty. They want to see a return, and will be hesitant to finance your product if it doesn't seem like you're going to be able to make it happen. They will not only want to see all of your plans, but will want to put some protection in place for their hard-earned dollars.

Erik Nilsson, the founder of Cubis, learned this lesson the hard way. He was working on his previous venture when he had a harrowing time with his founding team and investors. Erik had just left his two-decade career at a large and stable telecom giant. He joined a start-up that had just scored a huge VC backer. Though he didn't know it then, the VCs and the president didn't see eye to eye about the product and the company's growth. When the president made a bold push that failed, the company found itself underfunded for future moves.

When companies need more money, they look for more investors—and there were none to be had now. The VCs were up against a wall: wait for the company to burn through the finances, or get themselves out. So they got out—their terms let them keep the IP, bankrupt the company, and bail. The founders were left with nearly nothing: none of the tech they had developed, no stake in their company, and a few angry debtors to deal with. A cautionary tale: A cool product and a great plan are not enough; company founders need to have great relationships with their financiers.

The Perfect Business Plan

Now that you know who's holding the money, we have to capture your plan and distill it into a document that investors can use to understand your company. As an added challenge, we're going to create this document without taking our eye off the ball for our

Debate: Debt versus Equity

What if you had a choice not to give up anything to your financier? That might seem like getting something for nothing. A popular debate is whether it makes more sense to borrow the capital you need, and eventually pay it back, or take the capital in exchange for equity (which, while still paid back, doesn't hang on you like debt). The incentives are mixed, too—taking on an investment often comes with the expertise and network of your investors. A loan or line of credit does not.

In my opinion, the decision comes down to the stage of your project and the soundness of your plan, and what you plan on doing with the cash.

If you need cash for a near-term, well-defined event, or perhaps as a bridge while waiting for customers to pay you, a bank loan or line of credit will work. It will cost you 5 to 8 percent per year, but that means borrowing a thousand dollars for a month will cost you only $4 to $7.

On the other hand, if you need money for growth, for an investment that is good for the company, on a plan that stretches out over years, it might make more sense to seek an investor who shares your vision, who would be willing to help make it work.

If your project involves the need for physical assets, property, and equipment, you may be able to get a loan for these specific items that ties them up as collateral. If, on the other hand, your investments are needed in less tangible things like salaries, a web site, software, and specific inventory, that might be tough.

Lastly, if you need a lot of money—hundreds of thousands of dollars, a bank loan might be difficult without a relationship, a track record, and tying up anything you own in the deal. The right investor brings a wealth of knowledge, contacts, and skills to the table that make the loss of equity worth the risk.

foundling company. I've known too many people who spend time obsessing over their business plans that would be better spent building their brand. The truth is, an investor will be more impressed with a viable business than a shiny business plan (though it does help) and your plan will change every time you get a bit of customer feedback or learn something from a potential partner. Also, successful investors tend to be very sharp. They can read through your made-up facts a mile away, and can sense when you're uncertain about your claims. They usually have a fair idea on what makes for a successful product and what feels more like pie in the sky.

I certainly learned this lesson the hard way. In my first few investor meetings, I was sorely underprepared. My presentation was overly academic and not compelling. My business plan was unrealistic, and my product was not complete. I had no idea how to get to a fair valuation, what it meant to agree to nondilution, or even what fair terms were. Every investor I've met has asked for a plan, but all have been just as happy (or more so) with a one-pager as they've been with the 30-page monstrosity that I used to tote around. I'm sure they only read the first page of that one, too. The exception to this guidance is if you plan on competing in business plan competitions. These tend to be more academic, and are more likely to judge the merits of the plan document on its own.

I'm not suggesting operating blindly and without a plan of any kind. A sound and well-thought-through strategy can take you to the brink of success—but this could just as well be a whiteboard drawing that evolves with your experience. My advice is to write a strong one-to-three page summary and then consider the limited ways in which you can spend your time, and decide whether the perfect document is worth spending less time on your company. A good presentation, on the other hand, is a must.

The Compelling Investor Presentation

I've recently gotten fewer requests for my plan and more for my PowerPoint. This is a good document to have whenever meeting with a potential investor, and takes far less time to write than the business plan. It's often more compelling because you have more latitude for visuals, it is in color by default, and each page has to communicate a single discrete idea. It's tough to ramble in a discrete deck.

While there are many ways to assemble this presentation, I'll offer the recommendation from the New York Angels group, an active and well-respected group of angel investors. Keep it short— under 20 slides, and practice to run through them in under 15 minutes.

Open with a page for your company name and logo, and spend one slide capturing your business overview. Just one slide! It should feel a bit like your 60-second pitch. One page for the team, and one for the market before you get to the crux of the presentation.

Spend a slide on the product, and keep in mind that the investor wants to hear about your *company*—the product is just the way you're going to build your first success. Talk a bit about the business model on the next page: are you building a classic manufacturer-distributor-retailer business, or are you changing it in some way? How will you be paid? Who are your customers and how many are there?

Next, a few slides on how you make it happen. Do you bring any strategic relationships to the table? Who is the competition and how will you differentiate? Resist claiming that you have no competition just because you're pioneering a new category—there must be something else out there waiting for your customer's dollars, even if it is a bit different. Once you get there, what stops someone else from doing the same? Spend a slide discussing the barriers to entry that you will overcome and the ones that stand in the way of others who come after you.

After laying out the business, get to the finances. If you've made any money already, mention it here, and put down your forecast at least a few years forward. Even though investors may ignore your projections, its important to show that you're fiscally minded and looking out for them. On the next page, get to the deal—how much are you asking for and how will you use it? Where will you be because of this investment? Finally, fill them in on who else is at the table. Who all have invested (even if it's friends and family), who owns what, and at what valuation.

Think carefully through your last slide and summarize everything. Realistically yet optimistically, summarize your business, the investment opportunity, and the top three benefits of working with you.

Private Placement Memorandum

Somewhat different from a business plan, a private placement memorandum (PPM) is a document that summarizes your company as an investment. In some ways, it is similar to a business plan, but its focus is more on what your investors are buying, what they are getting, and the risks that stand in between. The focus is on the transaction that gets you an investor, rather than on your product or company itself.

The PPM isn't aimed at angels and VCs, but instead at retail investors. With a strong PPM, companies can raise capital from a wider market of investors than just those that might normally go for a start-up. The PPM serves to educate investors about what it is that they're buying (if you've ever bought into a mutual fund, or stocks of a company, you've probably seen one). It doesn't replace the business plan—that is a document that lays out your product and strategy. Instead, it supplements that by making your company easier to invest in.

A good PPM will have a complete description of what's offered for sale, now called a *security*. It has a summary of the investment—how much shares cost, how the company is set up, and what the terms of the offering are. If anything takes away from these, the disclaimers go here, too.

You will probably need to spell out what you're looking for in an investor. Often, you want a *sophisticated investor*—commonly defined as one who is worth more than $2.5 million or has made over $250,000 in the past two years. In some cases, you could get away with having an *accredited investor*—defined by the SEC as one who makes over $200,000 ($300,000 jointly with a spouse) or has a net worth over $1 million.

Similarly to your presentation, you'll want to summarize your financials, forecasts, and plan for spending investment. If you have different classes of stock (preferred, common, and so forth) you will want to lay them out here so that investors know what they are buying in to and what rights they get, especially if other investors have dividend restrictions or dilution protection.

Finally, you will want to include your plan for marketing this PPM document. If an investor believes you will be able to get other investors involved, they will feel less risk and may be more likely to invest. Also, your business plan or business plan summary becomes part of this document.

Valuation

Raising capital for your project is akin to selling a piece of it for some cash with a ton of strings attached. How much is that piece worth? Without a fair valuation, you aren't going to know whether you're being taken for a ride or not.

Market Value and Comps

The simplest and most compelling way to express value for your company is to put it in terms of market value. If comparable transactions have gone through and there are no important differences, you can claim pretty solid footing. For example, if your company sells notebooks and office supplies, and another company of similar size, in a similar market, with a similar management team raised $1 million against a $10 million valuation (that is, took $1 million in exchange for 10 percent in ownership), you could probably do the same.

Since true comps are usually rather difficult to come by—after all, it is unlikely that two companies are ever exactly the same—you could get to a valuation by getting as close as you can. To take the preceding example, suppose your company was not the same size, and your team was not of the same caliber. Perhaps your company has only 10 percent as much revenue, serves a slightly different customer, and your team is a bit less experienced. You might start by taking 10 percent of the valuation, adding a bit because your customers are more interesting, and then discounting it back a bit because your team is less experienced. You could then seek $100,000 or so in exchange for 10 percent, on reasonable grounds.

Revenue Multiple

In many industries, analysts use company revenues to get a quick ballpark of value using a multiple. It is what it sounds like—a multiplier that relates the company's value to its annual revenue.

Since public companies are required to report this information, we can take what we learn in the market and use it to supplement the other types of valuation you will come up with. Since we're talking about a product company, let's take a look at some of the big guys. Table 9.1 shows the price-to-earnings ratio for some publicly traded consumer products companies. These numbers are

Table 9.1: Public Multiples as Reported

Company	Price/Earnings Ratio
Procter and Gamble	14.9
Colgate-Palmolive	19.3
Coca-Cola	18.6
Mattel	16.0
Sara Lee	12.1

Source: Yahoo! Finance, April 2010.

Table 9.2: Private Multiples for Beverage Companies

Companies	Revenue Multiple on Acquisition	Details
Glaceau VitaminWater	11.5	$355 million sales > $4.1 billion price
Fuze	2.6	$90 million sales > $240 million price
Honest Tea	4.6	$23 million sales > $43 million price for 40 percent
Sweet Leaf	4.9	$12 million sales > $18 million price for 30 percent

Sources: rogocapital.com, Bevnet Live.

high—successful brands are worth more than 10 times the money they actually make.

This isn't just for public companies either—Table 9.2 shows a few recent transactions for beverage consumer product companies, which are often worth five times their actual revenues.

People get into product companies because of the multiples. Whereas a services business might be worth .5 to 1 × revenues, a strong product can be worth 5 to 10 × revenues.

Discounted Cash Flow

Whether or not any comps are available, a discounted cash flow (DCF) is another way that an investor will use to value your company, and indeed, is a popular method analysts use to value public companies. In a nutshell, DCF is a method to calculate the value today of all the money a company might make in the future. For example, if you had the option to take a dollar today, or a dollar a year from now—you would probably want the dollar today. It's the same amount of money, but the dollar today is actually worth more—since you could invest it and a year from now have made a profit.

The same is true of companies. If your company is going to make $10,000 a year for the next five years, it is certainly worth more than the $10,000 you make in year one—but how much more? By considering a few factors and making a few assumptions, we can estimate how much free cash the company will have around, and use that to discount back the answer. Five variables are:

1. *How quickly do we expect revenue to grow?* Mature companies grow painfully slowly—perhaps in the 10 percent ballpark.

Why Is Cash Flow Discounted?

A dollar in hand is worth two in the bush. That's the theory anyway—that capital has a time value to it. If you have a dollar now, you could invest it and have that interest rather than wait and get the money later. So if you have access to a risk-free investment like U.S. Treasuries, you could invest there with full confidence that you're going to get your money back (as opposed to stocks, with which you may or may not get your money back). If that rate is 3 percent, it means that $100 a year from now is not actually worth $100 to you; its worth is closer to $97.08.

That $3 may not seem like much, but imagine now a case in which we're talking about a company that makes millions of dollars each year, and is trying to talk you into investing in it. If it's going to make $10 million 10 years from now, does that mean you should pay that much for it? Keeping the 3 percent from before, this company is actually worth a bit over $7 million. In addition, this isn't an investment in T-bills; it's a company that takes risks. Depending on the kind of investor you are, that risk might be worth another 5 percent, and that $10 million company is now worth only close to $4.5 million.

Your company is a young, mobile start-up that is growing aggressively. Let's conservatively assume 50 percent growth.

2. *What are operating costs and what do we expect them to do?* I'll assume in the example that we have 60 percent operating costs, and that they grow by 5 percent each year as we face competition, labor inflation, and so on.

3. *What are the taxes?* After operating costs, taxes take a chunk out of our profits. While there is a lot we can do to legally minimize taxation, let's call the income tax 35 percent of operating profit (revenue minus operating cost).

4. *How much will you need to reinvest?* The revenue growth that we assume here doesn't come free. Your company must invest in the technology and equipment that it needs to grow. Each year, you'll make fresh investments, and some of your older equipment will likely depreciate. After all, factories, cars, and other equipment don't keep their value forever. We'll assume for this quick example that we reinvest 10 percent of revenue, and that old investments depreciate 5 percent each year.

5. *How much is your working capital?* Cash is free when you aren't using it for something else, so we also consider working

capital, the company's petty cash box. It's money tied up in inventory until it's sold, and tied up in receivables until you're paid. Since this number will grow with the company, that difference is considered against free cash flow, since it is taken off the table by the business.

Your money each year might look a bit like Table 9.3.

Combining the preceding five variables will give you the free cash flows for each year—but this is only half the picture. The other half returns to the question asked—how much is that money worth today? The Gordon growth model prescribes taking the final projected year free cash flow, the expected long-term growth rate and the discount rate, and squeezing them together to look like the following equation:

$$\text{Terminal value} + \frac{\text{Final year's projected cash flow} \times (1 + \text{Long} - \text{term expected growth})}{\text{Discount rate} - \text{Long} - \text{term expected growth rate}}$$

Both the long-term growth rate and the discount rate could be disagreed upon by any two people doing the same valuation. The discount rate is the result of a potentially complex calculation that I won't cover in a lot of detail here. It is meant to represent the cost of capital—after all, money isn't free. The discount rate is the weighted average cost of capital—a combination of the risk-free rate of return, and the premium for market risk in any investment, as well as other features—we'll estimate it to be 10 percent in this case. More than a home equity loan, less than a credit card advance.

Table 9.3: Simplified Discounted Cash Flow

	Year 1	Year 2	Year 3	Year 4	Year 5
Revenue	10,000.00	15,000.00	22,500.00	33,750.00	50,625.00
– Operating cost	6,000.00	9,450.00	14,175.00	21,262.50	31,893.75
– Taxes	1,400.00	1,942.50	2,913.75	4,370.63	6,555.94
– Investment	1,000.00	1,470.00	2,205.90	3,308.82	4,963.24
– Working capital changes	—	1,000.00	1,500.00	2,250.00	3,375.00
Free Cash flow	1,600.00	1,137.50	1,705.35	2,558.05	3,837.08

The long-term expected growth rate is the growth rate your company expects at maturity. It is likely a boring, single-digit number. We'll call it 5 percent—just a bit over inflation. In this case, the math looks a bit like the following equation:

$$\frac{\$3,800 \times (1.05)}{10\% - 5\%} = \$79,800$$

This means that if today you wanted to buy a company that is expected to make $10,000 per year over the next five years, it might be worth nearly $80,000, perhaps more if you are optimistic enough to hang your hat on a growth rate.

Remember that a discounted cash flow model will help you approximate only the fair value of your company. Ultimately, your stock is worth as much as you and an investor agree to make a deal over.

Intellectual Property/Intrinsic/Team

What if your company is still just a concept and a prototype? What if you have the most wonderful plan for a product that you absolutely cannot afford to produce? You will then need to rely on indicators other than the ones given in this example to get to a number.

The first pillar to hold on to is the *intellectual property* (or IP) that your concept represents. Is it an idea that you can protect with a patent? If not, a trademark or copyright will have to do.

The USPTO says a *patent* is "a property right granted by the Government of the United States of America to an inventor 'to exclude others from making, using, offering for sale, or selling the invention throughout the United States or importing the invention into the United States' for a limited time in exchange for public disclosure of the invention when the patent is granted." Patents were designed to incentivize innovation. In essence, granting the inventor a temporary monopoly, giving him enough room to recoup the time and expense of coming up with it. If your product has a structural, non-obvious innovation, you could file a utility patent. If not, you could almost always file a design patent. A patent on your product can offer you a level of protection against would-be copycats. What qualifies as non-obvious? It varies so much from one field to another that it's not always an easy question to answer.

Trademarks protect the representation of an idea, rather than a product itself. "A trademark protects words, names, symbols, sounds, or colors that distinguish goods and services from those manufactured or sold by others and to indicate the source of the goods. Trademarks, unlike patents, can be renewed forever as long as they are being used in commerce." If your product itself isn't patentable (either because it has minimal real innovation or because it isn't tangible), you can almost always trademark parts of the idea. Your company and brand names, taglines or slogans, logos and theme songs could all get an element of protection by filing a trademark. Unlike patents, trademarks can be renewed forever, and are easier to get. However, they apply only to the name and logo exactly as marked, whereas a patent will still hold as long as changes to it are obvious.

Copyrights are "a form of protection provided by the laws of the United States to the authors of 'original works of authorship,' including literary, dramatic, musical, artistic, and certain other intellectual works. This protection is available to both published and unpublished works." Unlike trademarks that protect the name or logo of a concept, copyrights protect the content of what you've created. Unless your product is a book or screenplay, a copyright may not directly protect your stuff. However, your business plan, web site, blog, and other messaging will benefit with some copyright protection. The cost is so minimal that it nearly always makes sense to file. Depending on your product, copyrights may or may not hold a lot of sway.

Trade secrets and the team are arguably most important. An investor will want to know about some of what can't be captured in formalized intellectual property. Is there something about your product that makes replicating it nearly impossible simply because you will keep it a secret and it can't easily be reverse-engineered? Does your team bring experiences that make success all but inevitable? These are just as important, and sometimes more so than IP in convincing an investor that your project is worth the investment.

The stories here are nearly too numerous to tell. When times are strong, as they were in the dot-com boom or the generally strong capital markets that followed the dot-com bust, an entrepreneur with a strong product could usually count on finding financing. In softer times, investors are looking for teams that go beyond just having a good product. A strong patent on an idea backed by strong demand is more likely to get financing than a strong idea that is easily copied. A team of seasoned product launchers (read: strong or blockbuster past successes) is more likely to get funded even with a weaker product.

Not all products are patentable, and not all trademarks will go through. The next thing an investor is going to look for is the strength and range of the management team. If your team is just you, as mine was, be ready for rather probing questions into what prepared you to launch this product, and what qualifies you to run this company. It feels a bit like interviewing for your own job—which, let's be honest—is exactly what you're doing. More than likely, the investor will want to know how you plan on filling your management team with capable, experienced individuals who will have the experience and context to execute on your needs as you grow.

If you've got a partner or a team, they are also going to want to know about your relationship, how you met, and how you work together. They will want to know what happens if one of you leaves as well as what the gaps are between skills the partners have and those needed to run your company when it is larger.

All else being equal, founders with past successful products and companies are much more likely to get funded. In fact, even founders with past failure, if accompanied by what lesson was learned, could also much more easily qualify for new funding. It is most challenging for founders with no experience.

Finally, there are other items intrinsic to the team, concept, and business that go on the table. If your product is nutritious, and a doctor is on the team, that's a plus. If one of the founders has ownership or access to the distribution or retail channels that will drive the product, that's a plus, too. If the model disrupts business as usual for your category—the way energy shots opened new channels and customer segments for the energy drinks category—that's a plus, too.

Before you go into your first investor meeting, do your homework on protectable IP, be honest about the gaps in your leadership team, and be creative about the intrinsic advantages of your concept. Remember that you represent an opportunity for your funder just as they do for you.

Understanding Terms

You'll know your investor discussions are going well when they want to talk terms with you. There are a lot of components that go into an investment, and each one is important to understand. It would be a huge mistake to walk in to an investment negotiation without knowing what each term means and what the trade-offs are.

- *Valuation/milestones/conditions/FROR:* For many people, the first and most important term is the volume of cash and the price it comes at. After all, a $1 million investment at a $5 million valuation means something much different from the same at $100 million valuation. However, since your company may not be ready right then for a ton of cash or the most favorable valuation, you can often set up milestones.

  Milestones or conditions can be in time or business terms, and both help reassure the investor that you're doing well, and bolster your valuation. For example, you might take $100,000 today at a $5 million valuation, another $300,000 when your business is producing a thousand orders a week at a $6 million valuation, and the last $600,000 when you've entered five markets successfully at a $10 million valuation. If you had taken the money all at once, it would have cost 20 percent of your company. By spreading it over milestones, you were forced to perform and gave up only 13 percent in equity.

  An FROR, or first rights of refusal, is an option that almost any investor will ask for. If and when you decide that you need more capital, your existing investors will want the first look to decide whether they are interested or not. If they think you're a strong investment, they will not want another investor to come to the table and potentially cause them issues. If they find you riskier, or if they are working on other companies in their portfolio, they may pass.

- *Preferred shares/co-investment:* The price of investment is more than just the raw dollars. An investor will often want to protect his interest through preferred shares or liquidation priority. From an investor's perspective, your business could be the most exciting project ever, but if he can't eventually exit, it may not be worth his while. If he's able to set up an exit in an IPO or in a sale to an acquirer, what happens if the sale amount is lower than what you thought your valuation was for? The preferred share owner gets his cash first.

For example, if you own 10 percent of a company that you think is worth a million bucks, and the investor owns 90 percent in preferred shares, they would get the first $900,000 in any sale of less than $1 million. So while you might think you're holding 10 percent, if the sale is $900,000 or less, you're actually holding zero percent.

Co-investment is a structure that allows the founders to get their hands on preferred shares. Normally, the founders do the work and get common stock while the investor puts down money in exchange for preferred stock. A co-investment clause would let the founders put money in themselves in exchange for preferred stock, just like their investors. In the preceding example, if the founders held 10 percent, half of which was preferred, while the investors held 90 percent in preferred stock, the same $900,000 sale would get the founders a little over $47,000. It sure beats zero percent, and if your investor will allow it, is a good clause to have.

- *Reverse vesting/noncompete:* The investors are often buying in to the team as much as the product. They want to make sure you stick around to see the deal through rather than disappearing if the opportunity suits you. For this reason, many investments come with a reverse vesting clause that essentially makes the founders earn back their company. Usually used in cases of larger investments, it could be asked for in any deal. For example, a $1 million investment on a $5 million valuation would leave you holding 80 percent of the company right then. However, if the investment came with reverse vesting, it might say that the founders hold 20 percent, and an additional 20 points will be vested each year over the next three years. This way, if the founders choose to quit, the investors aren't out a chunk of their capital.

  In addition, what good is their investment in this great company if the founders might leave when times get tough and just start over? A noncompete clause is almost always included, and will stop any of the founders from starting or working for a competing business in the future.

I met with a lot of investors when seeking financing for my recent product company. Some were not interested, and some offered a very low valuation. I even got an offer that included full reverse vesting at a valuation that would have left me holding less than 1 percent at the end of three years of vesting! I even met with an investor who insisted on paying in cash, in small installments, and all for preferred shares— one of the strangest people I've met to date (I didn't take the investment, don't worry). As you get started in your search for financing, you're sure to face some tough criticism and painful defeats. The best you can do is not to take the feedback to your company to heart. After all, if picking great companies was easy, investors would always make money.

- *Antidilution:* Investors will nearly always want to protect themselves against shares of the company going down in value. For example, suppose you get an investor to take 10 percent of your shares now. What happens if you issue more shares for your next investment? If they bought 10,000 shares out of 100,000 shares (at whatever price) and in your next round of investment you issue another 100,000 shares, they now have only 5 percent. Antidilution protection would mandate giving the original investor another 10,000 shares so they are still holding 10 percent. Put yourself in his shoes—without this protection, a company could take your money, and then issue so many new shares that the old ones are worth significantly less.

- *Dividend restriction:* When investors get involved with the operations of a new company, they will often want to make sure that at least some of the money produced (especially if it isn't a lot) goes back in to the company to fuel more growth. Dividend restriction will stop the founders from paying the cash out instead to other investors. This is a good thing— an investor that asks for dividend restriction is trying to enforce some fiscal discipline onto the company that could go a long way.

I found out that investors aren't the only ones who can ask for antidilution and dividends. Nearly every advisor that I considered wanted dilution protection as well. It made sense—they were offering a service that I found valuable but wasn't going to pay for. If I paid them in stock, they wanted to be sure it would keep its value. I ultimately ended up agreeing to three-year nondilution terms with my advisors, and in my discussions with others, have found that to be pretty normal. Dividends, on the other hand, are a different story. Investors can react in one of two ways to the risk they see in a company: on the one hand, asking for dividends would get them back a little bit of money and allow them to recoup part of the investment without giving up their stake. However, that pulls money out of the business that could otherwise be better spent. After all, if you're going to pay for financing, why not go to a bank? On the other hand, investors that are experienced with start-ups and want to see the company's money best spent, will often ask for dividend restriction, to make sure the cash stays in-house, where they can keep an eye on it. A sophisticated investor who believes in you won't ask for dividends. Beware of any who do.

- *Rep and warrant:* A new investor often takes a founder at his word for items that are difficult to check. Most often associated with IP or authority of any kind, a guarantee of representation and warrant asks you to confirm that you mean what you say. For example, if your project is a complicated mechanical product that uses ideas and materials that may be in other patents, it will take some homework to be sure you aren't infringing, or that you're allowed to use them. If your project involves using the assets of another company or person, you'll have to get permission and then be sure of its legitimacy. While it might sound simple, keep in mind that if it later comes out that you actually could not warrant your claims, your investors could pull out and leave you holding the bag.

- *Voting or a board seat:* Control is a tricky thing to share with an investor. One day you're a lone wolf, making decisions and shaping your company as you see fit, the next day you need to ask for permission, even though it's still your company. Although an investor will usually not buy in without accepting your vision, its possible that you'll disagree at times, and they want the ability to put in their vote. As part of the deal, they may ask that you establish a board of directors (often with three or five seats) and they will want one or two of them. This means you get to nominate your own board members for the other seats, and hopefully through them retain control over most of your business. Don't take this clause lightly—in every case that a founder has been thrown out of his own company, it is because he lost control of the board. The board reviews important decisions like key personnel hires, new lines of business, key investments, and will want to be generally informed.

- *Reporting:* The way your team and investors stay informed are through reports issued by your company. While not necessarily lengthy, these are bits of formal communication that you should send out periodically to keep everyone in the loop. In them, you can track whatever you think is important. They also usually include sales information, key decisions, and upcoming challenges.

Each Friday morning, I would sit down and tap out all the interesting things that happened that week in my weekly report. I started this to keep my advisors in the loop, and get their thoughts on where we were going. However, as we went along, I found that it was a useful way to communicate to my broader team. Soon, interns, salespeople, advisors, and board members were all getting my weekly e-mail in which I would summarize accomplishments, put down ideas for feedback, and point out upcoming challenges. It meant that anytime I had an issue, everyone knew what was going on, and when we had a success, people were able to see what we did to make it work. An informed team is a happy team, and a happy team is a productive team.

Summary

Financing can be difficult but does not need to be complex. If you're employed, tap yourself for funds, and, as you need it, put together a strong presentation and plan to shop around for money. Remember that investors are looking for your business and not your product—which means you need to be buttoned up about why people should invest in you and what they're getting back. When you're able to walk down the road of getting capital, talk to as many investors as you can, and if you get into discussing terms— congrats! You're only one step away from taking your dream to the next level.

! Challenge: Make it Happen

If you've been reading this book quietly without taking any action—stop. Put the book down, get up, and get out there. If you've got a product idea brewing away on your desk, make some more, share it with customers, and explore the distribution networks in your industry. Wherever you are, get to the next level.

Do some math about your business if you haven't already and make some educated guesses about how many customers are in your crosshairs, and how much money you might expect to make. Think about what you need to get there—production? marketing? sales? Knowing what you're going to need financing for makes asking easier.

Does the amount of money you're asking for make sense given how much you think you can make?

From here on out, you might feel like you're on your own. Fortunately, you're not. There are lots of people, just like you, who have ideas and want to bring them to life. Now, you've got the tools to make it happen.

Notes

Chapter 2

1. *The Gold Discovery*, Theodore Hittell (sfmuseum.org/hist6/impact.html).

Chapter 3

1. smallbusiness.aol.com/features/best-and-worst-company-names-of-all-time
2. Seth Stevenson, "The Cocktail Creationist," *New York* magazine, May 21, 2005. (http://nymag.com/nymetro/news/bizfinance/biz/features/10816/)

Chapter 5

1. fundinguniverse.com/company-histories/Red-Bull-GmbH-Company-History.html
2. *Bangkok Post*, 9/25/09, bangkokpost.com/news/local/155337/red-bull-owner-is-thailand-richest
3. Film: *Helvetica*, Gary Hustwit, Director. helveticafilm.com/.

About the Author

Vik Venkatraman is an entrepreneur, author, and student of life. He founded Star Power, a beverage company, and V Bespoke, a custom-tailored apparel company, both of which he took from concept to shelf. He graduated with honors from Columbia University in biomedical engineering, where he was also a brand manager for a leading energy drink company. As a management consultant, he has advised Fortune 500 retail and consumer product companies on issues ranging from operating and marketing strategies to international supply chain concerns.

Depending on the time of year, he enjoys snowboarding, motorcycling, photography, and lounging at the beach.

Index